Women's Fiction

Recent Titles in
Genreflecting Advisory Series

Diana Tixier Herald, Series Editor

Women's Fiction

A Guide to Popular Reading Interests

Rebecca Vnuk and Nanette Donohue

Genreflecting Advisory Series

Diana Tixier Herald, Series Editor

LIBRARIES UNLIMITED

AN IMPRINT OF ABC-CLIO, LLC
Santa Barbara, California • Denver, Colorado • Oxford, England

Library of Congress Cataloging-in-Publication Data

Vnuk, Rebecca.
  Women's fiction : a guide to popular reading interests / Rebecca Vnuk and Nanette Donohue.
      pages cm. — (Genreflecting advisory series)
  ISBN 978-1-59884-920-2 (hardback)   1. American fiction—21st century—Bibliography.
2. American fiction—20th century—Bibliography.   3. Women—Fiction—Bibliography.
4. American fiction—Women authors—Bibliography.   5. Women—Books and reading—United
States.   6. Fiction in libraries—United States.   7. Readers' advisory services—United States.
8. Public libraries—United States—Book lists.   I. Donohue, Nanette.   II. Title.
  Z1231.W85V589   2013
  [PS374.W6]
  016.3054'2—dc23   2013023685

ISBN: 978-1-59884-920-2

17 16 15 14 13   1 2 3 4 5

Libraries Unlimited
An Imprint of ABC-CLIO, LLC

ABC-CLIO, LLC
130 Cremona Drive, P.O. Box 1911
Santa Barbara, California 93116-1911

This book is printed on acid-free paper ∞
Manufactured in the United States of America

Contents

Introduction

Purpose and Scope

At first glance, women's fiction may seem easy enough to define. Books that women like to read, right? Well, it's not so simple. There are many different opinions of which books should or should not be classified as women's fiction. It's incredibly difficult to pin down exactly what women's fiction is (or what it isn't), because everyone seems to have a different take on it. It tends to be a catch-all term used by readers and by library staff to quickly identify a book—seemingly any book containing female characters written by a female author, or any book that might appeal to a female reader.

Women's fiction may be the least genre-y of all genres, mainly because books classified as women's fiction can also be thought of as romances, or literary fiction, or just plain old general fiction. (For the purpose of this book, let us settle on using the term "genre," even though it could easily be argued to be a "reading interest.") As a general definition, "women's fiction" reaches into most fiction genres and could easily lay claim to over half of all fiction—after all, it overlaps many genres and encompasses many time periods. It also does not hold to just one style—the books can be funny, weepers, literary, or gritty.

However, to simply classify any book that would be interesting to women as "women's fiction" does not do the genre justice. Studies show women outread men by a margin of 4 to 1,[1] and women read widely—book choices are, thankfully, not constrained by gender.

Librarians see this in action every day. Women read a wide variety of books, and calling something "women's fiction" just because the likely reader is a woman is not helpful to the readers' adviser or the reader herself.

Indeed, readers' advisory expert Joyce Saricks refers to the genre "Women's Lives and Relationships" in her book *The Reader's Advisory Guide to Genre Fiction*. She maintains that "these books that explore concerns faced by women in a specific age group or by women in general do not fall easily into a genre."[2]

For the purpose of this volume, a very specific definition is used. The hope is that this satisfies both librarians and readers and assists in leading them to their next great read. These criteria are an expanded version of rules that Rebecca initially developed as a readers' adviser and book reviewer.

The common threads that set women's fiction apart from other genres are that

- the central character (or characters) is female, and the story is character-driven;

- the main thrust of the story is something happening in the life of that woman (as opposed to the overarching theme being a romance, or a mystery of some sort),

- the setting is contemporary (defined, for the purposes of this volume, as after 1960);

- the author is female; and

- women's emotions and relationships are key elements of the plot.

Women's fiction explores the lives of female protagonists, with a focus on their many-layered relationships with spouses, parents, children, friends, and community. The woman (or women) is the star of the story, and her emotional development drives the plot.

A question that often comes up is, "Does a women's fiction author have to be a woman?" Our opinion is a resounding "yes." Nicholas Sparks, Nicholas Evans, and Chris Bohjalian are commonly mentioned as examples of men who write novels that could be classified as women's fiction. While some of their books (only some!) feature female protagonists, their stories fit more within romance, gentle reads, or literary fiction, or general fiction than they do within women's fiction. While these novels may appeal to readers of women's fiction, they don't have that nuance that gets into the character's head about what's going on in her life, and they don't delve into her relationships and her emotions.

Even writers themselves disagree on what falls under the umbrella of women's fiction. Author Amy Sue Nathan explains on her blog, "We write extraordinary yet realistic characters in realistic and extraordinary situations. If our main characters have love interests, it's a bonus. In our books, as in all books, the main character's journey leads to an ultimate goal. But in our books—the main character saves herself."[3]

The ultimate test? According to Kaite Mediatore Stover, Reader's Services Manager at Kansas City (Missouri) Public Library, if the main character could easily be swapped out for a male character, then it is general fiction.

What's Wrong with the Term "Women's Fiction"?

The notion that classifying a book as women's fiction is a negative is puzzling. There is plenty of derision out there in the publishing world and among the critics that a candy-colored cover is the kiss of death, or that women's fiction automatically equals fluff. Rebecca Traister, writing for Salon.com, says, "Beating on 'women's' fiction—and dismissing certain literary trends as feminine rubbish—has a history as long as the popular fiction itself."[4] And writer Hanne Blank points out, "The chick lit juggernaut of consumerist husband-hunting femme stereotypes is no less a pastiche (and in many ways no less a parody) of culture's directives to women than, say, Tom Clancy or Dean

Koontz novels are . . . of the cultural directives aimed at men. . . . The problem is that when critics (professional or otherwise) rip into chick lit, what they're really scoffing at most of the time isn't the worn clichés, the puerile plots, or the graceless prosody, it's women."[5]

As Neil Hollands, readers' advisory librarian at the Williamsburg (Virginia) Regional Library, was quoted on *Booklist*'s Book Group Buzz Blog, "I know from work experience that I'm not the only man in the world who dips into these novels, but the way the books get categorized leaves us out in the cold. . . . Sometimes I think the best step is to retreat from the genre categorizing, or if we're going to put books in categories, then stick with older, subject-based ideas like . . . 'coming-of-age', or even just 'contemporary fiction'. If we must use a genre label, I prefer 'women's lives'. At least that doesn't apply that the reader ought to be of the same sex."[6]

Though readers' advisers do not need to engage in lengthy discussions with readers about whether the term "women's fiction" is degrading or dismissive, it's important to understand why it could be seen that way, just as it's important to respect your readers' tastes, whatever they may be.

How Women's Fiction Differs from Romance Fiction

What distinguishes women's fiction from romance? Relationships and love stories are a key element of women's fiction, and boyfriends, husbands, and lovers show up as main characters as well. While women's fiction often incorporates romantic elements, there is more to the story than the love interest or sexual relationship. In women's fiction, a man may be waiting for the heroine of these novels at the end of her journey, but he does not usually get equal time or equal depth to his internal journey during the course of a book. In romance fiction, there is an expectation of a "happily-ever-after" ending, and that expectation doesn't exist in women's fiction. With a romance novel, a happy ending means that the protagonists fall in love and live happily ever after; in women's fiction, a happy ending might mean something entirely different—the protagonist escapes a bad relationship or starts a successful business, for example. More important, in addition to discovering the value of a loving relationship, in women's fiction the protagonist often usually discovers the value of loving herself. Personal growth is a common theme in women's fiction.

Another good way to look at it is that every single romance novel contains, well, a *romance.* There are many women's fiction titles that do not have any romantic elements at all. Danielle Steel, a grand dame of women's fiction, stated it best in an interview with CBS: "They're not really about romance. It's an element in life. But I think of romance novels as more of a category, and I write about the situations we all deal with. Loss and war and illness and jobs and careers, and good things, bad things, crimes, whatever. And I really write more about the human condition."[7]

All this hairsplitting about genres—does it really matter? As Diana Tixier Herald notes in the sixth edition of *Genreflecting*, "Whether women's fiction is a subgenre of romance fiction, as some romance publishers would have us believe, or romance fiction is in fact a subgenre of women's fiction is a question we will not attempt to answer. . . . Certainly a case could be made for either statement."[8] In this guide, selected popular romance authors with crossover appeal are noted in chapter 8, "Romantic Women's Fiction," as well as a description and list of selected popular romantic suspense authors.

For casual readers, it generally makes no difference whether we call it a romance or call it women's fiction—they just want something good to read. Placing an author in one genre or another is not a big deal, unless someone is an avid fan who specifically seeks out read-alikes, in which case grouping genre authors and titles together becomes valuable.

Characteristics and Appeal Factors

The primary appeal elements of women's fiction are character and story line. Character appeals because readers identify with women's fiction characters. When most readers pick up a women's fiction novel, they are looking for a sense of recognition—feeling as though they are that character, they know that character, or they understand just what that character is going through. From moments of sorrow to joyful celebrations to "thank goodness that never happened to me"—it's pleasurable and comforting to escape into a story that you can connect with. This does not mean that women's fiction characters are "stock." Indeed, it means that there are as many different characters as there are different types of women in the world.

Sometimes it's the opposite, though, and readers enjoy reading about the kinds of women they'd never be—in good ways and in bad! Glitz-and-glamour novels are appealing because it's nice to wish we were all rich and famous, but really, who wants all the troubles that crop up in those novels?

Some readers are especially interested in the story. Story line is hard to pin down as an appeal factor, since there is a wealth of different stories and plots that women's fiction takes on. For example, many women's fiction novels revolve around friendships and other relationships important to women. Others may concentrate on a woman's work or career. Many are family stories. Many stories still fall under the genre term "domestic fiction," concentrating on a woman's place in her surroundings, although the range of those surroundings are certainly broad in women's fiction—from Manhattan skyscrapers to California ranches, and all points in between. Setting may hold some interest for the reader—are they interested in a small town filled with eccentric characters, or life in the big bad city?

Finally, mood (or tone) cannot be discounted, although it is not usually the main appeal factor. However, because women's fiction can be laugh-out-loud funny, it can be tragic and sad, it can be sentimental or soap-opera dramatic, it's important to note what kind of book the reader seeks next. Are they looking to laugh? Do they want a comforting read, or something light or escapist? Or are they looking for something substantive to discuss with their book club? Of course, mood and tone are pretty subjective. Readers bring their own moods and perceptions into reading, and what's hilarious to one person might not be funny at all to another. One thing to keep in mind is that mood and tone are approached differently by different readers—some readers choose or enjoy a book to match the current mood they are in, while others choose or enjoy a book based on a mood they would like to be in—a very distinct difference.

In the end, there is very strong emotional appeal in women's fiction, and those emotions can run the gamut from happy, funny novels to tearjerker issue-driven fiction to comforting gentle reads.

Readers' Advisory for Women's Fiction

Because of the diverse nature of the books that can be termed women's fiction, the best way to perform any kind of readers' advisory for them involves getting back to basics. Find out what the reader is in the mood for—what other books have they enjoyed, and why? For readers' advisers, the key here is to really listen to what a patron says she is interested in, perhaps getting to know a book the patron has enjoyed before. Are they looking for something serious or something funny? Do they enjoy romantic suspense, or do they prefer chick lit? You can use this information to try and match the reader with similar books based on plot elements, such as locale, character's ages, and character's life circumstances.

It's nearly impossible to guess what a reader might like without asking them what they are in the mood to read, even if they state they are a fan of women's fiction in general. Women's fiction titles share common themes—women, their lives and relationships—but they most emphatically do not share the same tone. Many times the books are sassy and witty, other times they are sentimental, overdramatic, or tearjerkers. But as noted in the previous section, mood and tone are not always the definitive factor. Someone who has enjoyed fun, fast-paced chick lit might also be interested in a lengthy, cozy saga if what they are really in the mood for is a book featuring strong characters and their friends.

Readers of women's fiction are often looking for protagonists roughly their own age; though that's not to say that an older reader wouldn't like chick lit or a younger reader can't identify with characters older than herself. After all, the themes explored in women's fiction are truly timeless, and for the most part, readers will be able to identify with characters and scenarios no matter what their age.

Ultimately, becoming familiar with the various authors and styles found in women's fiction is one of the best ways to help lead patrons to their next read. Using lists found in this book and Rebecca's book *Read On . . . Women's Fiction: Reading Lists for Every Taste* (Libraries Unlimited, 2009), you can come up with read-alikes to match a reader with similar plotlines or characters.

Scope: What Was Included, What Was Not Included, and Why

The focus of this book is on contemporary women's fiction novels. Books by early writers such as Jane Austen and Louisa May Alcott make brief appearances in chapter 1 rather than throughout the chapters. Contemporary novels dominate this work—with the exception of classics of the genre or key novels by notable or prolific authors, the annotated selections have been published within the last ten years. Nearly 1,200 novels are identified here as women's fiction, and more than 600 of them are annotated, including appeal keywords. The edition information given is usually for the first edition. This work features novels published in English, in the United States. Short stories, both individual and collections, are excluded, as are novellas or graphic novels. Most of the books listed are currently in print and generally available in libraries.

An effort was made to keep romance fiction off of the lists, but due to the diverse nature of women's fiction, and its nebulous definition, some crossover could not be avoided, so there are chapters devoted to romantic women's fiction and authors with crossover appeal. Many romance novels feature women's full relationships, not just romantic relationships, at the heart of the story. Truly, there are a great number of authors who may or may not belong on these lists, and to avoid making this a multivolume work, some difficult decisions needed to be made! Jan Karon is a good example. Yes, she writes about women's lives, and her books appeal to female readers; but her main character is male, and her books are generally considered inspirational fiction. Since one of the defining characteristics of women's fiction is that the book must be written with a woman or women as the protagonist, Karon's novels fall outside our definition of women's fiction. In general, though contemporary inspirational fiction often shares some traits with women's fiction, it first and foremost falls under the "inspirational" or "Christian" genre, so such titles do not appear here, although some of the more popular authors are mentioned in chapter 9 on "Genreblends and Outliers."

Another good example is Barbara Kingsolver—she does not appear, because her books have a variety of characters and the stories are not limited to women's issues. This points to the need to clarify women's fiction as outside of general fiction featuring some female characters, or general fiction written by a female author. Again, chapter 9 delves further into this issue. Speaking of Kingsolver, literary fiction is another category that is difficult to distinguish from women's fiction. Some argue whether it is even a category or a useful descriptor. Can women's fiction take a serious tone, can it have lush language, or does that make it literary fiction? What makes this an especially thorny issue is that every reader has a different reaction to every book and its appeal characteristics. There is plenty of literary fiction that has heart and soul to the story, but just because a novel is written by a woman that has female protagonists, it doesn't mean it has the same style and appeal that would make it women's fiction. This is discussed further in chapter 1.

Organization of This Book and How to Use

Because there is so much variety in the world of women's fiction, this guide aims to explore the history, recent trends, and appeal factors of the genre. Chapters are divided into lists of subgenres, themes, or categories. Each chapter begins with a brief explanation of the subgenre or classification, explaining its appeal and identifying characteristics. The entries for each title include author, title, original publishing date, publisher, ISBN, and number of pages, followed by a brief plot summary or annotation. Entries are arranged alphabetically by author name within subgenre, with titles listed chronologically by publication date. In the case of series, only a general series description is provided, with titles listed in series order beneath. Although most titles fit neatly into a single category, some cut across several themes and appeal characteristics. When assigning a book to a specific chapter or section, we focused on the main characteristic or predominant themes of the story. The annotations are intended to give readers a good idea of what the story is about and why it is appealing. The effort was made to keep this guide simple and straightforward, because not all readers will use this book in the same way. Students may be interested in the background and history and trends, librarians and booksellers may be interested in read-alike choices or may want to know more about authors they are unfamiliar with, and general readers may be interested in what counts as a women's fiction book.

Our goal for this collection is a comprehensive overview of the women's fiction genre, as well as its most prominent offshoots. We focused on recent titles in the genre, as well as classic or genre-defining works by popular authors. We also consulted the lists for the awards and honors given to novels in the genre, including the American Library Association's Reading List Council award for women's fiction, the *Romantic Times* Reviewer's Choice Award for mainstream fiction, the Romance Writers of America's RITA for Novel with Strong Romantic Elements, the U.K.-based Romantic Novelists Association awards for contemporary romantic novels and comic romantic novels, and *Library Journal*'s annual list of best women's fiction. Novels that have won awards, are highlighted with a ribbon (🎗) and if a novel is deemed appropriate for book club discussions, it has been marked with an asterisk (*).

When women's fiction authors write in multiple genres, we've included the titles in the relevant chapter. For example, Jennifer Weiner's earliest novels were released at the height of the chick lit boom and were among the most popular (and widely imitated) books in the fledgling genre. These early books are included in the chick lit chapter, while her later books, which focus more on family relationships, are in the general women's fiction chapter. The author index provides locations for each author included in the book.

Keywords

We have included a selection of keywords intended to help readers locate materials that meet their needs. The keywords are general and focus on appeal terms relating to subgenre, character type, plot type, setting, or tone. The following keywords are used throughout the book:

- **Beach.** Novels that are beach reads—literally. These books are set in the sun and sand.

- **Coming-of-Age.** Novels featuring characters transitioning from youth to adulthood.

- **Emotional.** Novels that pack an emotional wallop. Sometimes called "tearjerkers."

- **Ensemble.** Novels featuring narration from multiple characters' point of view.

- **Family.** Novels where family relationships are at the forefront.

- **Friendship.** Novels where women's friendships are at the forefront.

- **Gentle.** Novels that meet the basic characteristics of gentle reads. See chapter 4 for more details.

- **Glitzy.** Novels focusing on the lives and loves of the rich and glamorous.

- **Grief.** Novels featuring women coping with loss.

- **Historical.** Novels featuring historical settings, loosely interpreted as pre-1950.

- **Humorous.** Novels that incorporate humor, from light romantic comedy to dark humor.

- **Marriage.** Novels where a woman's marriage is at the forefront of the plot.

- **Motherhood.** Novels about the struggles women face as parents.

- **Mothers and Daughters.** Novels about the complex and emotional relationships of mothers and daughters.

- **Older Women.** Novels featuring main characters who are fifty-five and older.

- **Romantic.** Novels where romantic relationships are at the forefront of the plot.

- **Saga.** Novels that follow characters or families over long spans of time.

- **Self-Actualization.** Novels where the main character learns about herself and moves toward realizing her full potential as a person.

- **Sisters.** Novels that explore the relationships between sisters.

- **Southern.** Novels set in the southern United States.

- **Thought-Provoking.** Novels featuring a plot that incorporates controversial issues, difficult dilemmas, or tough decisions.

- **Workplace.** Novels where a woman's professional life is at the forefront of the plot.

Notes

1. Eric Weiner, "Why Women Read More than Men," *NPR*, September 5, 2007, http://www.npr.org/templates/story/story.php?storyId=14175229, last accessed March 18, 2013.

2. Joyce Saricks, *The Readers' Advisory Guide to Genre Fiction*, 2nd ed. (Chicago: ALA Editions, 2009), 155.

3. Amy Sue Nathan, "About WFW," Women's Fiction Writers, http://womensfictionwriters.wordpress.com/about/, last accessed March 18, 2013.

4. Rebecca Traister, "Women's Studies," *Salon*, November 2005, http://www.salon.com/2005/11/01/chick_lit_3/, last accessed March 18, 2013.

5. Hanne Blank, "Don't Hate Me Because I'm Cute," *City Paper*, September 10, 2003, http://www2.citypaper.com/special/story.asp?id=5973, last accessed March 18, 2013.

6. Neil Hollands, commenting on *Book Group Buzz*'s post, "If Women Like it, It Must Be Stupid," August 7, 2010, http://bookgroupbuzz.booklistonline.com/2010/08/04/if-women-like-it-it-must-be-stupid/, last accessed March 18, 2013.

7. Danielle Steel, interview with Maggie Rodriguez, *CBS News*, September 21, 2010, http://www.cbsnews.com/stories/2010/09/21/earlyshow/leisure/celebspot/main6887539.shtml, last accessed March 18, 2013.

8. Diana Tixier Herald, *Genreflecting*, 6th ed. (Westport, CT: Libraries Unlimited, 2006), 494.

Chapter 1

Women's Fiction: A History

When talking about women's fiction, readers and librarians are generally thinking of contemporary writers. However, it's important to look at where the genre began. Early feminist writers and nineteenth-century writers of "domestic" fiction can be credited with the creation of this genre. These authors wrote about what was happening in the lives of women in their times, and even today, women's fiction tends to mirror the trends and issues of the period it was written in (unless, of course, it is specifically historical in nature).

Scholars and librarians use the term "domestic fiction" to define a certain type of novel that gained popularity with female readers during the middle of the nineteenth century, encompassing the domestic world (home, family, "woman's work") and centering on a woman going through some type of hardship. Today, the term is mainly applied to general fiction about everyday home or family life (it appears as a subject heading in library catalogs, though the term is rarely used by general readers). For the purposes of this guide, "domestic" fiction is used in the first sense, that is, to describe nineteenth-century novels rather than contemporary fiction. These are titles that can also be considered "classics," with many still in print and read by contemporary readers.

This chapter briefly covers early authors of domestic fiction, moving into the early twentieth century through the middle of the twentieth century—when women's fiction really began to take off as a marketable and identifiable genre, rather than general fiction that women enjoyed reading.

Early Forerunners

Susannah Rowson's *Charlotte Temple* (1794), largely considered the first "best seller" in America, is the tale of a young woman seduced by a soldier. Readers eager to hear all about Charlotte's fall and redemption readily embraced this sentimental, moral tale, and today the book is studied in universities as a novel that offers a glimpse into daily life during the post-Revolutionary War period. Jane Austen's novels, beginning with *Sense and Sensibility*, published in 1811, also feature heroines dealing with daily life and the morals of their times and can therefore be considered "women's fiction," although romance fans also claim her. Family plays a big role in her plots, as do the conventions of society.

In 1822 Catharine Maria Sedgwick solidified the genre of the domestic novel with *A New-England Tale*, the story of an orphaned girl who rises above her situation thanks to strong moral fiber (it doesn't hurt that she lands a wealthy husband).

Charlotte Bronte's *Jane Eyre* (1847) took the genre another step forward, as a multilayered coming-of-age story, a romance of sorts, and a social commentary. As protagonist, Jane is an intelligent, moral character who manages to overcome various trials and tribulations such as abuse and poverty to triumph in the end.

In 1851, Susan Warner's *The Wide, Wide World* became the first American book to sell over a million copies. The story follows heroine Ellen Montgomery, as she learns the values of hard work and self-sacrifice.

While Louisa May Alcott wrote her books in different styles, there is no doubt that *Little Women* (1880) is a classic example of early women's fiction. Following the trials and tribulations of the March sisters, it is a look at the strength of women, individuality, the importance of family, and a glimpse into daily life. Kate Chopin shocked readers in 1899 with *The Awakening*, where her protagonist Edna struggles to reconcile her increasingly nonconformist views on womanhood and motherhood with the prevailing social stances of the day. In a similar fashion, Miles Franklin's *My Brilliant Career* mirrors a time of political and social unrest. Sybylla is a young, spirited woman who rebels against convention of the times and the desire of her family that she be groomed to marry into a wealthy family. Instead, she heads off on her own, convinced that she will have a brilliant career.

While Virginia Woolf's *Mrs. Dalloway* (1925) is certainly more literary than domestic fiction, it deserves a mention here as well, because the main character, Clarissa Dalloway, spends the day depicted in the novel immersed in thoughts about the choices she's made in life and how they have affected her relationships and well-being.

In 1930, E. M. Delafield (Edmée Elizabeth Monica Dashwood) published her *Diary of a Provincial Lady*, a tongue-in-cheek look at a woman of the times dealing with her husband, children, and neighbors. Serialized in a magazine to great success, it was then published in novel form and followed by several sequels.

In 1936, Margaret Mitchell published *Gone with the Wind*. While some fans, particularly of the film version, would call it a romance, it is firmly in women's fiction territory. It's not all about the turbulent love story with Rhett, after all—the novel explores Scarlett's life during wartime and her emotions over not only the men in her life but also her family and homestead, and it takes an unflinching look at a women's role in times of crisis.

The 1940s to the 1960s: Women at Home, Women at Work

In the middle twentieth century, women's fiction began to evolve from domestic stories to full-on domestic dramas. In society, women were entering the workforce and times were beginning to change—there was life outside the home. Sexuality began to glimmer in fiction, as well. Nancy Mitford's trilogy consisting of *Pursuit of Love* (1945), *Love in a Cold Climate* (1949), and *Don't Tell Alfred* (1960) is the saga of an upper-crust British family, told in the voice of Fanny, the irrepressible narrator. Rona Jaffe should perhaps be credited with the original chick lit—her 1958 novel *The Best of Everything* is a fast-paced, sassy tale of New York secretaries enjoying sex, shopping, and cocktails while they attempt to climb the corporate ladder in the world of publishing.

Mary McCarthy's *The Group* follows a group of Vassar College friends from 1933 to 1940. The economic times allow these women to venture out for the first time, getting jobs and living on their own, reaching new social, professional, and personal heights. Grace Metalious's *Peyton Place* was published to much controversy in 1956, while the salaciousness of Jacqueline Susann's *Valley of the Dolls* was a huge hit in 1966. Elizabeth Cadell wrote from the 1940s through her death in the 1980s, but her books are sadly out of print. Sweeping sagas featuring eccentric characters were her hallmark.

The 1970s to the 1980s: The Rise of the Saga, Feminism, Glitz and Glamour

As feminism came to the forefront in the 1970s, women's novels followed the time. Sex sells, and Judy Blume's *Wifey*, Marilyn French's *The Women's Room*, and Erica Jong's *Fear of Flying* became huge hits as women discovered feminism and their sexuality. The "me decade" and the extravagance of the 1980s are perfectly mirrored in the soap opera-esque tales of glitz and glamour penned by Jackie Collins, Judith Krantz, and Danielle Steel. Strong women, power plays, plenty of money to throw around—these are all hallmarks of early 1980s popular women's fiction. Sagas, which also tend to have dramatic flourishes, become quite popular in this era. Authors such as Barbara Taylor Bradford, Judith Krantz, Judith Michael, and Helen Van Slyke were known for their long novels featuring beautiful, rich, and powerful women, sexy love scenes, and high levels of drama.

The New Millennium

The late 1990s through the middle of the 2000s saw the meteoric rise of chick lit. Helen Fielding's massive best seller *Bridget Jones's Diary* helped launch this trend, and the rise of sexy, single professional women in other areas of pop culture, including the hit television series *Sex and the City*, increased readers' appetites for chick lit.

Chick lit novels focus on young, single, protagonists trying to make their mark in life, in the big city or in a new fabulous career. Generally humorous and lighthearted, chick lit in its original fluffy, sexy form has been on the wane in recent years. Many of the publishers so prevalent in its heyday, including Downtown Press (Simon & Schuster), Strapless (Kensington), and Red Dress Ink (Harlequin) have been shuttered, but chick lit has not gone away entirely. Instead, it's simply grown up and branched out into subgenres such as Hen Lit (chicks grow up into hens), Mommy Lit, and Widow Lit.

Recent Trends in the Genre

It can be difficult to pinpoint trends in women's stories since many of the subjects and topics are consistent, real-life themes—family, friendship, love, marriage, and careers, to name just a few. What remains constant, and we can expect to see more of, are stories that continue to focus on women at all stages of life.

While chick lit came roaring out of the gate, as mentioned previously, the latest incarnation is "chick lit grows up." The books are still fun and humorous, but the characters have shifted—in the inevitable progression of chick lit, we've largely moved away from "Single in the City" books to young brides, young mothers, young divorcees, and even young widows. This shift accurately reflects the evolution of women's lives, and the changes that fans likely experience (similar to how the glitz-and-glamour novels of the 1970s and 1980s were a reflection of their over-the-top times).

At the time of this writing, many of the current crop of women's fiction books are what is often termed "ensemble fiction." These stories feature a cast of characters—there may or may not be one "main" character—sisters, friends, coworkers all share starring roles in the story. There has been a huge influx of women's fiction books with large casts of characters—books about sisters, books about college friends, books about reading groups, books about coworkers. Readers enjoy these ensemble stories because they can easily find a character within the group who they can identify with, or they can see their friends in. As a dovetail to this trend, another trend we're seeing is that many books feature crafts or cooking—knitting circles, quilting bees, scrapbooking groups, cupcake bakers, personal chefs. Again, a reflection of the times.

Another trend is issue-driven fiction: heavier books about heavy issues. While this trend really started in the late 1990s (thanks in part to Oprah's Book Club), it's exploded with "ripped-from-the-headlines" novels, such as those by Jacqueline Mitchard and Jodi Picoult. This mirrors what we're seeing in television and film, as well.

It's interesting to note that contemporary women's fiction is incredibly popular in the United Kingdom. It is fairly interchangeable with romance fiction there, and the fact that it is nearly all published as inexpensive trade paperbacks likely helps fuel the popularity. North American publishers have taken note of this and are starting to introduce American readers to the backlist titles of many established U.K. authors. Jilly Cooper, Freya North, and Fiona Walker are three authors who are huge in the United Kingdom, but surprisingly, have not yet really cracked the market in the United States. They write romance novels with strong female characters and a touch of soap-opera excitement (very much à la Jackie Collins). The rise of chick lit in the late 1990s did bring several U.K. authors stateside to wide popularity, including Jane Green and Marian Keyes. Selected notable authors are featured within this volume.

The "Franzen Flap" of 2011

In the summer of 2011, literary fiction author Jonathan Franzen published a new book and landed not only two separate *New York Times* book reviews but also the cover of *Time* magazine. (In 2009, only 38 percent of fiction reviewed in the *New York Times* was written by women.)[1] This caused quite a stir among women's fiction authors—notably, Jennifer Weiner and Jodi Picoult—who got lots of press for protesting, loudly, and in the media. Weiner started a Twitter campaign, using the hashtag "#franzenfreude," coining the phrase to mark her disgust at the fawning treatment Franzen's novel was getting. Then in 2011, V. S. Naipaul came along stating that no women writer, living or dead, could possibly be his equal, because of women's "sentimentality (and) narrow view of the world."[2]

As noted earlier in this chapter, this issue—the ongoing treatment of books written by women versus books written by men—is not new, nor is it over. It's been going on since George Eliot wrote her essay "Silly Novels by Lady Novelists" back in 1856 and will likely not stop any time soon. Writers may feel a need to be thought of as "serious," critics may decry that anything not termed literary fiction is all worthless, but the publishers are likely laughing all the way to the bank. And truly, it's the readers, not the critics, who matter here.

Notes

1. "Fact-Checking the Franzenfreude," *Slate*, September 2, 2010, http://www.slate.com/articles/double_x/doublex/2010/09/factchecking_the_franzenfreude.html, last accessed March 18, 2013.

2. Amy Fallon, "VS Naipaul Finds No Woman Writer His Literary Match—Not Even Jane Austen," *The Guardian*, June 1, 2011, http://www.guardian.co.uk/books/2011/jun/02/vs-naipaul-jane-austen-women-writers, last accessed March 18, 2013.

Chapter 2

Grand Dames
of Women's Fiction

All literary genres have their pioneers—those authors that helped define the genre or broke new, often controversial ground within an established genre. Romance fiction has authors like Katherine Woodiwiss or Rosemary Rogers, who brought steamy love scenes to romance fiction during the 1970s. Horror fiction has Edgar Allan Poe, H. P. Lovecraft, and Stephen King—all authors who took the genre in new and exciting directions. Women's fiction also has its pioneers, and we're calling them Grand Dames.

"Grand Dame" is a French phrase meaning "great lady," and this is an apt descriptor for the authors in this chapter. It's also a term of respect bestowed upon those women who are experts in their field. Each of the authors in this chapter has put an indelible mark on contemporary women's fiction, whether by pushing the genre in a new direction, by selling millions of novels worldwide, or by defining the conventions of the genre.

Defining characteristics of a grand dame of women's fiction include

- a career spanning multiple decades,

- multiple novels that have achieved bestseller status, and

- books that have helped to shape or define the women's fiction genre.

It seems fitting to put give these authors their own chapter, since they are classic, pioneering authors of the genre. You can't mention women's fiction without using one of their books as an example. From sagas to dramas to romantic tales, these authors have helped to define women's fiction.

Unlike the rest of this book, the author lists in this chapter are not annotated. After a brief biography, you'll find an unannotated, chronological list of each author's works. Recent works by each of our grand dames are listed in the appropriate chapter.

Binchy, Maeve.

Binchy's novels focus on family relationships, often featuring a large cast of characters, and are frequently set in Ireland. Her characters are often seeking independence or understanding. Though her early novels are classic examples of women's fiction, Binchy's later novels started to stray away from having women as her central characters, often featuring men in leading roles.

Light a Penny Candle. 1983.

The Lilac Bus. 1991.

Echoes. 1985.

Firefly Summer. 1988.

Silver Wedding. 1989.

Circle of Friends. 1991.

The Copper Beech. 1992.

The Glass Lake. 1995.

Evening Class. 1996.

Tara Road. 1998.

Scarlet Feather. 2001.

Quentins. 2002.

Nights of Rain and Stars. 2004.

Whitethorn Woods. 2007.

Heart and Soul. 2009.

Minding Frankie. 2011.

A Week in Winter. 2013.

Bradford, Barbara Taylor.

During the 1970s and 1980s, readers devoured Bradford's epic family sags, which feature strong women who overcome overwhelming obstacles. Bradford's Harte Family saga, which follows the life and fortune of department store magnate Emma Harte, is a classic of the women's fiction genre.

The hallmarks of Bradford's novels are strong female characters, often professional women in glamorous careers; hidden family secrets; and grand, epic love stories that span decades.

Voice of the Heart. 1983.

Act of Will. 1986.

The Women in His Life. 1990.

Remember. 1991.

Angel. 1993.

Everything to Gain. 1994.

Dangerous to Know. 1995.

Love in Another Town. 1995.

Her Own Rules. 1996.

A Secret Affair. 1996.

Power of a Woman. 1997.

A Sudden Change of Heart. 1999.

Where You Belong. 2000.

The Triumph of Katie Byrne. 2001.

Three Weeks in Paris. 2002.

Breaking the Rules. 2009.

Playing the Game. 2010.

Letter from a Stranger. 2011.

Secrets from the Past. 2013.

Harte Family saga.

A Woman of Substance. 1979.

Hold the Dream. 1985.

To Be the Best. 1988.

Emma's Secret. 2004.

Unexpected Blessings. 2005.

Just Rewards. 2006.

Ravenscar trilogy.

The Ravenscar Dynasty. 2006.

The Heir. 2007.

Being Elizabeth. 2008.

Brown, Sandra.

Like a number of women's fiction authors, Sandra Brown began her career writing category romance for Harlequin, Silhouette, and Loveswept. In the late 1980s, Brown made the move to single-title romance, often with a suspense element. Her prolific output spans traditional contemporary romance, romantic suspense, thrillers, and straightforward women's fiction, all featuring strong female leads. In recognition of her many career accomplishments, Brown received the Romance Writers of America's Lifetime Achievement Award in 1998. She also received the International Thriller Writers' Thrillermaster Award in 2008.

Because Brown's bibliography is so extensive and diverse, the titles are organized by genre, then chronologically within each genre.

Romantic Suspense/Thrillers

Slow Heat in Heaven. 1988.

Best Kept Secrets. 1988.

Mirror Image. 1990.

Breath of Scandal. 1991.

French Silk. 1992.

Where There's Smoke. 1993.

Charade. 1994.

The Witness. 1995.

Exclusive. 1996.

Fat Tuesday. 1997.

Unspeakable. 1998.

The Alibi. 1999.

The Switch. 2000.

Standoff. 2000.

Envy. 2001.

Seduction by Design. 2001.

The Crush. 2002.

Hello Darkness. 2003.

White Hot. 2004.

Chill Factor. 2005.

Ricochet. 2006.

Play Dirty. 2007.

Smoke Screen. 2008.

Smash Cut. 2009.

Tough Customer. 2010.

Lethal. 2011.

Low Pressure. 2012.

Deadline. 2013.

Contemporary Romance/Romantic Women's Fiction

Love's Encore. 1981.

A Treasure Worth Seeking. 1982.

Not Even for Love. 1982.

Eloquent Silence. 1982.

Hidden Fires. 1982.

Love Beyond Reason. 1982.

A Secret Splendor. 1983.

A Kiss Remembered. 1983.

Prime Time. 1983.

Shadows of Yesterday. 1983.

Tempest in Eden. 1983.

Tomorrow's Promise. 1983.

Temptation's Kiss. 1983.

Breakfast in Bed. 1983.

Heaven's Price. 1983.

Bittersweet Rain. 1984.

Tiger Prince. 1984.

Words of Silk. 1984.

In a Class by Itself. 1984.

Send No Flowers. 1984.

Another Dawn. 1985.

Sunset Embrace. 1985.

Led Astray. 1985.

Sweet Anger. 1985.

Thursday's Child. 1985.

Above and Beyond. 1986.

Honor Bound. 1986.

The Rana Look. 1986.

22 Indigo Place. 1986.

The Devil's Own. 1987.

Two Alone. 1987.

Demon Rumm. 1987.

Sunny Chandler's Return. 1987.

Fanta C. 1987.

The Silken Web. 1988.

Tidings of Great Joy. 1988.

Hawk O'Toole's Hostage. 1988.

Adam's Fall. 1988.

The Thrill of Victory. 1989.

Long Time Coming. 1989.

Temperatures Rising. 1989.

A Whole New Light. 1989.

Riley in the Morning. 1989.

Texas! Trilogy. 1992.

Rainwater. 2009.

Collins, Jackie.

Collins began titillating and shocking readers with the publication of her first novel, *The World Is Full of Married Men*, in 1968. Her debut set the stage for her later works, which feature lavish settings, over-the-top characters with glamorous and extravagant lifestyles, and steamy sex scenes. Collins's career peaked in the 1980s with two blockbuster series that captured the zeitgeist of the decade. Though the mania for glitz-and-glamour novels has faded, Collins continues to write in the genre.

The World Is Full of Married Men. 1968.

The Stud. 1970.

Sinners. 1971.

The Love Killers. 1974.

The World Is Full of Divorced Women.
    1975.

Lovers and Gamblers. 1977.

The Bitch. 1979.

Chances. 1981.

Hollywood Wives. 1983.

Sinners. 1984.

Lucky. 1985.

Hollywood Husbands. 1986.

Rock Star. 1988.

Lady Boss. 1990.

American Star: A Love Story. 1993.

Hollywood Kids. 1994.

Vendetta: Lucky's Revenge. 1996.

Thrill! 1997.

L.A. Connections. 1998.

Dangerous Kiss. 1999.

Lethal Seduction. 2000.

Hollywood Wives: The New Generation. 2001.

Deadly Embrace. 2002.

Hollywood Divorces. 2003.

Lovers and Players. 2006.

Drop Dead Beautiful. 2007.

Married Lovers. 2008.

Poor Little Bitch Girl. 2010.

Goddess of Vengeance. 2011.

The Power Trip. 2013.

Michaels, Fern.

Fern Michaels is the pen name of Mary Ruth Kuczkir. She began writing in the mid-1970s, when her youngest child entered kindergarten and her (now ex-) husband told her she needed to get a job. Like many of the other grand dames of women's fiction, Fern Michaels got her start in romance fiction. She describes herself as "a hell of a storyteller" and has written books in a number of genres, including category romance, historical romance, contemporary romance, mystery, romantic suspense, thrillers, and women's fiction.

Pride and Passion. 1975.

Captive Passions. 1977.

Valentina. 1978.

Whitefire. 1978.

Captive Embraces. 1979.

Captive Splendors. 1980.

Delta Ladies. 1980.

Golden Lasso. 1980.

Sea Gypsy. 1980.

Beyond Tomorrow. 1981.

Captive Innocence. 1981.

Paint Me Rainbows. 1981.

Whisper My Name. 1981.

Without Warning. 1981.

Nightstar. 1982.

Panda Bear Is Critical. 1982.

Wild Honey. 1982.

All She Can Be. 1983.

Free Spirit. 1983.

Tender Warrior. 1983.

Cinders to Satin. 1984.

Texas Rich. 1985.

Texas Heat. 1986.

To Taste the Wine. 1987.

Sins of Omission. 1989.

Texas Fury. 1989.

Sins of the Flesh. 1990.

Captive Secrets. 1991.

For All Their Lives. 1991.

Texas Sunrise. 1993.

Desperate Measures. 1994.

Seasons of Her Life. 1994.

Serendipity. 1994.

To Have and to Hold. 1994.

A Gift of Joy. 1995.

Dear Emily. 1995.

A Joyous Season. 1996.

Vegas Rich. 1996.

Wish List. 1996.

Heart of the Home. 1997.

Heartbreak Ranch. 1997.

Homecoming. 1997.

Vegas Heat. 1997.

Vegas Sunrise. 1997.

Finders Keepers. 1998.

Sara's Song. 1998.

Annie's Rainbow. 1999.

Celebration. 1999.

Split Second. 1999.

Through the Years. 1999.

Yesterday. 1999.

Five Golden Rings. 2000.

Guest List. 2000.

Listen to Your Heart. 2000.

Picture Perfect. 2000.

What You Wish For. 2000.

Charming Lily. 2001.

Kentucky Rich. 2001.

Plain Jane. 2001.

The Future Scrolls. 2001.

Kentucky Heat. 2002.

Kentucky Sunrise. 2002.

No Place Like Home. 2002.

About Face. 2003.

Crown Jewel. 2003.

Late Bloomer. 2003.

Let It Snow. 2003.

Maybe This Time. 2003.

Trading Places. 2003.

Weekend Warriors. 2003.

Deck the Halls. 2004.

Dream of Me. 2004.

Family Blessings. 2004.

Jingle All the Way. 2004.

Payback. 2004.

The Real Deal. 2004.

Pretty Woman. 2005.

The Jury. 2005.

The Nosy Neighbor. 2005.

Vendetta. 2005.

Fool Me Once. 2006.

Hey, Good Looking. 2006.

Lethal Justice. 2006.

Sugar and Spice. 2006.

Sweet Revenge. 2006.

Comfort and Joy. 2007.

Free Fall. 2007.

Hide and Seek. 2007.

Hokus Pokus. 2007.

The Marriage Game. 2007.

Up Close and Personal. 2007.

Collateral Damage. 2008.

Fast Track. 2008.

Final Justice. 2008.

Promises. 2008.

Silver Bells. 2008.

Mr. and Miss Anonymous. 2008.

Razor Sharp. 2009.

Snow Angels. 2009.

The Scoop. 2009.

Under the Radar. 2009.

Vanishing Act. 2009.

Crossroads. 2010.

Deadly Deals. 2010.

Déjà vu. 2010.

Exclusive. 2010.

Game Over. 2010.

Holiday Magic. 2010.

I'll Be Home for Christmas. 2010.

Return to Sender. 2010.

Betrayal. 2011.

Christmas at Timberwoods. 2011.

Home Free. 2011.

Late Edition. 2011.

Southern Comfort. 2011.

A Winter Wonderland. 2012.

Breaking News. 2012.

Coming Home for Christmas. 2012.

Deadline. 2012.

Fancy Dancer. 2012.

Tuesday's Child. 2012.

Gotcha! 2013.

Pilcher, Rosamunde.

Pilcher's storied career began in 1949, when she published her first novel with the British romance fiction publisher Mills & Boon under the pseudonym Jane Fraser. Though she began publishing under her own name in 1955, she didn't achieve mainstream success in the United States until 1988, when her novel *The Shell Seekers* was released. Although she stopped writing in 2000, Pilcher maintains a steady fan base for her gentle novels, which feature large casts of characters, often families; English and Scottish settings; and gentle, comfortable romance.

A Secret to Tell. 1955.

On My Own. 1965.

Sleeping Tiger. 1967.

Another View. 1969.

The End of Summer. 1971.

Snow in April. 1972.

The Empty House. 1973.

The Day of the Storm. 1975.

Under Gemini. 1976.

Wild Mountain Thyme. 1978.

The Carousel. 1982.

Voices in Summer. 1984.

The Shell Seekers. 1988.

September. 1990.

Coming Home. 1995.

The Key. 1996.

Shadows. 1999.

Winter Solstice. 2000.

Plain, Belva.

Known for her sweeping, multigenerational historical sagas, Plain's courageous and independent heroines balance romance with family tragedies and triumphs. Many of her novels are set in different historical time periods such as the Civil War era and the early twentieth century.

Evergreen. 1978.

Random Winds. 1980.

Eden Burning. 1982.

Crescent City. 1984.

Golden Cup. 1986.

Tapestry. 1988.

Blessings. 1989.

Harvest. 1990.

Treasures. 1992.

Whispers. 1993.

Daybreak. 1994.

The Carousel. 1995.

Promises. 1996.

Secrecy. 1997.

Homecoming. 1997.

Legacy of Silence. 1998.

Fortune's Hand. 1999.

After the Fire. 2000.

Looking Back. 2001.

Her Father's House. 2002.

The Sight of the Stars. 2003.

Crossroads. 2004.

Heartwood. 2011.

Roberts, Nora.

Best known for her romantic suspense novels, Nora Roberts's prolific, decades-spanning career began in category romance, and she continues to write single-title and series contemporary romance, often organized into trilogies. Though they have strong romantic elements and span a variety of subgenres of women's fiction, her novels always maintain a strong focus on women's lives. In recognition of her many accomplishments and innovations in romance fiction, the Romance Writers of America gave Roberts its Lifetime Achievement Award in 1997. Roberts is also a member of the Romance Writers of America Hall of Fame for winning multiple awards in the long contemporary romance, romantic suspense, and contemporary single-title romance categories. Many of Roberts's early category romances have been repackaged and republished several times; this list reflects the original titles and publication dates for her novels.

As J. D. Robb, she writes a futuristic romantic suspense series featuring police inspector Eve Dallas. Since those novels fit more within the suspense/police procedural genre, they are not included in this list.

Irish Thoroughbred. 1981.

Blithe Images. 1982.

Song of the West. 1982.

Search for Love. 1982.

Island of Flowers. 1982.

The Heart's Victory. 1982.

From This Day. 1983.

Her Mother's Keeper. 1983.

Once More with Feeling. 1983.

Reflections. 1983.

Tonight and Always. 1983.

Dance of Dreams. 1983.

Untamed. 1983.

This Magic Moment. 1983.

Endings and Beginnings. 1984.

Storm Warning. 1984.

Promise Me Tomorrow. 1984.

Sullivan's Woman. 1984.

First Impression. 1984.

A Matter of Choice. 1984.

Less of a Stranger. 1984.

The Law Is a Lady. 1984.

Rules of the Game. 1984.

Opposites Attract. 1984.

Playing the Odds. 1985.

The Right Path. 1985.

Partners. 1985.

Tempting Fate. 1985.

Night Moves. 1985.

All the Possibilities. 1985.

One Man's Art. 1985.

Boundary Lines. 1985.

Summer Desserts. 1985.

Dual Image. 1985.

Second Nature. 1986.

The Art of Deception. 1986.

One Summer. 1986.

Affaire Royale. 1986.

Lessons Learned. 1986.

Treasures Lost, Treasures Found. 1986.

Risky Business. 1986.

A Will and a Way. 1986.

Home for Christmas. 1986.

For Now, Forever. 1987.

Mind over Matter. 1987.

Command Performance. 1987.

Hot Ice. 1987.

Temptation. 1987.

The Playboy Prince. 1987.

Sacred Sins. 1987.

Local Hero. 1988.

Irish Rose. 1988.

The Last Honest Woman. 1988.

Brazen Virtue. 1988.

Dance to the Piper. 1988.

Rebellion. 1988.

Skin Deep. 1988.

The Name of the Game. 1988.

Sweet Revenge. 1988.

Loving Jack. 1989.

Best Laid Plans. 1989.

Lawless. 1989.

Impulse. 1989.

Gabriel's Angel. 1989.

The Welcoming. 1989.

Time Was. 1989.

Times Change. 1990.

Public Secrets. 1990.

Taming Natasha. 1990.

Without a Trace. 1990.

In from the Cold. 1990.

Night Shift. 1991.

Night Shadow. 1991.

Courting Catherine. 1991.

A Man for Amanda. 1991.

For the Love of Lilah. 1991.

Genuine Lies. 1991.

Suzanna's Surrender. 1991.

Luring a Lady. 1991.

Carnal Innocence. 1991.

Unfinished Business. 1992.

Honest Illusions. 1992.

Captivated. 1992.

Divine Evil. 1992.

Entranced. 1992.

Charmed. 1992.

Falling for Rachel. 1993.

Private Scandals. 1993.

Nightshade. 1993.

Convincing Alex. 1994.

The Best Mistake. 1994.

Hidden Riches. 1994.

Night Smoke. 1994.

Born in Fire. 1994.

All I Want for Christmas. 1994.

The Return of Rafe MacKade. 1995.

Born in Ice. 1995.

True Betrayals. 1995.

The Pride of Jared MacKade. 1995.

Born in Shame. 1996.

The Heart of Devin MacKade. 1996.

Montana Sky. 1996.

The Fall of Shane MacKade. 1996.

Daring to Dream. 1996.

Megan's Mate. 1996.

Holding the Dream. 1997.

Waiting for Nick. 1997.

Sanctuary. 1997.

Finding the Dream. 1997.

Hidden Star. 1997.

The MacGregor Brides. 1997.

Captive Star. 1997.

Sea Swept. 1998.

Secret Star. 1998.

Homeport. 1998.

Rising Tides. 1998.

The Reef. 1998.

The Winning Hand. 1998.

The MacGregor Grooms. 1998.

Inner Harbor. 1999.

The Perfect Neighbor. 1999.

River's End. 1999.

Enchanted. 1999.

Jewels of the Sun. 1999.

Carolina Moon. 2000.

Irish Rebel. 2000.

Tears of the Moon. 2000.

Night Shield. 2000.

Heart of the Sea. 2000.

Considering Kate. 2001.

The Villa. 2001.

Dance upon the Air. 2001.

Midnight Bayou. 2001.

Heaven and Earth. 2001.

Cordina's Crown Jewel. 2002.

Three Fates. 2002.

Face the Fire. 2002.

Chesapeake Blue. 2002.

Birthright. 2003.

Remember When. 2003.

Key of Light. 2003.

Key of Knowledge. 2003.

Key of Valor. 2004.

Northern Lights. 2004.

Blue Dahlia. 2004.

Black Rose. 2005.

Blue Smoke. 2005.

Red Lily. 2005.

Angels Fall. 2006.

Morrigan's Cross. 2006.

Dance of the Gods. 2006.

Valley of Silence. 2006.

High Noon. 2007.

Blood Brothers. 2007.

The Hollow. 2008.

Tribute. 2008.

The Pagan Stone. 2008.

Vision in White. 2009.

Black Hills. 2009.

Bed of Roses. 2009.

Savor the Moment. 2010.

The Search. 2010.

Happy Ever After. 2010.

Chasing Fire. 2011.

The Next Always. 2011.

The Witness. 2012.

The Last Boyfriend. 2012.

The Perfect Hope. 2012.

Whiskey Beach. 2013.

Dark Witch. 2013.

Steel, Danielle.

Danielle Steel published her first novel in 1972, and has published over eighty best selling novels for adults, as well as several volumes of nonfiction and a series of books for children. Steel's novels feature both contemporary and historical settings, as well as wealthy, glamorous women caught up in dramatic situations. Though her novels frequently have strong romantic elements, the main focus is on the lives and relationships of women.

Going Home. 1973.

Passion's Promise. 1977.

Now and Forever. 1978.

The Promise. 1978.

Season of Passion. 1980.
Summer's End. 1980.
The Ring. 1980.
To Love Again. 1981.
Loving. 1981.
Palomino. 1982.
Crossings. 1982.
A Perfect Stranger. 1983.
Once in a Lifetime. 1983.
Thurston House. 1983.
Changes. 1983.
Full Circle. 1984.
Family Album. 1985.
Secrets. 1985.
Wanderlust. 1986.
Fine Things. 1987.
Kaleidoscope. 1987.
Zoya. 1988.
Star. 1989.
Daddy. 1989.
Message from Nam. 1990.
Heartbeat. 1991.
No Greater Love. 1991.
Jewels. 1992.
Mixed Blessings. 1992.
Vanished. 1993.
Accident. 1994.
The Gift. 1994.
Wings. 1994.
Lightning. 1995.
Five Days in Paris. 1995.
Malice. 1996.
Silent Honor. 1996.
The Ranch. 1997.
Special Delivery. 1997.
The Ghost. 1997.
The Long Road Home. 1998.

The Klone and I. 1998.
Mirror Image. 1998.
Bittersweet. 1999.
Granny Dan. 1999.
Irresistible Forces. 1999.
The Wedding. 2000.
The House on Hope Street. 2000.
Journey. 2000.
Lone Eagle. 2001.
Leap of Faith. 2001.
The Kiss. 2001.
The Cottage. 2002.
Sunset in St. Tropez. 2002.
Answered Prayers. 2002.
Dating Game. 2003.
Johnny Angel. 2003.
Safe Harbour. 2003.
Ransom. 2004.
Second Chance. 2004.
Echoes. 2004.
Impossible. 2005.
Miracle. 2005.
Toxic Bachelors. 2005.
The House. 2006.
Coming Out. 2006.
H. R. H. 2006.
Sisters. 2007.
Bungalow 2. 2007.
Amazing Grace. 2008.
Rogue. 2008.
A Good Woman. 2008.
One Day at a Time. 2009.
Matters of the Heart. 2009.
Southern Lights. 2009.
Big Girl. 2010.
Family Ties. 2010.
Legacy. 2010.

44 Charles Street. 2011.

Happy Birthday. 2011.

Hotel Vendome. 2011.

Betrayal. 2012.

Friends Forever. 2012.

The Sins of the Mother. 2012.

Until the End of Time. 2013.

Chapter 3

Contemporary Women's Fiction

This is the lengthiest chapter in this book, and for good reason—"contemporary women's fiction" covers a lot of ground, and this chapter is our catchall chapter. (We'll cover a variety of subgenres, including issue-driven women's fiction, chick lit, and multicultural women's fiction later in the book.)

The novels annotated in this chapter were generally published within the last twenty years and share the same general appeal factors: contemporary times and places and the realistic portrayal of modern women with modern issues. Twenty years may seem like a long span of time, but many contemporary women's fiction novels from the 1990s have held up well and continue to be popular with readers. Since the stories tend to revolve around universal themes of relationships, there isn't much in them that dates them.

In addition to the contemporary setting, the novels listed in this chapter all share the characteristics we identified in the introduction as the hallmarks of women's fiction:

- the central character (or characters) is female, and the story is character driven;

- the main thrust of the story is something happening in the life of that woman (as opposed to the overarching theme being a romance or a mystery of some sort);

- the setting is contemporary (defined, for the purposes of this volume, as after 1960);

- the author is female; and

- women's emotions and relationships are key elements of the plot.

Humorous fiction does have a separate section in this chapter because it reflects a strong appeal characteristic that is often requested specifically by readers.

Trends in Contemporary Women's Fiction

If chick lit was the trend of the late 1990s and the early 2000s, then beach house novels are the trend of the early 2010s. These books, which tend to have soft-focus covers showing a woman walking on a beach and feature plots centered on women escaping from their daily lives—often with friends or family—to the shore. The style of these novels ranges from light and escapist to serious and literary.

Another trend in contemporary women's fiction is ensemble novels. These books often include alternating points of view, allowing the story to be told from the perspective of several different women. The characters in ensemble novels tend to be friends or family, but this technique is occasionally used to tell a story from the perspective of a wife and a mistress, or a birth mother and an adoptive mother.

General Contemporary Women's Fiction

This is the catchall category within the catchall chapter, and the novels included here represent a broad spectrum of the genre. Included are novels featuring diverse character types and backgrounds, as well as a wide variety of personal, professional, and romantic issues.

Allen, Sarah Addison.

Allen's Southern fiction explores themes of family, friendship, and love with a touch of magic and the supernatural.

Garden Spells. 2007. Bantam. ISBN 9780553805482. 290p.
Sisters Claire and Sydney Waverly couldn't be more different. What they share is their family's legacy, a garden that seems to have magical powers. When Sydney returns to the family's hometown of Bascom, North Carolina, she and her sister must learn to coexist—and to accept all the things that being a Waverly means.

Keywords: Sisters, Southern.

The Sugar Queen. 2008. Bantam Dell. ISBN 0553805495. 288p.
Quiet, quirky Josey prefers being a homebody living at her mother's house, even though her mother treats her like dirt most of the time. That's okay with Josey though: she doesn't expect much else and is fine retreating to her room where she can gorge herself on her hidden cache of sweet treats. When outspoken wild child Della Lee appears, hiding out in Josey's closet, she convinces Josey to stand up for herself and seek the truth about her family.

Keywords: Family, Self-Actualization, Southern.

The Girl Who Chased the Moon. 2010. Bantam. ISBN 9780553807219. 269p.
Emily Benedict arrives in Mullaby, North Carolina, hoping to learn something about her mother, who is in many ways a mystery. But instead of finding answers, Emily finds more questions, as well as an eccentric cast of characters with mysteries of their own.

Keywords: Family, Self-Actualization, Southern.

The Peach Keeper. 2011. Bantam. ISBN 9780553807226. 273p.

Willa Jackson and Paxton Osgood may have grown up together in Walls of Water, North Carolina, but that doesn't mean they're friends. The two women couldn't be more different. Paxton, raised in the lap of luxury by her wealthy family, is renovating a mansion that belonged to Willa's family until they lost it in the 1930s. When a skeleton is dug up on the property and strange events begin happening around town, both women are forced to come to terms with long-buried family secrets.

Keywords: Family, Friendship, Romantic, Southern.

Anshaw, Carol.

Lucky in the Corner. 2002. Houghton Mifflin. ISBN 0395940400. 245p.

Permanent student Fern, her lesbian mother Nora and her lover Jeanne, and her cross-dressing (but straight) uncle Howard are featured in this fun novel, a look at a slightly dysfunctional but very loving family. The most stable family member is Lucky, Fern's dog. When Fern discovers her mother is cheating on Jeanne, the family dynamic is rocked.

Keywords: Family, Mothers and Daughters, Thought-Provoking.

Carry the One. 2012. Simon & Schuster. ISBN 9781451636888. 272p.

Siblings Carmen, Nick, and Alice are followed over the course of twenty years. The novel opens on Carmen's wedding night, when a tragic car accident leaves a young girl dead. The characters are never able to shed their guilt and responsibility.

Keywords: Emotional, Family, Thought-Provoking.

Arsenault, Emily.

Miss Me When I'm Gone. 2012. Morrow. ISBN 9780062103109. 356p.

Jamie is shocked when her best friend from college, Gretchen, dies in a suspicious accident. The two women's trajectories diverged after college—Gretchen became a best-selling author, and Jamie got stuck in a dead-end job—but following Gretchen's death, Jamie becomes Gretchen's literary executor. In the course of her duties, Jamie finds an unfinished manuscript, which hints that her friend's death may not have been an accident.

Keyword: Friendship.

Bache, Ellyn.

The Art of Saying Goodbye. 2011. William Morrow. ISBN 9780062033680. 352p.

Five friends find themselves having to say goodbye when one of them is stricken with cancer. The women draw closer than ever and help each other find the strength to embrace and cherish their lives with acceptance and gratitude.

Keywords: Emotional, Ensemble, Friendship.

Bagshawe, Tilly.

British author Bagshawe writes sexy glitz-and-glamour novels updated for the millennium, in the style of Jackie Collins. In 2009, Bagshawe published the first of four novels based on notes left by Sidney Sheldon, whose glitz-and-glamour potboilers were best sellers in the 1970s and 1980s.

Adored. 2005. Warner. ISBN 0446576883. 560p.

Siena McMahon is the glamorous granddaughter of Hollywood movie legend Duke McMahon. Gorgeous, talented, and ambitious, Siena is on the path to stardom, but obstacles such as illegitimate relatives, jealousy, and true love keep getting in her way.

Keywords: Glitzy, Romantic.

Fame. 2013. Montlake Romance. ISBN 9781612184630. 462p.

A film remake of *Wuthering Heights* sets the stage for this Hollywood-themed glitz-and-glamour novel featuring a child star turned bad-girl grown-up, a sexy British leading man, and a legendary director with a tarnished reputation.

Keywords: Glitzy.

Flawless. 2013. Montlake Romance. ISBN 9781612186948. 468p.

Love triangles, steamy sex, and the glamorous diamond industry anchor the story of Scarlett Drummond Murray, a model-turned-jewelry designer whose outspoken criticism of conditions faced by diamond miners places her at the center of controversy and scandal.

Scandalous. 2013. Montlake Romance. ISBN 9781612184647. 380p.

Sasha Miller is a driven young college student who falls prey to Theo Dexter, a sleazy professor who seduces her, then steals her work and passes it off as his own. Years later, she's the wealthy, powerful head of her own corporation, but she hasn't forgiven Theo for what he did to her. She teams up with Theo's ex-wife, and they plan the revenge of a lifetime.

Keyword: Glitzy.

Baker, Tiffany.

The Gilly Salt Sisters. 2012. Grand Central. ISBN 9780446194235. 372p.

Raised on their parents' salt farm on Cape Cod, the two Gilly sisters, Jo and Claire, navigate life differently. Jo's childhood friend Whit, heir to the fortune of the town's wealthiest family, falls in love with (and marries) Claire, offering her an escape from the drudgery of home. Years later, the revelation of family secrets brings Claire back to the island and forces both sisters to face their family's history.

Keywords: Family, Sisters.

Bank, Melissa.

The Wonder Spot. 2005. Viking. ISBN 0670034118. 336p.

Sophie, a witty, self-deprecating suburban child, grows up into an astute young woman. Over the course of twenty years she struggles to define herself throughout Hebrew school, college, and her first job. Her family plays a big role in the story as well, from her grandmother's descent into senility, her quiet father and high-strung mother, and her two brothers.

Keywords: Coming-of-Age, Family, Self-Actualization.

Barbieri, Heather.

The Cottage at Glass Beach. 2012. Harper. ISBN 9780062107961. 320p.

When her politician husband has a very public affair, Nora Cunningham escapes with her two daughters to an island off the coast of Maine to regroup and heal. As mysterious events begin to occur on the island, the locals are reminded of the long-ago disappearance of Nora's mother, and Nora is forced to confront her family's past in order to figure out what her future will hold.

Keywords: Emotional, Family, Mothers and Daughters.

Barry, Brunonia.

*The Map of True Places. 2010. Morrow. ISBN 9780061979217. 416p.

Zee, a psychologist, has just lost a bipolar patient to suicide. This hits too close to home—Zee's mother also suffered from bipolar disorder and committed suicide when Zee was younger. Needing a break from her life, Zee escapes to Salem, Massachusetts, to take care of her father, who is rapidly deteriorating from Parkinson's. Zee uncovers family secrets and comes to terms with many issues in her life.

Keywords: Family, Self-Actualization, Thought-Provoking.

Bass, Elizabeth.

Wherever Grace Is Needed. 2011. Kensington. ISBN 9780758235121. 352p.

Grace returns to her hometown of Austin, Texas, to care for her ailing father. Things are worse than she realized—he is in the early stages of Alzheimer's, and has been taking care of the two abandoned teenagers who live next door to him.

Keywords: Family, Thought-Provoking.

Bauer, Ann.

The Forever Marriage. 2012. Overlook. ISBN 9781590207215. 320p.

Carmen's marriage has been little more than a sham, so when her husband dies, she's relieved—but also shocked by her grief. The most surprising outcome of Carmen's widowhood is the way it forces her to take a critical look at herself and the choices she's made with her life, and she isn't satisfied with what she finds.

Keywords: Family, Marriage, Thought-Provoking.

Bauermeister, Erica.

The School of Essential Ingredients. 2009. Berkley. ISBN 9780425232095. 261p.
Lillian has a gift for cooking, and she shares her gift with others via a series of Monday night cooking classes at her restaurant. The eight students in the class each come bearing their own burdens, and all seek—and find—release through the act of making and enjoying gourmet food.

Keywords: Ensemble, Friendship.

Joy for Beginners. 2011. Putnam. ISBN 9780399157127. 288p.
Breast cancer survivor Kate challenges her six best friends to each do something meaningful—and in some cases, terrifying. From whitewater rafting to getting a tattoo to finally clearing the house of an ex-husband's belongings, the women help each other achieve these small but gratifying goals.

Keywords: Emotional, Ensemble, Friendship.

Berentson, Jane.

Miss Harper Can Do It. 2009. Viking. May 2009. ISBN 9780670020775. 322p.
Annie Harper's boyfriend David is deployed to Iraq in 2003, and she begins a journal for herself, envisioning a blockbuster memoir. Instead of a sappy tell-all, however, she ends up using the journal to vent, fantasize, clear her head, and figure out what she wants from her relationship. She alternates between missing David deeply and being angry with him for leaving. To quell her loneliness, she volunteers at a nursing home, becoming friends with a woman whose husband may have been a World War II hero. Meanwhile, her best friend, Gus, becomes more and more attractive, and Annie has to determine whether or not this is a symptom of missing David.

Keywords: Emotional, Thought-Provoking.

Berg, Elizabeth.

Berg writes about everyday life, tragedies large and small, and the search for happiness in its many forms.

*Durable Goods. 1993. Random House. ISBN 0679422080. 192p.
Set in the early 1960s, Berg's debut follows Katie, a twelve-year-old Army brat who is still reeling over her mother's death from cancer. Katie copes with the trials and triumphs of growing up without the loving care of her mother. Her guides through this difficult time are her older sister, Diane, and her best friend, Cherylanne.

Keywords: Family, Friendship, Self-Actualization.

Joy School. 1997. Random House. ISBN 0345423097. 208p.

> Berg revisits Katie Nash, the heroine of *Durable Goods*, in this sequel, which explores Katie's life after her family relocates to Missouri. Katie's quest for her place in the world continues, as she befriends a variety of misfit characters, develops a crush on a kindred spirit, and struggles to gain the acceptance of her father. Followed by *True to Form* (2002).
>
> **Keywords:** Coming-of-Age, Family, Friendship, Self-Actualization.

Open House. 2000. Random House. ISBN 0375501002. 201p.

> Samantha's husband walks out after twenty years of a crumbling marriage, leaving her with no job, a house to pay for, and a preteen son. To help with the mortgage, she decides to open her house to roomers. The various people she meets and becomes friends with boost her self-confidence; and she discovers there really is life after divorce.
>
> **Keywords:** Family, Marriage, Thought-Provoking.

The Year of Pleasures. 2005. Random House. 2005. ISBN 1400061601. 206p.

> After the death of her husband, Betta Nolan relocates to a small town with the hope of starting a new life. In her new home, Betta finds unexpected friendships with her new neighbors, including a ten-year-old boy and a young adult who is just beginning to learn who he is.
>
> **Keywords:** Friendship, Thought-Provoking.

The Last Time I Saw You: A Novel. 2010. Random House. ISBN 9781400068647. 244p.

> Berg takes a crack at the high school reunion trope with this exploration of four men and women attending their fortieth reunion. Each character brings elements of his or her past, and each has hopes for what might happen, whether it's reconnecting with a classmate or resurrecting a lost love.
>
> **Keyword:** Friendship.

Once Upon a Time, There Was You. 2011. Ballantine. ISBN 9780345517326. 304p.

> Irene knew on her wedding day that her marriage to John would not work out. Years later, divorced and having moved on long ago, they are still connected by their daughter, Sadie. When a tragedy strikes, they must come together to support her.
>
> **Keywords:** Family, Thought-Provoking.

Tapestry of Fortunes. 2013. Random House. ISBN 9780812993141. 240p.

> Cecilia Ross may make her living as a motivational speaker, but she has a difficult time sorting her own life out. After she receives a postcard from the one who got away, she makes the sort of bold, life-altering decision she's always avoided and goes on an unforgettable road trip in hopes of changing her life.
>
> **Keywords:** Friendship, Thought-Provoking.

Bernier, Nichole.

The Unfinished Work of Elizabeth D. 2012. Crown. ISBN 9780307887801. 320p.
Kate mourns the unexpected death of her best friend, Elizabeth. When she receives a trunk full of Elizabeth's old journals, Kate realizes there was a side of Elizabeth that she never knew—that possibly, no one knew. As Kate reads on, she discovers her friend was deeply discontent with life and starts to question the choices she's made herself.

Keywords: Self-Actualization, Thought-Provoking.

Bird, Sarah.

The Boyfriend School. 1989. Ballantine. ISBN 9780345460097. 368p.
Photographer Gretchen is sent to cover the annual Luvboree, a romance writer's convention. There she meets Juanita and Lizzie, who think she needs to make over her love life. Lizzie sets her up with her nerdy brother, but he's quickly tossed aside as Gretchen becomes obsessed with a hunky mystery man.

Keywords: Humorous, Romantic.

The Gap Year. 2011. Knopf. ISBN 9780307592798. 301p.
When teenage Aubrey discovers romance with a popular classmate, single mom Camilla doesn't quite know how to handle things. Their relationship becomes further muddied when Camilla's long-estranged ex-husband contacts Aubrey in secret.

Keywords: Coming-of-Age, Mothers and Daughters.

Block, Ellen.

The Language of Sand. 2010. Bantam. ISBN 9780440245759. 276p.
When a tragic accident kills Abigail Harker's husband and son, the life she loved collapses. In an attempt to heal, she relocates to Chapel Isle, along North Carolina's outer banks, where she encounters a cast of colorful characters, all struggling to make sense of their lives just as she is. Followed by *The Definition of Wind* (2011).

Keywords: Emotional, Family, Friendship, Southern.

Blume, Judy.

Summer Sisters. 1998. Delacorte. ISBN 0385324057. 400p.
Caitlin and Vix are "summer sisters," who meet up every year for summer vacation in New England. Caitlin is wealthy and beautiful, while Vix comes from a poor, troubled home. They grow up together over several summers, testing the limits and strengthening their intense bond. An older title, but perennially popular with readers.

Keywords: Beach, Friendship.

Bockoven, Georgia.

The Year Everything Changed. 2011. Morrow. ISBN 9780062069320. 416p.
Jessie Reed's dying wish is to reunite with his four daughters, who he abandoned. All four women are affected in different ways by their absent father, who has cast a pall over their lives and influenced the choices they have made. As the sisters get to know one another and reacquaint themselves with their father, they are forced to make choices that will impact their lives forever.

Keywords: Emotional, Family, Sisters.

Bradford, Barbara Taylor.

Bradford's early sagas helped shape the women's fiction genre, and spawned many imitators, especially during the saga craze of the 1980s.

Harte Family saga.

Born to a poor family in Yorkshire, Emma Harte is expected to live a life of poverty and servitude. Emma's drive, ambition, and desire to rise above her family's station help her establish Harte's, a world-renowned department store. The novels in the Harte Family saga follow the lives of Emma and her descendants as they manage both the Harte business empire and their rocky but romantic personal lives.

A Woman of Substance. 1979.

Hold the Dream. 1985.

To Be the Best. 1988.

Emma's Secret . 2004.

Unexpected Blessings. 2005.

Just Rewards. 2006.

Ravenscar trilogy.

Bradford's Ravenscar trilogy is a modern retelling of the story of the Wars of the Roses, with contemporary characters standing in for the Yorks, Plantagenets, and Tudors. Like the Harte Family saga, the Ravenscar trilogy follows a family through the major events of the twentieth century.

The Ravenscar Dynasty. 2006.

The Heir. 2007.

Being Elizabeth. 2008

Playing the Game. 2010. St. Martin's. ISBN 0312578083. 400p.
Art dealer Annette Remington is at the peak of her career. A self-made woman, she rose to prominence in the high-stakes world of art dealers thanks to her persistence—and some help from people in high places. When Annette auctions off a rare, long-lost Rembrandt, it's a career-making move,

but it also puts her in touch with journalist Jack Chalmers, whose connection with Annette sets off a chain of events that could destroy both her marriage and her career.

Keywords: Family, Marriage.

Letter from a Stranger. 2012. St. Martin's. ISBN 0312631685. 432p.

Justine was always close to her late grandmother, Gabriele, and a return to her childhood home brings Justine's loss back to the forefront of her life. When Justine discovers a mysterious letter, it sends her on a quest to uncover her grandmother's secrets and set right the mistakes of the past.

Keywords: Family, Romantic.

Secrets from the Past. 2013. St. Martin's. ISBN 9780312631666. 368p.

Second-generation war photographer Serena Stone has always gone to great lengths to get to the heart of a story, but when her father dies unexpectedly, she must reevaluate her priorities. In the aftermath of his death, she is drawn to a former lover and fellow journalist, and the two heal from their wounds together. As Serena delves into her father's body of work, she discovers that her family is not what it seemed.

Keywords: Family, Grief, Romantic.

Brashares, Ann.

The Last Summer of You and Me. 2007. Riverhead. ISBN 1594489173. 320p.

Sisters Alice and Riley fight for the affection of their best childhood friend, Paul. Alice likes him romantically, while Riley remains platonic but doesn't want to give him up to her sister. When Riley falls seriously ill, must Paul and Alice give in to her wishes and remain only friends?

Keywords: Emotional, Family, Sisters.

Brown, Eleanor.

🎗 *The Weird Sisters.* 2011. Amy Einhorn Books. ISBN 9780399157226. 320p.

The three Andreas sisters are daughters of an eccentric Shakespeare professor who named his girls after the playwright's most famous characters. Each woman has a personal problem that brings her back to her childhood home, and they must learn to navigate their pasts as well as come to terms with their parents' complicated legacy.

Keywords: Family, Sisters.

Buchan, Elizabeth.

Buchan's novels feature strong women and realistic story lines about the ups and downs of relationships. Her focus is on middle-aged women, generally in their forties and fifties.

Revenge of the Middle-Aged Woman. 2003. Viking. ISBN 0670032069. 368p.

London editor Rose has admirably juggled being a wife, mother, and career woman for the last twenty-five years. Then she discovers her husband is leaving her for a much younger woman—her assistant, to add insult to injury. As she picks up the pieces of her shattered life, she begins to realize that living well is the best revenge. Followed by *Wives Behaving Badly* (2006).

Keywords: Humorous, Older Women.

The Good Wife Strikes Back. 2004. Penguin. ISBN 0143034499. 304p.
Fanny Savage has spent almost twenty years being the ideal wife to her politician husband, but she craves a change. Before she married, she had a successful career in her family's wine business, and she longs to return to her old life. But is it too late to go back?

Keywords: Humorous, Older Women, Self-Actualization.

Everything She Thought She Wanted. 2005. Penguin. ISBN 0143037005. 350p.
Chic Siena Grant is a successful fashion consultant with an enviable life and a stable marriage. Her husband wants to start a family and move to the country, but Siena worries about what the change will mean for her career—and her happiness. Siena's story is juxtaposed with the story of Barbara Beeching, a 1950s housewife with two children who has a passionate affair with a much younger man. Have times changed, or are women still stuck in predetermined roles?

Keywords: Humorous, Older Women, Self-Actualization.

Separate Beds. 2011. Viking. ISBN 0670022365. 484p.
Annie is pretty sure her marriage to Tom is over, and she's ready to ask for a divorce when Tom's mother is diagnosed with dementia and must move in with them. To compound things, their son Jake is also moving back home with his baby daughter in tow. Despite their differences, they must all learn to be a family in now-cramped quarters.

Keywords: Family, Older Women.

Buxbaum, Julie.

After You. 2010. Dial. ISBN 9780385341257. 368p.
When her best friend Lucy is murdered, Ellie drops everything and travels to England to help Lucy's family, especially Lucy's eight-year-old daughter Sophie, who witnessed the crime. Unable to cope with the loss of her mother, Sophie has stopped speaking and retreated into herself, and it is up to Ellie to find a way to reach the troubled young girl. As she works with Sophie, Ellie discovers startling secrets about the best friend she thought she knew.

Keywords: Friendship, Grief.

Carter, Mary.

The Things I Do For You. 2012. Kensington. ISBN 9780758253378. 375p.
Bailey Jordan's life is shaken up when her husband is seriously injured in an automobile accident. The accident causes the couple to reevaluate their priorities, and Brad decides to make his dream of converting a lighthouse

into a bed-and-breakfast into a reality. As Bailey and Brad work together to renovate the lighthouse, a secret is revealed that causes Bailey to question her marriage.

Keywords: Marriage, Family.

Chamberlin, Holly.

Chamberlin writes emotional, often romantic women's fiction featuring families and friendships.

*One Week in December. 2009. Kensington. ISBN 9780758214058. 352p.

Becca became pregnant when she was sixteen, and her parents convinced her to allow her brother and sister-in-law to adopt the baby. Unhappy with this decision, Becca has distanced herself from the family. Now thirty-two, she has decided it's time to reclaim her daughter, much to the dismay of the rest of the family.

Keywords: Emotional, Family.

The Family Beach House. 2010. Kensington. ISBN 9780758235060. 352p.

The McQueen siblings gather at Larchmere, the family's beach house on the Maine coast, to commemorate the death of their mother. Tensions rise when the siblings realize that their father's plan to marry his younger girlfriend could cause them to lose the house that they believe to be their birthright, and they are forced to confront their family's past—and their shared future.

Keywords: Beach, Ensemble, Family.

The Summer of Us. 2012. Kensington. ISBN 9780758277336. 480p.

This novel explores the personal lives of three women who become unexpected roommates on a summer vacation: Gincy, who escaped her poor upbringing and is now happy with her career and loving the single life in Boston. When a single dad catches her eye, her fear of commitment might stop their relationship before it gets off the ground. Danielle is used to the good life, with high society and frills, so why is she falling for a fisherman? Meanwhile blue-blooded Clare lets her boyfriend take charge of pretty much everything, and she's finally growing tired of it.

Keywords: Beach, Ensemble, Romantic.

Last Summer. 2012. Kensington. ISBN 9780758235084. 318p.

Jane and Frannie are best friends, and so are their daughters, Rosie and Meg. During the girls' freshman year of high school, Rosie is targeted by a group of bullies, and Meg abandons her. When Rosie suffers a breakdown, Jane blames Frannie and Meg for not standing by Rosie, and all four women are unsure if the friendships can be salvaged.

Keyword: Friendship.

Close, Jennifer.

The Smart One. 2013. Knopf. ISBN 9780307596864. 352p.

Weezy's parents always called her "the smart one," while her sister was "the pretty one." She has defied her family's expectations, marrying well and raising three lovely children, who are now grown up. But now Weezy's adult children are facing personal and professional crises of their own, and as they return to the once-empty nest, Weezy has to find a way to cope with their perpetual childhood—and her own, too.

Keywords: Ensemble, Family.

Collins, Jackie.

Though Collins's writing career stretches back into the late 1960s, her novels epitomize the glitzy excesses of the 1980s.

Santangelo Family series.

Collins's best-known series follows the Santangelo family, including patriarch Gino Santangelo, a former gangster, and his "dangerously beautiful" daughter, Lucky. Expect sex, drugs, and violence—and lots of it.

Chances. 1981.

Lucky. 1985.

Lady Boss. 1990.

Vendetta: Lucky's Revenge. 1996.

Dangerous Kiss. 1999.

Drop Dead Beautiful. 2007.

Goddess of Vengeance. 2011.

Hollywood series.

Collins's sex-and-scandal-soaked series was originally intended as an expose of the darker side of the glamour capitol of the world. Though each novel stands alone, there are recurring characters throughout the series.

Hollywood Wives. 1983.

Hollywood Husbands. 1986.

Hollywood Kids. 1994.

Hollywood Wives: The New Generation. 2001.

Hollywood Divorces. 2003.

Dave, Laura.

The Divorce Party. 2008. Viking. ISBN 9780670018598. 244p.
Gwyn and Thomas Huntington have brought their friends and family together at their storied Long Island home for an unusual occasion—a celebration of their divorce. At the same time, their son Nate is introducing his fiancée Maggie to the family for the first time, and Maggie learns of a family secret that could forever change her relationship with Nate.

Keywords: Ensemble, Family, Humorous, Marriage.

The First Husband. 2011. Viking. ISBN 9780670022670. 246p.
>   Annie's orderly life is thrown into chaos when her boyfriend leaves her for a woman from his past. When a rebound relationship gets serious, Annie marries her new beau, thinking she's made the right decision. Then Nick reappears, looking for a second chance, and Annie finds herself unmoored yet again—and forced to make a difficult decision between the two men.
>
>   **Keywords:** Humorous, Marriage.

Dawson, Maddie.

The Stuff That Never Happened. 2010. Shaye Areheart. ISBN 9780307393678. 325p.
>   After thirty years, Annabelle and Grant's perfect-on-the-outside marriage is in crisis. A betrayal that took place when the couple first married has come back to haunt them, and Annabelle wonders what might have happened if she had made different choices. A chance encounter brings Annabelle and her former lover back together, and she must choose between her steady, stable marriage and the potential for romance and excitement.
>
>   **Keywords:** Family, Marriage.

de los Santos, Marisa.

De los Santos writes contemporary women's fiction featuring themes of friendship and family.

Love Walked In. 2005. Dutton. ISBN 0525949178. 320p.
>   Cornelia becomes part of a dysfunctional family when she falls for handsome Martin. Martin seems like an old-time movie star and things are pretty perfect until one day he shows up at Cornelia's café with the secret he's been hiding—his ten-year-old daughter, Claire. Although Cornelia never thought she had it in her to be a parent or role model, she finds herself relishing the role of mom, even as her relationship with Martin loses its luster.
>
>   **Keywords:** Family, Mothers and Daughters.

*Belong to Me. 2008. Morrow. ISBN 0061240273. 400p.
>   Cornelia and Teo, best friends since childhood and now happily married, move to the suburbs to start a family. When Cornelia meets the beguiling and mysterious free spirit Lake, the two women become fast friends. Unfortunately, Lake has an ulterior motive and is keeping a big secret from her new friend.
>
>   **Keywords:** Family, Friendship, Thought-Provoking.

*Falling Together. 2011. William Morrow. ISBN 9780061670879. 368p.
>   Pen, Cat, and Will meet on their first day of college and seem destined for lifelong friendship, but the realities of adulthood get in the way. After years of estrangement, Cat contacts Pen and Will with an urgent request to meet up at their college reunion. Pen's suspicious, but agrees, and she and Will discover Cat's been hiding something that she desperately needs help with.
>
>   **Keywords:** Ensemble, Friendship.

Drake, Abby.

The Secrets Sisters Keep. 2010. William Morrow. ISBN 0061878324. 320p.
Ellie, Amanda, Babe, and Carleen are extremely dissimilar sisters who tend to stay away from one another's drama. When their eccentric and vaguely famous uncle throws himself a blockbuster birthday party and then disappears just as the guests are arriving, the women are forced to reconnect and help each other out.

Keywords: Ensemble, Family, Sisters.

Evans, Harriet.

Evans writes contemporary British women's fiction with a romantic feel.

The Love of Her Life. 2009. Downtown Press. ISBN 1439113157. 448p.
Londoner Kate needs to escape her life after it all shatters, so she runs away to live with her mother and stepfather in New York. When her father falls ill, she must return to London and confront her past.

Keywords: Emotional, Grief, Thought-Provoking.

I Remember You. 2010. Downtown Press. ISBN 1439182000. 464p.
Tess Tennant relocates from bustling London to her childhood home in English countryside for the job of her dreams. Life in Langford is much slower than life in London, but Tess finds comfort with Adam, her best friend from childhood. Old feelings are rekindled, and a confrontation between the two friends leads Tess to Rome and a fling with an American journalist.

Keywords: Emotional, Romantic, Self-Actualization.

Love Always. 2011. Gallery Books. ISBN 9781451639629. 480p.
When Natasha returns to Cornwall for her grandmother's funeral, she discovers her large extended family is harboring many secrets. Her grandfather shows her the diary of her aunt Cecily, who died in a tragic accident as when she was just a teenager. Within the diary's pages, Natasha finds a tale of forbidden love and heartbreak.

Keywords: Family, Grief, Romantic.

Happily Ever After. 2012. Gallery Books. ISBN 9781451677263. 474p.
Elle Bee gets her start in publishing during the early years of the British chick lit boom, and she's a bit like a chick lit heroine herself—prone to silly errors on professional correspondence, overindulgence in cocktails, and dubious romantic choices. When a relationship with her boss goes wrong, Elle flees to a job swap in New York City and finds herself. But is she being true to herself, or is she running from her past and her family?

Keywords: Family, Romantic, Self-Actualization, Workplace.

Fay, Juliette.

Shelter Me. 2009. Avon. ISBN 9780061673399. 415p.

Grief rules Janie LaMarche's life. Her husband died four months ago, and she is still coming to terms with her loss. When a contractor unexpectedly shows up to add a porch to her suburban Boston house, she realizes that it's a final gift from her husband—and an opportunity to heal.

Keywords: Emotional, Family.

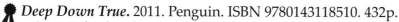 *Deep Down True.* 2011. Penguin. ISBN 9780143118510. 432p.

A year after her divorce, Dana still isn't quite over it. Her children are not coping well, and her ex can't keep up with his child support payments. When her teenage niece runs away from home and begs Dana to take her in, it just might be the shake-up she needs to get her life back on track.

Keywords: Family, Self-Actualization.

Fishman, Zoe.

Balancing Acts. 2010. HarperCollins. ISBN 0061711802. 384p.

Four women who haven't seen each other since college meet again at their ten-year reunion and join the new yoga studio that one of them is starting. Charlie has left her high-stress banking job to open the studio, Naomi used to be a hot photographer and media darling but is now a struggling single mom, Sabine is a frustrated writer, and Bess has a job at a tabloid but dreams of working on real news.

Keywords: Ensemble, Friendship.

Saving Ruth. 2012. Morrow. ISBN 9780062059840. 280p.

Nineteen-year-old Ruth Wasserman is a fish out of water in her Alabama town. During her freshman year of college, she lost a substantial amount of weight, which changes the way others look at her—but not the way she sees herself. Ruth's summer job as a lifeguard opens her eyes about her hometown and helps her to face some of her body-image issues and repair her problematic relationship with her family.

Keywords: Coming-of-Age, Friendship, Self-Actualization.

Frank, Dorothea Benton.

Frank's novels take place in the coastal towns of South Carolina and feature everyday women in realistic situations, often dealing with family and friends.

Sullivan's Island: A Lowcountry Tale. 1999. Berkley. ISBN 0739408372. 383p.

Susan Hayes isn't sure how she ended up in her current situation. Her marriage is collapsing, her teenage daughter is distant, and her work is unfulfilling. But her memories are strong, and she returns to her childhood home (now occupied by her sister) on South Carolina's Sullivan's Island to heal and to rebuild her life.

Keywords: Emotional, Family, Self-Actualization, Southern.

Return to Sullivan's Island. 2009. Morrow. ISBN 0061438456. 400p.

Beth Hayes has just graduated from college, and she has returned home to South Carolina's Lowcountry to spend a year house-sitting at her family's beachfront home. Beth's quirky, sprawling extended family help make her year at Island Gamble unforgettable.

Keywords: Coming-of-Age, Family, Southern.

Folly Beach. 2011. Morrow. ISBN 9780061961274. 368p.

After her husband's suicide, Cate returns to her family's beach house on Folly Beach to pick up the pieces of her shattered life. Cate discovers the house's interesting past—a husband and wife helped Gershwin write *Porgy and Bess* there. Interested in this history, Cate discovers she has a talent for writing that she must nurture.

Keywords: Emotional, Grief, Romantic, Self-Actualization, Southern.

Porch Lights. 2012. Morrow. ISBN 9780061961298. 324p.

When Jackie's husband, a New York City firefighter, is killed in the line of duty, she and her grieving son return to Jackie's childhood home on Sullivan's Island, in the South Carolina Lowcountry. As her family and friends help her grieve and regroup, she and her son spend a magical summer exploring the history and nature of the South Carolina coast.

Keywords: Emotional, Family, Friendship, Grief, Southern.

Frankel, Laurie.

The Atlas of Love. 2010. St. Martin's. ISBN 9780312595387. 336p.

When grad student Janey becomes unexpectedly pregnant, her boyfriend splits, leaving her on her own. When Janey's two closest friends (and grad-school colleagues) learn of Janey's predicament, they band together to help her raise her son, even though their approaches to life are often very different.

Keywords: Friendship, Family, Motherhood.

Goodbye for Now. 2012. Doubleday. ISBN 9780385536189. 288p.

Sam Elling is a genius computer programmer whose first invention, an algorithm that helps single people find their soul mates, brought him love and lost him his job with an Internet dating site. When Meredith, Sam's partner, loses her beloved grandmother, Sam sets his mind on a way to give Meredith one last chance to talk to her. The results are surprising, and as the two get further into developing Sam's newest invention, they learn as much about love and loss as they do about themselves.

Keywords: Emotional, Romantic.

Gaffney, Patricia.

Gaffney's novels feature smart and mature women and revolve around their friendships and family relationships. Her characters and situations are realistic.

Circle of Three. 2000. HarperCollins. ISBN 0060193751. 421p.

Recently widowed, Carrie struggles to raise her teenage daughter, Ruth, despite her grief. It doesn't help that just before her husband died, he moved the family back to the town Carrie grew up in—and couldn't wait to escape, thanks to her disapproving mother, Dana. Ruth is having trouble dealing with the loss of her father as well, and Dana is unsure how to handle Carrie's homecoming.

Keywords: Ensemble, Family, Grief, Mothers and Daughters.

Mad Dash. 2007. Crown. ISBN 0307382117. 355p.

Dash and her husband, Andrew, are going through a rocky patch when Dash impulsively leaves him, to live in their vacation cabin in rural Virginia. Coping with both the recent death of her mother and the reality of an empty nest now that their daughter is gone at college, Dash wants freedom from the predictability of life with her somewhat boring spouse.

Keywords: Family, Grief, Marriage, Self-Actualization.

Giffin, Emily

Giffin follows in the footsteps of Jane Green and Jennifer Weiner, with her earlier novels more in the chick lit vein. Her writing matures with each subsequent novel.

Something Borrowed. 2004. St. Martin's. ISBN 031232118X. 336p.

Shy Rachel falls in love with her best friend Darcy's fiancé, Dex. Rachel and Dex knew each other first, but bossy Darcy swooped in and took him over. Turns out Dex was always interested in Rachel, and they embark on an affair. Followed by *Something Blue* (2006), which tells Darcy's side of the story.

Keywords: Friendship, Romantic.

*Baby Proof. 2007. St. Martin's. ISBN 9780312348649. 352p.

Claudia and Ben agreed that they didn't want to have children. After a few years of marriage though, one of their biological clocks starts ticking . . . and surprise, its Ben's. Claudia decides that kids are a deal breaker and consents to a divorce despite being very much in love with her husband. Will either one give in?

Keywords: Marriage, Romantic, Self-Actualization, Thought-Provoking.

Heart of the Matter. 2010. St. Martin's. ISBN 0312554168. 384p.

Stay-at-home mom Tessa thinks she's got a perfect life, until she suspects her husband, Nick, a renowned pediatric specialist, is cheating on her with the mother of one of his young patients. As Nick finds himself getting in deeper and deeper with single mother Valerie is an affair inevitable?

Keyword: Emotional.

*Where We Belong. 2012. St. Martin's. ISBN 9780312554194. 384p.

Marian has a dream job as a TV producer in New York and has convinced everyone, including herself, that her life is perfect. When the daughter she gave up in secret eighteen years ago shows up at her doorstep, things change completely.

Keywords: Emotional, Family, Mothers and Daughters.

Glass, Julia.

*I See You Everywhere. 2008. Pantheon. ISBN 0375422757. 304p.

Cautious and artistic Louisa and her restless, adventurous sister Clem are complete opposites—Louisa owns an art gallery in New York, while Clem is a wildlife specialist working with endangered species. This episodic novel follows the past twenty-five years of their lives, from joys to sorrows, culminating in a reunion at a family funeral.

Keywords: Family, Sisters.

Godwin, Gail.

Godwin's literary novels feature creative and intellectual women dealing with adversity, often in family relationships and issues.

The Odd Woman. 1974. Knopf. 419p.

Jane Clifford is a successful professor of English literature, but beneath her professional success lies a woman plagued by uncertainty. The death of her grandmother brings Jane back home to the South, where she confronts the family and friends who helped shape her.

Keywords: Grief, Self-Actualization.

A Mother and Two Daughters. 1982. Viking. ISBN 0670490210. 564p.

The lives of three very different women (the titular mother and her two daughters) intersect in the context of grief and loss. The daughters, Cate and Lydia, face middle age in very different ways, while their mother tries to process her feelings for her children and her late husband.

Keywords: Ensemble, Mothers and Daughters, Self-Actualization.

Evensong. 1999. Ballantine. ISBN 0345372441. 405p.

Margaret Bonner is the pastor of an Episcopal church in the Smoky Mountain town of High Balsam. As a pastor, she's at the center of her community, which puts her into contact with a variety of local personalities who lead her to self-reflection and questioning of her own life.

Keyword: Self-Actualization.

Unfinished Desires. 2009. Random House. ISBN 9780345483201. 416p.

The antics of three classmates, survivors of an all-girls boarding school in the 1950s, are chronicled here when the prickly headmistress decides to record her memoirs fifty years later.

Keyword: Ensemble.

Goldsmith, Olivia.

The late Goldsmith's novels feature strong, sassy women, often with troubled pasts or secrets.

The First Wives Club. Reprint, 2008. Pocket. ISBN 9781416562832. 576p.

Annie, Brenda, and Elise find themselves dumped for younger models after they have helped their husbands achieve success. When another friend commits suicide after her divorce, the three band together to form the First Wives Club, set on helping each other get revenge.

Keywords: Ensemble, Friendship.

Goudge, Eileen.

Goudge's women's fiction features women dealing with relationships, often broken friendships or family secrets. Several of her novels are pure romances, while others have romantic suspense elements.

Garden of Lies. 1989. Viking. ISBN 9780670824588. 544p.

Sylvie Rosenthal is pregnant, but her husband isn't the father. Afraid that her deception will be discovered, Sylvie takes advantage of a disaster at the hospital and switches her baby with another woman's baby. Her natural daughter is raised in relative poverty, while the other woman's daughter enjoys all the luxuries that Sylvie can provide. When the two girls meet as adults, a dramatic chain of events is set in motion that will force all of the women to confront the truth about their lives.

Keywords: Emotional, Glitzy, Saga.

Immediate Family. 2006. Gallery. ISBN 9780743483193. 352p.

Four college friends reunite at their fifteen-year class reunion, only to find that their lives have taken them in unexpected directions. Despite their glamorous careers, they realize that they rely on their friends to help them solve their problems and find the happiness that has escaped them.

Keywords: Emotional, Ensemble, Friendship.

The Diary. 2009. Vanguard. ISBN 1593155298. 224p.

When Emily and Sarah Marshall discover their mother's old diary, they are especially shocked by one of the secrets within: their father was not the true love of their mother's life. As the sisters delve further into their mother's past, they are forced to confront painful truths about her life.

Keywords: Emotional, Mothers and Daughters.

Once in a Blue Moon. 2009. Vanguard. ISBN 9781593155346. 336p.

When their emotionally unstable mother is sent to prison, sisters Lindsay and Kerrie Ann are sent to separate foster homes. The girls grow up under very different circumstances—Lindsay was placed with a loving couple and becomes a successful bookstore owner, while Kerrie Ann was shuffled from one bad foster home to the next and ends up a drug-addicted single mother. The sisters reunite when Kerrie Ann needs help regaining custody of her daughter.

Keywords: Family, Thought-Provoking.

Green, Jane.

Green's novels feature young women dealing with friendships, jobs, family issues, and romantic relationships, and most are set in Great Britain. She successfully blends witty dialogue and humorous situations with more serious issues, such as infidelity and loss. Her first three novels were at the forefront of the chick lit movement and are included in chapter 6.

To Have and to Hold. 2004. Broadway. ISBN 0767912268. 432p.
> Alice has let herself be molded into a perfect wife by her cheating boor of a husband. When he gets caught philandering at work, his London firm sends him to the United States. She hopes it will be a new beginning for them—but it really turns into a new beginning for her.

Keywords: Family, Thought-Provoking.

The Other Woman. 2005. Viking. ISBN 0670034045. 400p.
> When Ellie becomes engaged to Dan, the man of her dreams, his mother, Linda, becomes her worst nightmare. Needy and controlling, Linda knows exactly what buttons to push in order to get her way. When things with Linda go from bad to worse after Ellie and Dan have a baby, it puts Ellie's whole marriage in jeopardy.

Keywords: Family, Thought-Provoking.

Promises to Keep. 2010. Viking. ISBN 9780670021796. 343p.
> Callie has the kind of life that many women dream of—professional success in a job that she loves, a supportive husband, happy children, and a sister and best friend who provide emotional support. But then tragedy strikes when Callie's breast cancer returns, and this time, it's incurable. Determined to live her last days to the fullest, Callie leans on friends and family to get her through.

Keywords: Family, Friendship.

*Another Piece of My Heart. 2012. St. Martin's. ISBN 9780312591823. 352p.
> Andi has finally found the perfect man, after spending most of her twenties and thirties searching. Ethan, a single dad with two daughters, seems perfect, and Andi is excited to be a stepmother. But the girls have a different opinion on that matter.

Keywords: Family, Mothers and Daughters.

Family Pictures. 2013. St. Martin's. ISBN 9780312591830. 344p.
> Sylvie and Maggie don't know each other—yet. But when their daughters Eve and Grace become friends during their freshman year of college, a secret that will change both families forever is revealed, and both women must right the wrongs of their pasts.

Keywords: Ensemble, Family, Friendship.

Hall, Emylia.

The Book of Summers. 2012. Mira. ISBN 9780778314110. 348p.
> Nine-year-old Erzsi goes on the summer vacation of a lifetime to Hungary, her mother's home country. When summer is over, her parents separate, and her mother stays behind. Each summer, Erzsi visits her mother, but when she is sixteen years old, a family secret destroys their relationship. Years later, Erzsi receives a scrapbook chronicling the summers she spent with her mother, which steers her onto a path of reconciliation and forgiveness.

Keywords: Family, Mothers and Daughters.

Hannah, Kristin.

Hannah's novels are often considered romances (and her early paperback releases truly are); however, the family relationships and the issues that her characters must overcome are hallmarks of women's fiction. She writes about love and loss, complicated relationships, and family secrets, and her novels are often "tearjerkers."

🎗 *Firefly Lane.* 2008. St. Martin's. ISBN 9780312364083. 496p.

Since the mid-1970s drama queen Tully and shy, stable Kate have been inseparable best friends. When they grow up, move into careers, and fall in love, life has different plans for them. Kate falls in love with Tully's ex, and Tully gets her revenge publicly years later. Followed by *Fly Away* (2013).

Keyword: Friendship.

True Colors. 2009. St. Martin's. ISBN 9780312364106. 393p.

Though their personalities could not be more different, Winona, Aurora, and Vivi Ann Grey became inseparable after the death of their mother, but dramatic circumstances and relationships gone wrong threaten their close bond. When Vivi Ann's husband is arrested for murder, the sisters must band together to heal old wounds and forgive those who have hurt them.

Keywords: Ensemble, Sisters.

🎗 *Winter Garden.* 2010. St. Martin's. ISBN 9780312364120. 394p.

Sisters Meredith and Nina Whitson have always followed different paths, both as children and as adults. The one thing that they do have in common is their love for their father, who is dying. His death brings Meredith and Nina back together, along with their mother, who tells them a love story so unexpected and shocking that it leads the sisters on a quest for the truth about their family.

Keywords: Family, Sisters.

🎗 *Night Roads.* 2011. St. Martin's. ISBN 9780312364427. 385p.

Jude Farraday is completely devoted to—and perhaps slightly overprotective of—her teenage twins, Mia and Zach. When a troubled young woman named Lexi enters their lives, Jude embraces her as one of her own, but a tragic accident changes everything.

Keywords: Emotional, Family, Motherhood.

Home Front. 2012. St. Martin's. ISBN 9780312577209. 400p.

Jolene, a National Guard pilot, fears her marriage to Michael is falling apart. Then an unexpected deployment sends Jolene to Iraq and leaves Michael at home, unaccustomed to being a single parent to their two little girls.

Keywords: Emotional, Family, Thought-Provoking.

Harding, Robyn.

Unraveled. 2008. Berkley. ISBN 9780425224625. 308p.

After a bad breakup, Beth is coerced into joining a knitting circle as way to "get over it"—something she's not sure she needs to do. It turns out that her new hobby is just what she needed to jump-start her life. But when her new boyfriend is not all that he seems, Beth leans on her new friends for support.

Keyword: Friendship.

Chronicles of a Midlife Crisis. 2010. Berkley. ISBN 9780425236475. 326p.
Lucy and Trent's marriage has collapsed, and each has a different idea of what the return to single life will entail. At first, Lucy is devastated, but now she's just angry, and her girlfriends are helping to fan the flames of her anger. Trent, meanwhile, realizes that being a middle-aged bachelor isn't quite what he expected.

Keywords: Ensemble, Humorous, Marriage.

Harmel, Kristin.

 The Sweetness of Forgetting. 2012. Gallery. ISBN 9781451644296. 368p.
Hope McKenna-Smith's life is falling apart. She's still grieving her mother's death, her marriage has fallen apart, and now her beloved grandmother Mamie is slowly dying of Alzheimer's. Before Mamie forgets everything, she tells Hope her deepest secrets and sends her to Paris to uncover the truth about her family's past.

Keywords: Emotional, Family, Grief.

Higgins, Lisa Verge.

The Proper Care and Maintenance of Friendship. 2011. 5 Spot. ISBN 9780446563512. 344p.
When Rachel dies of cancer at the age of thirty-eight, she leaves behind challenges for her three closest friends—challenges that will help them overcome their grief and get past roadblocks that are threatening to destroy their lives. Stay-at-home mom Kate takes a literal plunge by skydiving, hardworking nurse Sarah is challenged to confront her troubled relationship with a longtime lover, and businesswoman Jo faces the greatest challenge of all—adopting Rachel's daughter and confronting her troubled past.

Keywords: Emotional, Friendship, Grief, Self-Actualization.

One Good Friend Deserves Another. 2012. 5 Spot. ISBN 9781455500307. 338p.
When they were younger, friends Dhara, Kelly, Marta, and Wendy invented a list of rules for future relationships. The intent was to keep each other from getting hurt, and the rules seem to be working. Then each woman finds herself in the midst of a relationship in crisis, and they must rely on each other's love and support to get them through.

Keywords: Ensemble, Friendship, Romantic.

Hilderbrand, Elin.

Hilderbrand's novels are set on Nantucket and feature women on the brink of change and life lessons.

Barefoot. 2008. Little, Brown. ISBN 9780316018586. 403p.

Sisters Vicki and Brenda are joined by their friend Melanie for what should be a summer escape to a charming Nantucket cottage. But their peace is shattered by the devastating secrets that each woman brings with her: Vicki has lung cancer, Brenda has been fired from her job as a college professor, and Melanie's husband is having an affair. Enter townie Josh Flynn, who seems to provide an escape for all three women, but at what cost?

Keywords: Beach, Ensemble, Family.

A Summer Affair. 2008. Little, Brown. ISBN 9780316018609. 408p.

Claire gave up a promising career as a glassblower to care for her four children—a choice she is growing to regret. When she is offered the opportunity to chair a lavish benefit for a Nantucket charity, Claire jumps at the chance—and soon finds herself in the midst of a torrid affair with the charity's director. Her guilt soon overwhelms her and threatens to destroy her relationship with her nice-guy husband and her best friend.

Keywords: Family, Marriage.

The Castaways. 2009. Little, Brown. ISBN 9780316043892. 359p.

The MacAvoy marriage is in tatters, and the couple hopes to rekindle their relationship with an anniversary trip on their sailboat. The couple drowns in a mysterious accident, leaving behind two children. As their friends try to sort out what happened, they discover numerous secrets that show just how troubled the MacAvoys' relationship really was.

Keywords: Ensemble, Marriage.

The Island. 2010. Little, Brown. ISBN 978031604387-8. 416p.

Two generations of women come together off the coast of Nantucket as they spend the summer in the family beach cottage. They're all there for different reasons: Chess is trying to mend her broken heart after her ex-fiancé dies in a tragic accident; her sister, Tate, is eager to escape boredom and figure out what she really wants from life; their mother, Birdie, is still coming to terms with her divorce; and Birdie's sister, India, is trying to help them all—while dealing with her own secret pain.

Keywords: Beach, Ensemble, Family, Friendship.

Silver Girl. 2011. Little, Brown. ISBN 9780316099660. 400p.

When Meredith's husband is nabbed by the feds for orchestrating a Ponzi scheme, she flees to Nantucket hoping to stay with her oldest friend, even though they've been estranged for several years. As the press and her husband's victims start to track her down, she soon finds she can't hide out forever. Things get complicated when Connie's older brother, Meredith's high school sweetheart, shows up for the summer.

Keywords: Friendship, Romantic.

Summerland. 2012. Little, Brown. ISBN 9780316099837. 392p.

After the tragic death of her daughter and the serious injury of her son in an automobile accident, Zoe Alistair questions her role as a mother. But one person involved in the accident knows why it happened—Penny's friend Demeter, whose secrets, if revealed, would answer a number of questions but would devastate an entire community.

Keywords: Family, Friendship.

Holton, Cathy.

Holton's Southern women's fiction titles are fine examples of ensemble fiction showcasing multiple characters—sisters, friends.

Revenge of the Kudzu Debutantes. 2007. Ballantine. ISBN 9780345479280. 288p.

Lavonne, Nita, and Eadie have been best friends for years, since their high-powered attorney husbands all work together at a Georgia law firm. When they discover that their hubbies' annual hunting trip means the men are on the hunt for mistresses, not game, the trio decide to take matters into their own hands. Followed by *The Secret Lives of the Kudzu Debutantes* (2008).

Keywords: Ensemble, Friendship, Southern.

Beach Trip. 2010. Ballantine. ISBN 9780345505996. 406p.

Four college friends, now in their forties, travel to coastal North Carolina for an idyllic week in a beach house, but old secrets and resentments threaten to destroy their friendship.

Keywords: Beach, Ensemble, Friendship, Southern.

Summer in the South. 2011. Ballantine. ISBN 9780345506016. 352p.

Ava, an author, decides to spend a summer in Tennessee caring for a friend's elderly aunts, Josephine and Fanny. Little does she know that she's about to be drawn into some family secrets and a sixty-year-old murder mystery.

Keywords: Family, Southern.

Hood, Ann.

Hood's women's fiction features women dealing with family issues, enjoying friendships, and dealing with the triumphs and tragedies of life.

The Knitting Circle. 2007. W. W. Norton. ISBN 9780393059014. 384p.

When Mary loses her young daughter to a sudden illness, she turns to a knitting circle for distraction. The people she meets there help her to come to terms with her tragedy—as she goes through the stages of mourning, she learns a new stitch from each person and also learns something about their past.

Keywords: Emotional, Ensemble, Friendship.

The Red Thread. 2010. W. W. Norton. ISBN 9780393070200. 304p.

To cope with her grief after losing her infant daughter in a freak accident, Maya decides to open the Red Thread, an adoption agency that specializes in China-to-America adoptions. She interacts with six diverse couples who share their journeys toward family.

Keywords: Emotional, Ensemble, Thought-Provoking.

Isaacs, Susan.

Isaacs has been giving her wry take on society and women's issues since the 1970s and continues with contemporary stories, some tinged with suspense.

Compromising Positions. 1978. Times Books. ISBN 0812907361. 248p.

The life of a housewife is slowly killing sharp-as-nails Judith Singer—she's desperately in need of an adventure to liven up her days. When a local dentist is found dead, Judith is intrigued, and when the blame shifts to her neighbor, she starts investigating what happened. Judith quickly uncovers the dentist's shameful secret—he's quite the lothario—and she also finds herself falling for the sexy police detective assigned to the case. Judith returns in *Long Time No See* (2001).

Keyword: Humorous.

As Husbands Go. 2010. Scribner. ISBN 9781416573012. 352p.

Wife and mother Susie thinks she has a perfect life, until her husband is found stabbed to death in a prostitute's apartment. Unhappy with the too-fast resolution by the district attorney, Susie is suspicious and is determined to unearth the truth about her husband's killer.

Keyword: Humorous.

The Goldberg Variations. 2012. Scribner. ISBN 9781451605914. 336p.

Eighty-year-old Gloria Garrison summons her three grandchildren—movie editor Daisy, baseball PR manager Matt, and Legal Aid lawyer Raquel—to her palatial home to answer a pressing question: who should inherit Gloria's booming beauty-products empire? The problem is that none of her grandchildren are interested, nor are they willing to forgive Gloria her trespasses.

Keywords: Family, Humorous, Older Women.

Jackson, Joshilyn.

Jackson's fractured family stories are full of eccentric characters and strong female heroines dealing with interesting situations.

Gods in Alabama. 2005. Warner. ISBN 0446524190. 288p.

How's this for an opener? When Arlene runs away from home she makes three promises to God—she will stop sleeping around, she will never tell another lie, and she will never return to Alabama. All He has to do in return is keep the body hidden. When a former classmate comes knocking on her door looking for answers, Arlene decides she needs to return home for some damage control.

Keywords: Family, Thought-Provoking, Southern.

*Backseat Saints. 2010. Grand Central. ISBN 9780446582346. 344p.

On the outside, Ro Grandee is flawless, but that perfect veneer hides a devastating secret. When a tarot reader tells her that her abusive husband will kill her unless she kills him first, Ro goes on the run, digging up old family secrets along the way.

Keywords: Family, Thought-Provoking, Southern.

🎖 **A Grown Up Kind of Pretty.* 2012. Grand Central. ISBN 9780446582353. 336p.

Three generations of women are torn apart by a devastating secret. Fifteen-year-old Mosey discovers a small grave in the backyard and is determined to figure out why it's there. Liza, her ill mother, is haunted by choices she made as a teenager. Jenny, Liza's mother, will stop at nothing to protect her family.

Keywords: Coming-of-Age, Ensemble, Family, Mothers and Daughters, Thought-Provoking.

Jacobs, Kate.

Comfort Food. 2008. Putnam. ISBN 9780739496404. 336p.

Popular TV chef Augusta, a widow who thinks she's aging gracefully, is surprised when she gets a new co-host: the hot young Carmen. It's soon apparent on the set that this pairing isn't working, so the two are packed off on a team-building retreat.

Keywords: Family, Romantic, Workplace.

Friday Night Knitting Club series.

Georgia runs a Manhattan yarn shop and begins a Friday night knitting club where she becomes friends with the diverse group of women who join up.

The Friday Night Knitting Club. 2006. Putnam. ISBN 9780399154096. 352p.

Knit Two. 2008. Putnam. ISBN 9780399155833. 320p.

Knit the Season. 2009. Putnam. ISBN 9780399156380. 260p.

Johnson, Diane.

Johnson's contemporary novels have been finalists for both the Pulitzer Prize and the National Book Award and are well received by critics. Her books often feature American women living in, or visiting, France.

Le Divorce. 1997. Dutton. ISBN 0525942386. 309p.

Stepsisters Isabel and Roxy are reunited in Paris during tumultuous times: Isabel has dropped out of film school, and Roxy is pregnant and her husband has left her for another woman. Soon, Isabel is romantically involved with two very different Frenchmen, and Roxy is in the midst of a tangle involving a wedding gift that she gave to her soon-to-be ex-husband.

Keywords: Family, Humorous, Romantic.

Kelly, Cathy.

Kelly's novels feature a variety of female characters, of all ages and backgrounds, all dealing with families and friendship, always set in Ireland.

Best of Friends. 2005. Downtown Press. ISBN 0743490258. 528p.

Four Irish best friends band together in this charming novel. Divorced Lizzie worries about being alone; TV star Abby frets about growing older; beauty salon owner Sally is always too busy; and Erin is obsessed with family secrets. When Sally is diagnosed with breast cancer, the women realize their problems are insignificant.

Keywords: Ensemble, Friendship.

Homecoming. 2011. Gallery. ISBN 9781451616767. 464p.

Elderly Eleanor returns home to Ireland after her self-exile to America some seventy years ago. She finds herself drawn into the lives of three younger local women, Megan, Rae, and Connie. Actress Megan is on the run from publicity hounds, restaurateur Rae is always there for everyone else but finds few are there for her when she needs them, and Connie, a schoolteacher, has given up on love.

Keywords: Ensemble, Friendship.

The House on Willow Street. 2013. Gallery. 9781451681406. 496p.

Danae is the postmistress of a small Irish town, and as the postmistress she knows more about Avalon's residents than most. But nobody knows Danae's secret, which she has spent eighteen years carefully hiding. When her niece Mara arrives, the truth is slowly revealed. Meanwhile, sisters Tess and Suki have pasts of their own to overcome before they can move forward with their lives.

Keywords: Ensemble, Family.

Kendrick, Beth.

Kendrick's charming and light novels feature women dealing with humorous situations. She is another author who began her career in chick lit, and her early novels can be found in chapter 6.

Second Time Around. 2010. Bantam. ISBN 9780385342247. 336p.

Five friends, all former English majors, are called back to their university when one of them passes away and leaves the remaining four all of her money—with the stipulation that they must use it to pursue a dream and revisit a missed chance. The group buys the dilapidated house they once shared off-campus and work together to turn it into a bed-and-breakfast.

Keywords: Ensemble, Friendship, Humorous.

The Bake-off. 2011. NAL. ISBN 0451233107. 336p.

Two wildly different sisters team up to enter a national baking contest in order to win money. Suburban mom Amy and former child prodigy Linnie put their differences aside to work with their feisty grandmother, who is beyond thrilled that the sisters have reunited.

Keywords: Family, Humorous, Sisters.

The Lucky Dog Matchmaking Service. 2012. NAL. ISBN 9780451236661. 336p.

Dog trainer Lara Madigan is a genius at matching homeless dogs to their perfect companion, but she can't find her own perfect match. After her long-term relationship ends (he's just not that into dogs), she moves in with her pampered mother, and her equally pampered friends bring her business in directions she never expected.

Keywords: Family, Humorous, Mothers and Daughters.

Keyes, Marian.

Keyes's novels are very humorous, and feature everyday young Irish and British women navigating work issues, family problems, and relationships—making her earlier novels great choices for readers who enjoy chick lit. Several of her novels (*Watermelon, Rachel's Holiday, Angels, Anybody Out There?*), while not a series, revolve around the sisters from the loving and funny Walsh family.

Watermelon. 1995. Avon. ISBN 038097617X. 417p.

Claire is shocked, to say the least, when her seemingly perfect husband walks out on her the day she gives birth to their first child. She takes refuge in her quirky but loving family back in Dublin and figures out how to reconstruct her life, new baby in tow. When her hubby comes back contrite, what will Claire do?

Keywords: Family, Humorous, Marriage.

Rachel's Holiday. 1998. Morrow. ISBN 9780688180713. 576p.

Rachel Walsh loves her fast-paced, glitzy New York life—but too much overindulging has left her with some serious problems. After a series of personal losses, Rachel goes on a binge that lands her in the hospital—and after an intervention from her loving family, she ends up in rehab. Released at the height of the chick lit boom, Rachel's story shows the dark side of the extravagant lifestyles embraced by chick lit heroines, but Keyes manages to keep the tone light (and not preachy).

Keywords: Family, Self-Actualization.

Anybody Out There? 2006. Morrow. ISBN 9780060731304. 464p.

Anna Walsh's enviable life is brought to a screeching halt by a disfiguring car accident. Recovery brings her back to her close-knit Irish family. Though she can't wait to return to New York and her loving husband, she has much to work through before her world can return to normal.

Keywords: Family, Marriage.

This Charming Man. 2008. Morrow. ISBN 9780061124020. 563p.

Paddy de Courcy is a womanizing politician nicknamed "The J.F.K. Jr. of Dublin." As he's ascended the ranks of the politically powerful, he's left a trail of broken hearts behind. The reality, though, is that he's not the nice young man he seems to be, and four of the women he's wronged band together to exact their revenge.

Keywords: Ensemble, Friendship.

The Brightest Star in the Sky. 2010. Viking. ISBN 9780670021406. 468p.

The inner lives of the residents of a London townhouse are revealed when a mysterious spirit begins to visit them all. The spirit is on a mission to change someone's life, but it's not sure which neighbor that will be until the end. It could be Matt and Maeve, newlyweds with a terrible secret. Or Lydia, who spends most of her time worrying about her mother. Perhaps it's Katie, who has a seemingly perfect career and boyfriends but feels unfulfilled.

Keywords: Ensemble, Romantic.

The Mystery of Mercy Close. 2013. Viking. ISBN 9780670025244. 352p.
Helen, the youngest of the Walsh sisters, is a private investigator charged with tracking down a missing member of a 1990s boy band. During the investigation, Helen's depression returns, and her close-knit family helps her find her way again.

Keywords: Family, Humorous.

Kibler, Julie.

Calling Me Home. 2013. St. Martin's. ISBN 9781250014528. 325p.
Hairdresser Dorrie Curtis is shocked when one of her elderly clients asks her for a very strange favor. Isabelle McAllister wants Dorrie to accompany her on a trip from their small Texas town to a funeral in the Cincinnati area. While on the trip, Isabelle confesses a stunning secret: as a young girl in the 1930s, she had an affair with a young black man—an affair that had far-reaching consequences. Dorrie must rethink everything she thought she knew about Isabelle, and in the process, she is able to help herself work through her own problems.

Keyword: Friendship.

Kidd, Sue Monk.

The Secret Life of Bees. 2002. Viking. ISBN 9780670032372. 302p.
Set in South Carolina in 1964, this coming-of-age tale is the story of teenage Lily, who misses the mother she never knew. It's also the story of Lily's black nanny, Rosaleen, as the two women decide to run away from Lily's abusive father, and the three sisters who take them in.

Keywords: Coming-of-Age, Emotional, Self-Actualization, Southern.

King, Cassandra.
King's Southern fiction focuses on strong and memorable women.

The Same Sweet Girls. 2005. Hyperion. ISBN 1401300383. 416p.
Six college friends who have met up twice a year for thirty years are preparing for a trip to Alabama when one of them becomes terminally ill, testing the strength of their bond. Nearing fifty, they realize they are not really the "Same Sweet Girls" they always thought they'd stay.

Keywords: Ensemble, Friendship, Older Women, Southern.

Queen of Broken Hearts. 2007. Hyperion. ISBN 1401301770. 432p.
Claire, a divorce therapist, has to deal with her own life when her husband passes away. She's also helping her best friend and her daughter deal with their marital problems, which is an excellent way for Claire to avoid her own issues.

Keywords: Family, Grief, Mothers and Daughters, Self-Actualization, Southern.

Kline, Christina Baker.

The Way Life Should Be. 2007. William Morrow. ISBN 0060798912. 288p.

Angela is dissatisfied with her job, Manhattan, and life in general. On a whim after finding a man on an online dating site, she packs it all up and moves to the coast of Maine, only to discover both the man and the area were not what she was expecting. Determined to make the best of things, she rents a cottage, takes a job at the local coffee hangout, and begins teaching cooking classes.

Keyword: Romantic.

*Bird in Hand. 2009. William Morrow. ISBN 9780688177249. 288p.

Two couples, friends since college, find their marriages crumbling. Allison and Charlie have been struggling to keep up appearances, but when Allison is involved in a car crash that kills a young child, she discovers she cannot count on her husband to support her emotionally—mainly because he's been having an affair with her best friend, Claire. Claire, an author, is married to Ben, who tries hard but can never seem to keep up with Claire, and their marriage may not be able to survive an affair.

Keywords: Family, Marriage, Thought-Provoking.

Lamb, Cathy.

Lamb's contemporary novels feature women dealing with family relationships and self-discovery.

Such a Pretty Face. 2010. Kensington. ISBN 9780758229550. 352p.

Stevie loses half her body weight—a staggering 170 pounds—after having a heart attack at age thirty-two. Unfortunately, she still struggles with trying to lose the many emotional demons that haunt her, including a bad childhood. Struggling to come to terms with her new image, she seeks a new happiness she's never had before.

Keyword: Self-Actualization.

*The First Day of the Rest of My Life. 2011. Kensington. ISBN 9780758259387. 480p.

Life coach Madeline inspires hundreds of women to change their courses but can't manage to keep her own life in check. Hiding behind a carefully constructed facade, she finds her world is threatened when a reporter begins reinvestigating the crime that put Madeline's mother behind bars.

Keywords: Family, Mothers and Daughters, Self-Actualization.

Lansens, Lori.

*The Wife's Tale. 2010. Little, Brown. ISBN 0316069310. 368p.

Lethargic Mary, overweight and suffering from depression, is finally moved to action when her husband doesn't come home the night of their twenty-fifth wedding anniversary. She pretends everything is fine for a bit and then decides to go out and find him—without having a clue where he might be. Her travels take her from rural Canada to glitzy California, where she makes interesting new friends and discovers herself.

Keywords: Older Women, Self-Actualization.

Letts, Billie.

*Where the Heart Is. 1995. Warner. ISBN 0446519723. 358p.
Teenage Novalee, pregnant and abandoned by her boyfriend, finds herself
stranded in a Walmart in tiny Sequoyah, Oklahoma. When the eccentric locals
discover her, they take her in as one of their own. A quirky and loveable cast of
characters round out this story of unexpected family and the powerful bonds that
can form between strangers.

Keywords: Family, Friendship.

Lewis, Kristyn Kusek.

How Lucky You Are. 2012. 5 Spot. ISBN 9781455502035. 340p.
Three close friends find their relationship challenged as they face personal crises
that test every aspect of their lives. Waverly's small business is foundering (and
so is her marriage), Kate is unsure about her future with her husband, and stay-
at-home mom Amy harbors a secret that could destroy all that she has come to
love. Each woman envies the others' life, but their friendship may be the only
thing that will sustain them through difficult times.

Keywords: Ensemble, Friendship.

Lipman, Elinor.

Lipman's novels feature realistic, everyday women and comic humor. They often
deal with family and social issues. While two of her books do feature men as
the main characters (*The Ladies' Man* and *The Family Man*), women are on equal
footing in those novels, and family issues are at the heart of the stories.

Isabel's Bed. 1995. Pocket. ISBN 0671881604. 387p.
Harriet is unceremoniously kicked out by her longtime boyfriend, so he can marry
his new, younger girlfriend. Homeless and unsure of her path in life, she retreats
to Cape Cod to ghostwrite the autobiography of a woman who was involved in
a scandalous murder case. The two women become friends, and Harriet learns
more about herself and who she wants to be.

Keywords: Friendship, Humorous.

The Family Man. 2009. Houghton Mifflin. ISBN 0618644660. 320p.
Harry, a gay man who was once married with a stepdaughter, Thalia, now wants
to reconnect with that young woman. Thalia, a budding actress, is happy to have
the family connection with Harry back in her life, and her mother, Denise, who
has missed him, is also thrilled.

Keyword: Family.

Livesey, Margot.

The House on Fortune Street. 2008. HarperCollins. ISBN 9780061451522. 320p.

> This literary novel is the story of Dara, a young therapist. Dara and her best friend, Abigail, an actress, have remained friends through thick and thin and are now flatmates in London. As their respective romantic relationships begin to show signs of trouble, will the women remain friends or turn on one another out of spite and jealousy?
>
> **Keywords:** Friendship, Thought-Provoking.

Lovelace, Sharla.

The Reason Is You. 2012. Berkley. ISBN 9780425247120. 336p.

> Single mom Dani and her sixteen-year-old daughter Riley return to Dani's tiny Texas hometown after Dani loses her high-powered corporate job. Dani's memories of Bethany, Texas, aren't the fondest—her childhood was troubled, to say the least. When a person from Dani's past unexpectedly returns, secrets are revealed, and Dani must rethink everything important about her life.
>
> **Keywords:** Family, Mothers and Daughters.

Before and Ever Since. 2012. Berkley. ISBN 9780425253052. 327p.

> Emily Lockwood is doing all right—her daughter is an adult, her relationship with her ex-husband is undramatic, and her work is fulfilling. Then an old flame returns to town, unearthing a long-buried secret that has the potential to hurt the people Emily loves the most.
>
> **Keyword:** Family.

Mansell, Jill.

> Mansell's British women's fiction is just starting to be reprinted here in the United States and features charming, romantic story lines.

An Offer You Can't Refuse. 2009. Sourcebooks. ISBN 9781402218330. 416p.

> Middle-class Lola is offered a large sum of money to break up with her boyfriend, Doug. Seems that Doug's mother doesn't think Lola's quite good enough for him. Lola's ready to refuse when her father turns up desperate for money, so she takes the bribe. Ten years later, Lola and Doug run into each other again, and the sparks are ready to fly.
>
> **Keywords:** Humorous, Romantic.

Rumor Has It. 2010. Sourcebooks. ISBN 9781402237508. 416p.

> Tilly Cole trades in her fast-paced London life for a small town in the Cotswolds, where she finds a job as the assistant to a well-known interior designer. Tilly soon finds her best friend Erin is the subject of some not-so-nice rumors—just as Tilly herself is falling for the local Lothario.
>
> **Keywords:** Humorous, Romantic.

To the Moon and Back. 2011. Sourcebooks. ISBN 9781402243851. 448p.

> Even though Ellie's husband Jamie was killed in an accident over a year ago, she still speaks to him regularly. Worried that she's about to lose her mind, she resolves to start over—moving to a new town and taking on a new job. She finds a kindred spirit in a new neighbor, who also has some secrets of her own.
>
> **Keyword:** Romantic.

Nadia Knows Best. 2012. Sourcebooks. ISBN 9781402265167. 480p.

> When Nadia meets Jay, she's already involved in a serious relationship so she doesn't give him a second thought. Several months later, they meet again, and now she's been unceremoniously dumped, so is it time to give him a chance? Nadia's over-the-top mother, grandmother, and sister also want to have their say.
>
> **Keyword:** Romantic.

A Walk in the Park. 2012. Sourcebooks. ISBN 9781402269943. 448p.

> At age sixteen, Lara Carson left her family and her boyfriend with no explanation and a big secret to hide. Eighteen years later, Lara and her teenage daughter return to Bath, and there's a lot of catching up (and explaining) to be done. Will her friends forgive her for abandoning them, and will her ex-boyfriend Flynn understand why she left?
>
> **Keywords:** Friendship, Romantic.

Mapson, JoAnn.

> Mapson's folksy, family-centered novels feature everyday people dealing with extraordinary events.

Bad Girl Creek trilogy.

> Beryl, Nance, Phoebe, and Ness come together to help Phoebe when she inherits a flower farm. As they work to overcome the farm's problems, they support each other to defeat their personal problems.

Bad Girl Creek. 2001.

Along Came Mary. 2003.

Goodbye, Earl . 2004.

🏵 ****Solomon's Oak.*** 2010. Bloomsbury. ISBN 1608193306. 384p.

> Young widow Glory Solomon, fears losing her California farm after losing her husband. To make ends meet, she hosts weddings in the chapel her husband had built under their two-hundred-year-old white oak tree, known locally as Solomon's Oak. To add to her stress, Glory is unsure she can handle the teenage runaway who appears on her doorstep, even though she and her husband used to be foster parents. Can she go it alone? Followed by ***Finding Casey*** (2012).
>
> **Keyword:** Thought-Provoking.

Mars, Julie.

Anybody Any Minute. 2008. St. Martin's. ISBN 9780312378691. 352p.

When Ellen impetuously buys a farm in upstate New York, she decides it's time to leave New York City and her husband. She takes up organic gardening and butts her way into the locals' lives. When her beloved sister suddenly must go out of the country, Ellen, who's deliberately avoided responsibility all her adult life, must care for her toddler nephew.

Keywords: Family, Thought-Provoking.

Maynard, Joyce.

*The Good Daughters. 2010. Morrow. ISBN 9780061994319. 288p.

The story of two girls, born on the same day, to entirely different families. Ruth is sensitive and artistic and can't seem to understand her farmer father and cold mother. Dana, who grows up to be a scientist, is constantly seeking grounding and stability, thanks to her flighty parents and her loosey-goosey childhood. The girls are friends of a sort, mainly thrust together in the "isn't-it-cute-they-share-a-birthday" sense. As they grow up and find their places in the world, family secrets come to light and their worlds slowly begin to make sense.

Keywords: Family, Friendship, Thought-Provoking.

McBride, Susan.

Little Black Dress. 2011. William Morrow. ISBN 9780062027191. 320p.

Toni has a perfect career and the perfect boyfriend—at least that's what she keeps telling herself. In reality, she's overworked and underappreciated. When her estranged mother has a stroke, Toni drops everything to be by her side, and as she is getting her mother's house back in order, Toni discovers a mysterious black dress at the center of some very interesting family controversy.

Keywords: Family, Romantic.

McComas, Mary Kay.

What Happened to Hannah. 2012. William Morrow. ISBN 9780062084781. 352p.

Hannah ran away as a teenager, determined to never return to her unloving family. Twenty years later, she is jolted back to her past when her mother and sister die, leaving Hannah the sole guardian of the teenage niece she's never met.

Keywords: Family, Grief, Self-Actualization, Thought-Provoking.

McDonough, Yona Zeldis.

A Wedding in Great Neck. 2012. NAL. ISBN 9780451237941. 315p.

The Silversteins have gathered for the fairy-tale wedding of youngest daughter Angelica, but their dysfunctional family threatens to spoil Angelica's careful plans. Her divorced parents are fighting, her teenage niece is acting out, and her siblings are wrapped up in their own problems. Can this wedding be saved?

Keyword: Family.

McHenry, Jael.

The Kitchen Daughter. 2011. Gallery. ISBN 9781439191699. 352p.

When Ginny's parents die unexpectedly, she is left on her own for the first time in her twenty-six-year-old life. Unable to cope with what's happening, Ginny turns her focus to cooking various recipes from the family collection. When the ghosts of the recipe's creators start to appear, seemingly called forth by the rich aromas of Ginny's cooking, does it mean she's going crazy or is it just her private way of seeking advice and comfort?

Keywords: Family, Grief, Thought-Provoking.

McInerney, Monica.

The Alphabet Sisters. 2005. Ballantine. ISBN 034547953X. 437p.

The three Quinlan sisters were child stars, but a romance gone wrong ruined their relationship. When their beloved grandmother Lola wants them to reunite for her eightieth birthday, the sisters see an opportunity to heal old wounds. Followed by *Lola's Secret* (2012), which continues the family's story.

Keywords: Family, Friendship.

The Faraday Girls. 2007. Ballantine. 9780345490230. 562p.

After their mother died, the five Faraday sisters were raised by their father—and each other. When youngest sister, Clementine, gets pregnant at sixteen, it changes everything for the entire family. Twenty years later, the sisters have scattered, and it's up to Clementine's daughter, Maggie, now an adult, to bring the Faraday women back together.

Keyword: Family.

At Home with the Templetons. 2011. Ballantine. ISBN 9780345518651. 496p.

The eccentric Templeton family relocates from England to a familial home in Australia, and father Henry comes up with a get-rich-quick scheme: they'll operate their home as a tourist attraction, with the family in historical costume. Naturally, the neighbors find them odd, and the family soon finds itself dealing with a variety of crises, while mother Eleanor tries to hold everything together.

Keyword: Family.

McLaren, Kaya.

How I Came to Sparkle Again. 2012. St. Martin's. ISBN 978125013873. 337p.

After her pregnancy comes to a tragic end and she catches her husband in bed with another woman, Jill Anthony flees to her safe haven—the ski resort town of Sparkle, Colorado, where she grew up. She finds a job as a babysitter for Cassie, a ten-year-old girl whose mother recently died of breast cancer. As she helps Cassie grieve the loss of her mother, Jill also grieves her own losses and finds love in the process.

Keywords: Family, Friendship, Grief, Romantic.

McQuestion, Karen.

The Long Way Home. 2012. Amazon Publishing. ISBN 978161283565. 327p.
   Four women meet in a grief support group and find not only support but also unexpected friendship. Marnie is devastated by the death of her husband but is dealt an even bigger blow when custody of her stepson, Troy, is given back to his birth mother. Desperate to reconnect with her beloved child, Marnie enlists the help of four of her support-group colleagues, who join Marnie on a road trip to Las Vegas.

Keywords: Ensemble, Family, Friendship, Grief.

Meacham, Leila.

Roses. 2010. Grand Central. ISBN 0446550000. 609p.
   Spanning most of the twentieth century, this multigenerational novel is written in the grand tradition of classic romantic sagas from Belva Plain and Catherine Cookson. When her brother defects after World War I, Mary Toliver inherits her family's Texas cotton plantation at a tender age and is determined to never, ever let the neighboring Warwick family get any of her land for their competing timber business—even though the heir, Percy, stands to be the love of her life.

Keywords: Historical, Romantic, Saga.

Tumbleweeds. 2012. Grand Central. ISBN 9781455509249. 480p.
   Already grieving the death of her parents, eleven-year-old Cathy Benson experiences major culture shock when she moves from California to a small town in the Texas panhandle. Two young men, orphans themselves, help Cathy adjust to her new life. As the three grow up together, romantic entanglements bring them together, and the resulting love triangle has far-reaching repercussions.

Keywords: Friendship, Romantic, Saga.

Meaney, Roisin.

Semi-Sweet: A Novel of Love and Cupcakes. 2011. 5 Spot. ISBN 9780446570114. 385p.
   Hannah Robinson should be having the time of her life. She's in a wonderful relationship, and she's about to realize her dream of opening a cupcake bakery in her picturesque Irish hometown. But then her boyfriend leaves her, and she realizes that starting and running a business on her own isn't as easy as she thought it would be. Her friend Patrick gives her

an ultimatum: take seven months to make the business a success, or give up. Hannah's friends and family both help and hinder her progress, and Hannah soon realizes how much she depends on the people around her.

Keywords: Friendship, Family.

Life Drawing for Beginners. 2012. 5 Spot. ISBN 9781455504084. 420p.
Audrey Matthews isn't sure what to make of the students in her adult-education life drawing class. Brought together from a variety of backgrounds, it seems like the only thing that they share is an interest in art. As the class progresses, friendships are formed, and the students learn as much about life and love as they do about drawing the human form.

Keywords: Friendship, Romantic.

Medoff, Jillian.

Good Girls Gone Bad. 2002. Morrow. ISBN 0066212693. 288p.
Neurotic thirty-something Janey Fabre joins a group therapy session to help her work through her issues, which include stalking her ex-boyfriend and despairing that she will never marry or have children. As she befriends the women in her therapy group, she finds both support and unexpected solutions to her problems.

Keywords: Friendship, Humorous.

I Couldn't Love You More. 2012. Five Spot. ISBN 9780446584623. 410p.
Eliot Gordon is satisfied with her life as a working mother to three daughters—one biological daughter, and two stepdaughters. When her first love abruptly returns, tragedy strikes, and Eliot is forced to reevaluate what motherhood and her relationship with her partner mean to her.

Keywords: Emotional, Family, Motherhood.

Medwed, Mameve.

Medwed's novels are contemporary and humorous, and feature everyday, mature women dealing with family relationships.

Of Men and Their Mothers. 2008. William Morrow. ISBN 9780060831219. 304p.
When Maisie and Rex divorce, Maisie finds she's still not free of her mother-in-law, Ina, who was a big factor in the breakup of the marriage. Ina is determined to have her say in how Maisie raises her teenage son, Tommy. Meanwhile, Tommy brings home a less-than-suitable girlfriend, prompting Maisie to contemplate what kind of mother-in-law she'll make someday.

Keywords: Family, Humorous.

Meier, Diane.

The Season of Second Chances. 2010. Henry Holt. ISBN 9780805090819. 285p.
After fifteen years teaching at Columbia University, Joy Harkness is offered a position at Amherst—a change that will force her to let go of both her physical and her emotional baggage and start fresh. Joy moves into a dilapidated Victorian,

and the challenge of rebuilding the house becomes intertwined with the challenge of rebuilding her life.

Keywords: Older Women, Self-Actualization.

Meister, Ellen.

The Smart One. 2008. Avon. ISBN 0061129623. 384p.

Bev, tired of an endless string of entry-level jobs, decides to become a teacher and moves back into her parents' home in order to save money. She's drawn back into the family drama, however, when her older sister Clare's marital problems surface and her younger sister Joey's struggle to stay sober seems doomed. Why does Beth have to be the stable one?

Keywords: Ensemble, Family, Sisters.

The Other Life. 2011. Penguin. ISBN 0399157131. 323p.

Quinn Braverman has something very unusual in the basement of her Long Island home: a portal to another world, one where she's made very different decisions. She's avoided the temptation of her alternate life thus far, but when she receives devastating news about her unborn child, she takes a peek—and what she discovers could drive her toward the other path.

Keywords: Family, Thought-Provoking.

Farewell, Dorothy Parker. 2013. Putnam. ISBN 9780399159077. 320p.

In writing, movie critic Violet channels the scathing wit of her hero, Dorothy Parker, but in person, she's a bit of a pushover. After a visit to the Algonquin Hotel, one of Parker's legendary haunts, Violet finds Parker's spirit—literally. As the two interact, both are challenged to overcome their fears, and the results are life-changing.

Keywords: Humorous, Self-Actualization.

Michaels, Anna.

The Tender Mercy of Roses. 2012. Gallery. ISBN 9781439180990. 326p.

When Jo Beth Dawson discovers the body of Pony Jones in the Alabama woods, she is driven to solve the mystery of the young rodeo star's murder. But getting back to her former career as a detective means confronting her personal demons, and an encounter with Pony's father, Titus, unearths family secrets that provide clues to unlock the mystery.

Keyword: Family.

Michaels, Fern.

Godmothers series.

Four women of a certain age, led by ringleader Teresa "Toots" Loudenberry, embark on a variety of adventures, including purchasing a tabloid from a corrupt publisher, investigating a spouse's murder, and helping to plan a wedding.

The Scoop. 2009.

Exclusive. 2010.

Late Edition. 2011.

Deadline. 2012.

Breaking News. 2013.

Classified. 2013.

Moore, Meg Mitchell.

The Arrivals. 2011. Little, Brown. ISBN 9780316097710. 324p.
Empty-nesters Ginny and William Owens are used to their quiet life. Then their three adult children—stay-at-home mom Lillian, freelance writer Stephen, and casting director Rachel—return home, each bearing serious emotional baggage. The reunited family must learn to navigate their new relationship, while leaning on each other for support.

Keywords Family.

So Far Away. 2012. Little, Brown. ISBN 9780316097697. 322p.
Thirteen-year-old Natalie, whose parents' divorce has left her feeling wounded; archivist Kathleen, whose personal losses are unbearable; and Bridget, an Irish maid in service to a wealthy family circa 1920, couldn't be more different. Yet these three lives intersect in an unusual way when Natalie finds Bridget's old diary in her mother's basement, and Bridget's experiences help both Natalie and Kathleen overcome their grief.

Keywords: Family, Self-Actualization.

Moriarty, Liane.

 *What Alice Forgot.* 2011. Amy Einhorn Books. ISBN 9780399157189. 426p.
Alice leads what appears to be a charmed life—she's happily married, lives in a charming (albeit rundown) house, and is expecting her first child. But when Alice awakens on the floor of a gym, it's ten years later, and nothing is the same. Her home is a mess, her relationship with her husband is on the rocks, and she barely recognizes her own body. With ten years of her life missing, can she reconstruct how everything changed?

Keywords: Family, Marriage.

The Hypnotist's Love Story. 2012. Amy Einhorn Books. ISBN 9780399159107. 416p.
Ellen O'Farrell's life has always been complicated. From her unorthodox childhood to her unorthodox career (she's a hypnotherapist), nothing in her world has ever been typical—until her relationship with Patrick. Ellen is thrown for a loop when Patrick tells her that his ex-girlfriend is stalking him, and Ellen soon realizes that she's been seeing the ex as one of her clients.

Keywords: Humorous, Romantic.

Netzer, Lydia.

Shine Shine Shine. 2012. St. Martin's. ISBN 9781250007070. 308p.

On the outside, Sunny Mann looks like a typical upper-middle-class suburban housewife with perfect grooming, an immaculate home, a genius husband, and spots on the most prestigious charity boards. But when her wig falls off during a minor automobile accident, the truth of her life begins to seep out. Her mother is dying, her autistic son is overmedicated, and her husband may never return from his mission to space.

Keywords: Family, Grief, Thought-Provoking.

Noble, Elizabeth.

Noble's women's fiction runs the gamut from ensemble stories to romance to weepers.

Things I Want My Daughters to Know. 2008. William Morrow. ISBN 9780061122194. 384p.

Four sisters deal with the death of their beloved mother in this tearjerker. Barbara has written letters to her daughters, ages fifteen to thirty-eight, and left them behind for the girls to read after she succumbs to cancer. Each daughter has a personal problem to overcome, and Mom's words of wisdom guide the girls through a difficult year.

Keywords: Ensemble, Family, Grief, Sisters.

When You Were Mine. 2011. Touchstone. ISBN 1439154856. 352p.

Susannah has had a series of doomed-to-fail relationships. When her first love, Rob, comes back into her life, their old flame is rekindled . . . but he's married. They decide to just remain friends, but will the stress of helping her dearest friend deal with cancer push Susannah to another doomed love affair?

Keywords: Friendship, Romantic.

Noble, Shelley.

Beach Colors. 2012. Morrow. ISBN 9780062103086. 356p.

After fashion designer Margaux Sullivan's husband betrays her, she flees her fast-paced New York life to regroup in Crescent Cove, a small coastal community in Connecticut. A chance encounter with Nick Prescott, a "townie" whose childhood crush on Margaux was known to all, gives her the opportunity to reevaluate her priorities and see her home in a different light.

Keywords: Beach, Romantic, Self-Actualization.

O'Neal, Barbara.

Prolific romance author Barbara Samuel writes contemporary women's fiction under the pen name O'Neal. Her food-themed books may appeal to chick lit fans, as well.

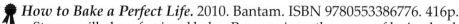 *How to Bake a Perfect Life.* 2010. Bantam. ISBN 9780553386776. 416p.
Strong-willed professional baker Ramona is on the verge of losing her house and her business when her daughter Sofia needs assistance. Sofia's husband has been injured in Iraq and when she goes to his side, she asks Ramona to care for her teenage stepdaughter.

Keyword: Family.

The Garden of Happy Endings. 2012. Bantam. ISBN 9780553386783. 416p.
Elsa, shaken by a crisis, returns to her hometown and begins working at the local soup kitchen. When her sister Tamsin's life crumbles around her and she returns home as well, the two women take over a neglected community garden and watch their lives flourish along with the plants.

Keyword: Family, Sisters.

Packer, Ann.

The Dive from Clausen's Pier. 2002. Knopf. ISBN 0375412824. 369p.
Carrie is about to break her engagement to Mike when he has a diving accident that leaves him paralyzed. Stricken with guilt and indecision, she spends the summer by his side but then runs away to New York City, where she discovers her talent for clothing design—plus a new romance.

Keywords: Coming-of-Age, Thought-Provoking.

Page, Jean Reynolds.

Safe Within. 2012. Morrow. ISBN 9780061876943. 325p.
Carson Forsyth is terminally ill, and his dying wish is to spend his final days in his idyllic North Carolina hometown. But the family's peace is shattered by Carson's mother, Greta, whose misadventures have landed her in trouble with the law. After Carson's death, his widow, Elaine, must make peace with Greta and come to terms with the secrets that haunt her family.

Keywords: Family, Grief, Southern.

Palmer, Liza.

More Like Her. 2012. Morrow. ISBN 9780062007469. 309p.
Frances's longtime boyfriend has just dumped her. When she meets Emma Dunham, the new headmistress at her school, she aspires to be just like her: poised, professional, and together. Then a tragic event exposes Emma's seemingly perfect life as a sham, and Frances and her friends are forced to take stock of their own lives.

Keyword: Friendship.

Plain, Belva.
One of the grand dames of women's fiction. Plain's specialty is sprawling family sagas.

Werner Family saga.

Plain's breakout novel, *Evergreen*, is the first volume in this long-running family saga, which follows the fortunes of Anna, a Polish Jewish immigrant who arrives in New York City at the turn of the twentieth century and finds her fortune—and love—in her new home. Anna's story continues in the three following volumes, and Plain's final novel, the posthumously published *Heartwood*, concludes the story with the third generation of Werners.

Evergreen. 1978.

The Golden Cup. 1986.

Tapestry. 1988.

Harvest. 1990.

Heartwood. 2011.

Radish, Kris.

Radish is best known for her ensemble fiction, which is charming and emotional.

Annie Freeman's Fabulous Traveling Funeral. 2006. Bantam. ISBN 0553382640. 352p.

When Annie dies of ovarian cancer, she leaves a package for her best friend, Katherine. The package contains her ashes (enclosed in red high-top sneakers) and instructions to gather her four best friends from across the country for a road trip, to scatter her ashes in meaningful places.

Keywords: Ensemble, Friendship, Grief.

Hearts on a String. 2010. Bantam. ISBN 9780553384758. 336p.

Five wildly different women are stuck together in a Florida hotel room after a terrible storm shuts down the entire area. Overtly sexy Cathy, stressed-out Nan, Vegas lounge singer Patti, stay-at-home-mom Margo, and shy hairdresser Holly have nothing in common but decide to bunk together anyway. Over the next few days, as the storm rages outside, so do tempers inside as the women drop their facades and get to know one another.

Keywords: Ensemble, Friendship.

Tuesday Night Miracles. 2012. Bantam. ISBN 9780553384765. 496p.

Four women meet in an anger management class. Grace is a struggling single working mother. Jane is a high-profile realtor who is watching her business dry up thanks to the recession. Kit is trying to deal with fifty years of dysfunctional family history, while young mother Leah, is trying to recoup after ending a bad relationship. Can these unlikely friends help each other while also learning to help themselves?

Keywords: Ensemble, Friendship.

Ray, Jeanne.

Ray's novels take a humorous look at romance among the middle-aged and older generations. The stories portray loving families and realistic situations.

Julie and Romeo. 2000. Harmony. ISBN 9780609606728. 240p.

These star-crossed lovers are just what you'd expect, only they're in their sixties, not teenagers. Julie, newly divorced, runs her family's flower shop. She's known forever about the family feud with the Cacciamanis, the other florist in town, but no one's really sure how the generations-long fight started. When she meets recently widowed Cacciamani heir Romeo at a floral convention, love blooms. Followed by *Julie and Romeo Get Lucky* (2005).

Keywords: Gentle, Older Women, Romantic.

Eat Cake. 2002. Shaye Areheart Books. ISBN 060961004X. 240p.

Ruth finds baking a relaxing escape from the troubles of everyday life. Her husband just lost his job, her estranged father is coming to live with them while he recuperates from an injury, and her teen daughter is getting moodier by the minute. Baking is the one thing she can indulge in, and she often pretends she's looking at the world from inside a nice, soft layer of cake.

Keywords: Family, Gentle.

*Calling Invisible Women. 2012. Crown. ISBN 9780307395054. 256p.

In this quirky allegory, middle-aged Clover has long felt metaphorically invisible—men are no longer interested in her, her family only notices her when she doesn't do something—and wakes up one morning actually, physically invisible. She meets up with a group of similar women who are determined to be recognized.

Keywords: Older Women, Self-Actualization, Thought-Provoking.

Rayner, Sarah.

One Moment, One Morning. 2010. St. Martin's Griffin. ISBN 9781250000194. 407p.

Lou, Karen, and Anna are commuting to work on the train (as they do every morning) when Karen's husband collapses suddenly and unexpectedly and dies. This tragic event brings the three women together and forces them to reconsider their path in life and their priorities.

Keywords: Friendship, Self-Actualization.

The Two Week Wait. 2012. St. Martin's Griffin. ISBN 9781250021489. 423p.

Lou, the thirty-something youth worker from Rayner's debut novel, reappears in this semi-sequel, which features her quest to have a baby. Lou desperately wants children, but her partner is indifferent. Miles away, Cath also wants to start a family, but infertility may change her plans. With the help of in vitro fertilization—and their newfound friendship—both may get their wish.

Keywords: Friendship, Motherhood.

Reichs, Kerry.

The Best Day of Someone Else's Life. 2008. Avon ISBN 9780061438578. 430p.

Despite her masculine name, Kevin "Vi" Connelly is a girly-girl—a hopeless romantic who dreams of her wedding day. At age twenty-seven, she's been a bridesmaid in eleven different weddings but she's never been a bride, and her boyfriend doesn't seem to be the Mr. Right she's looking for. As Vi begins to scrutinize the romantic choices that she's made, she realizes that something has to change—and that she has to take charge of her own destiny.

Keywords: Humorous, Romantic.

Leaving Unknown. 2010. Avon. ISBN 9780061808135. 356p.
Maeve Connelly is on the road trip of a lifetime. But when her car breaks down en route to Los Angeles, she finds herself in the small town of Unknown, Arizona, with some very expensive repairs in her future. Soon, her temporary layover starts to feel more permanent than she expected, and Maeve finds herself reevaluating her priorities in life.

Keywords: Humorous, Romantic, Self-Actualization.

What You Wish For. 2012. Morrow. ISBN 9780061808142. 408p.
Dimple Bledsoe, a television actress from a popular medical drama, feels her biological clock ticking. Though her biography on *Wikipedia* says she's in her late thirties, she's on the wrong side of forty, and her desire to become a mother is beginning to overshadow her interest in her career. Maryn Windsor froze her embryos prior to breast cancer treatment, but her divorce means that her husband has to agree—and he won't. Eva Lytton doesn't want children, but her new boyfriend might; and Eva's cousin Wyatt really wants a child but is having trouble adopting as a single man. The characters' lives intersect as they navigate a messy maze of fertility clinics, adoption, and the politics of conception.

Keywords: Family, Humorous.

Rice, Luanne.
Rice's novels feature mature, strong female characters. Homecomings, facing responsibilities, and the importance of family are also frequent themes.

The Perfect Summer. 2003. Bantam. ISBN 9780553584042. 464p.
Bay McCabe has a seemingly perfect life—a successful banker husband and three beautiful children—but one day, her life is shattered. Her husband Sean goes missing and shortly after, the FBI shows up to tell her that he is under investigation for embezzlement. Suddenly, Bay and her children are hunted by the press, shunned by their community, and completely broke.

Keywords: Marriage, Mothers and Daughters, Thought-Provoking.

Beach Girls. 2004. Bantam. ISBN 9780739445334. 277p.
Childhood friends Emma, Maddie, and Stevie are all grown up. When a tragic accident kills Emma, her distraught husband and daughter retreat to Hubbards Point, the summer resort where the three women met. As Jack sorts through his feelings, he and his daughter are drawn to Stevie, who has personal troubles of her own. Can the three lonely people make a new life together?

Keywords: Emotional, Friendship, Grief.

The Geometry of Sisters. 2009. Bantam. ISBN 9780553805130. 336p.

Maggie returns to her New England hometown with a lot of baggage—her husband has drowned and her oldest child, Carrie, has run away. She's confronted with more problems, as her estranged sister still lives there, as does the man who drove them apart. Characters from this novel return in *The Deep Blue Sea for Beginners* (2010).

Keywords: Family, Sisters, Thought-Provoking.

The Silver Boat. 2011. Viking. ISBN 9780670022502. 304p.

Three sisters must deal with the family home on Martha's Vineyard before it has to be sold for taxes. As the sisters reunite to get the house in order, they unearth their parents' love letters, and decide to finally uncover the mystery of why their father disappeared when they were young.

Keywords: Ensemble, Family, Sisters.

Little Night. 2012. Viking. ISBN 978-0670023561. 336p.

Claire tries to save her sister, Anne, from an abusive marriage and ends up in jail after she assaults Anne's husband. When Anne chooses to testify against Claire in favor of her spouse, can the sisters ever regain their bond?

Keywords: Emotional, Family, Sisters.

Riggle, Kristina.

Riggle's fiction features dysfunctional (yet often happy) families and realistic characters.

*Real Life and Liars. 2009. Avon. ISBN 0061706280. 252p.

Free-spirited Mirabelle decides to not follow through with treatment when she's diagnosed with breast cancer. Needless to say, her biggest hurdle with that plan is how her family is going to take the news, consisting of her grown children who have returned to their hometown for Mirabelle and her husband's thirty-fifth wedding anniversary. From her drama queen youngest to her self-absorbed eldest, no one is ready to deal with Mirabelle's illness or her decision.

Keywords: Family, Mothers and Daughters, Older Women, Thought-Provoking.

Things We Didn't Say. 2011. William Morrow. ISBN 9780062003041. 352p.

Casey's hiding something big from her fiancé, Michael, and his children—she's a recovering alcoholic. Michael would never get into another relationship with an addict again, as that was what destroyed his first marriage. When his teenage daughter, who hates Casey, thinks she's uncovered Casey's secret, all hell is ready to break loose, but Casey gets a reprieve when Michael's young son goes missing.

Keywords: Family, Thought-Provoking.

*Keepsake. 2012. William Morrow. ISBN 9780062003072. 352p.

Trish thinks of herself as just a distracted, messy housekeeper—but when her young son, Jack, suffers a broken collarbone after a pile of papers falls on him, Child Protective Services comes calling, forcing her to deal with the fact that she has inherited her mother's hoarding habits. Much to Trish's chagrin, her estranged sister, Mary, comes to help her get her house (and life) in order so that Jack is not removed from the home. Meanwhile, Trish's ex-husband and her older teenage son are not sure they want any part of this family anymore. And Trish knows exactly what has driven her to this compulsion—but refuses to share her pain.

Keywords: Family, Self-Actualization, Thought-Provoking.

Riley, Lucinda.

The Girl on the Cliff. 2012. Atria. ISBN 9781451655827. 416p.
After suffering a miscarriage, Grania leaves her life in New York for her family's home on the rustic Irish coast. On one of her walks down the coast, Grania meets Aurora, the youngest of the Lisles, a mysterious family living in a storied local house. As Grania and Aurora become friends, long-buried secrets are uncovered, changing both women's lives forever.

Keywords: Family, Grief, Thought-Provoking.

Rosenfeld, Lucinda.

I'm So Happy for You. 2009. Little, Brown. ISBN 9780316044509. 268p.
Wendy has always been the smart one and Daphne has always been the pretty one, and their friendship has revolved around these two basic truths. Wendy depends on Daphne to make her feel better about herself—Daphne is a disaster with men and lives a life full of drama. When Daphne gets pregnant and engaged, Wendy finds herself consumed with jealousy—and determined to sabotage her best friend.

Keywords: Friendship, Humorous.

Saffran, Lise.

Juno's Daughters. 2011. Penguin. ISBN 9780452296732. 352p
Jenny, a single mom of two teenage daughters, is gearing up for the annual summer theatre festival. This year, it's a production of Shakespeare's *The Tempest*, and Jenny finds herself getting involved with one of the professional actors brought in from New York. Trouble is, her elder daughter, Lily, likes him as well. To add to the stress of the summer, Jenny's younger daughter, thirteen-year-old Frankie, decides to get away from all of the literal and figural drama and runs away.

Keywords: Family, Mothers and Daughters.

Satran, Pamela Redmond.

The Possibility of You. 2012. Gallery. ISBN 9781451616422. 384p.
Three women—one in 1916, one in 1976, and one in 2012—make choices that will change their lives forever. Bridget feels responsible for the death of her young charge, Billie tracks down family secrets, and Cait finds herself in the midst of a bad affair. As each story line progresses, it becomes clear that these three women are faced with eerily similar dilemmas.

Keyword: Self-Actualization.

Scotch, Allison Winn.

Scotch's contemporary women's fiction showcases a talent for realistic characters.

The Department of Lost and Found. 2007. William Morrow. ISBN 0061161411. 320p.
Natalie, an ambitious senior aide to a senator from New York, is ditched by her cheating boyfriend right after she's diagnosed with breast cancer. As if that weren't enough, she loses her job soon after and finds her carefully cultivated world falling apart. Natalie's battle with cancer is portrayed with humor and grace, and the story also deftly portrays a young woman surviving a terrible illness and growing as a person after cancer.

Keyword: Thought-Provoking.

Time of My Life: A Novel. 2008. Crown. ISBN 0307408574. 288p.
Jillian appears to have the perfect suburban life—a fabulous home, a successful lawyer husband, and a beautiful baby girl. Yet for some reason, she can't help constantly wondering, "What if ?" After learning that her last boyfriend, Jackson, is engaged, she wishes she could go back and see what might have been. And then she wakes up—seven years in the past.

Keywords: Family, Marriage, Romantic, Thought-Provoking.

The One That I Want. 2010. Crown. ISBN 9780307464507. 288p.
Tilly loves her seemingly perfect life, until she realizes it's not so perfect after all. When her husband leaves her to follow his basketball-coaching bliss, Tilly stumbles through life until a psychic pal grants her the gift of clarity—the ability to flash forward into the future and see where life is going to take her.

Keywords: Family, Self-Actualization.

The Song Remains the Same. 2012. Putnam. ISBN 9780399157585. 320p.
Nell survives a plane crash but wakes up in the hospital with no memory of the crash—or any other memory, for that matter. She sorts through the pieces of her life, hoping something will jog her memory. As she slowly begins to remember, she realizes that not all of the people in her life want to help her—worst of all, her own mother and her husband may be lying to her about her past.

Keywords: Family, Thought-Provoking.

Seidel, Kathleen Gilles.

A Most Uncommon Degree of Popularity. 2006. St. Martin's. ISBN 0312333269. 304p.
Lydia doesn't quite know how to deal with her tween daughter's newfound popularity. A sixth-grader at a posh D.C. private school, Erin is a likable girl, and her close childhood friends suddenly make up the school's popular clique. When a new queen bee takes over and Erin's friends all join an afterschool vocal group without her, she becomes sullen and difficult, and Lydia discovers her own social status has dropped as well, as the girls' mothers adopt the same pettiness as their teenage daughters.

Keywords: Family, Mothers and Daughters, Self-Actualization.

Shaffer, Louise.

Shaffer, a former actress, writes contemporary, funny novels featuring friends and families.

The Three Miss Margarets. 2003. Random House. ISBN 037550852X. 324p.

Three Margarets—better known as Li'l Bit, Maggie, and Peggy—share a tight friendship and dark secrets. As upstanding Georgia ladies, they'd never admit to involvement in any scandal—they said all that was needed to be said long ago. When an old murder case comes back to haunt them, they must stand united to see the truth come out. The sequel is *The Ladies of Garrison Gardens* (2006).

Keywords: Ensemble, Family, Southern.

Family Acts. 2007. Ballantine. ISBN 9781400060634. 336p.

Complete strangers Katie and Randa find themselves joint inheritors of a famous but crumbling theater, the Venerable Opera house, in small-town Georgia. As they unravel their mysterious shared history and the history of the theater, readers are treated to a rich, delightful backstory involving a talented acting family, love, betrayal, and secrets.

Keywords: Family, Southern.

Siddons, Anne Rivers.

Siddon's main focus is women's fiction with a Southern setting, often involving privileged families with hidden secrets.

Islands. 2004. HarperCollins. ISBN0066211115. 374p.

Anny Butler has spent most of her life caring for others, often at her own expense. When she marries an older man, she finds herself adopted by her husband's circle of friends, affectionately nicknamed the Scrubs. As the Scrubs endure tragedy and the ravages of time, they rely on each other for love and emotional support.

Keywords: Friendship, Southern.

Sweetwater Creek. 2005. HarperCollins. ISBN 9780066213354. 356p.

Raised by a distant father and ignored by her older brothers, Emily Parmenter has spent much of her young life fending for herself. When spoiled rich girl Lulu turns up at Emily's family plantation, ostensibly to help with the family's dogs, her father hopes that Lulu's influence will help transform Emily into the young lady her wants her to be. Instead, it sets a chain of events in motion that will he all of the Parmenters, as well as Lulu.

Keywords: Family, Southern.

Off Season. 2008. Grand Central. ISBN 0446527874. 368p.

Lilly Constable has strong memories of her carefree childhood summers at her family's home in Maine—but those days came to an abrupt end following a tragic boating accident as well as her mother's death from cancer. Lilly retreats into herself, forming a close relationship with her father. When

Lilly meets Cam, a confident, wealthy young architect, her life expands, and their whirlwind courtship leads to a quick marriage. Years later, Cam's abrupt death leads Lilly back to Maine, where she uncovers long-buried family secrets.

Keyword: Grief, Family, Marriage.

Burnt Mountain. 2011. Grand Central. ISBN 9780446527897. 325p.

Thayer Wentworth was raised in the lap of luxury, but her childhood was tragic— her father died in an automobile accident when she was a child, and her mother's love was stifling. Her escape to an idyllic summer camp in the mountains of North Carolina sustained her through a number of difficult years. As an adult, Thayer is happily married and settled in a family home near the mountain that was the site of her father's car accident. The proximity to Burnt Mountain, combined with her husband's newfound love of the area, force Thayer to reconsider the events of her youth, as well as her marriage.

Keywords: Family, Marriage, Southern.

Sittenfeld, Curtis.

*Prep: A Novel. 2005. Random House. ISBN 1400062314. 416p.

In this coming-of-age story, Lee is a student at a prestigious New England prep school who is having a hard time fitting in. A scholarship student from the Midwest, she doesn't have much in common with her wealthy, snobbish classmates, nor does she care to be friends with most of them. When a popular young man takes an interest in her but wants to keep it a secret, she makes some very grown-up choices and deals with a broken heart.

Keywords: Coming-of-Age, Self-Actualization.

Smith, Haywood.

Smith started out writing historical romances but is now best known for her contemporary fiction featuring sassy older women, particularly her Red Hat Club trilogy.

Red Hat trilogy

Southern queens and lifelong friends Diane, Georgia, Linda, SuSu, and Teeny band together and help each other deal with lousy husbands, sobriety, and dysfunctional family issues.

The Red Hat Club. 2003.

The Red Hat Club Rides Again. 2005.

Wedding Belles. 2008.

Wife In Law. 2011. St. Martin's. ISBN 9780312609771. 384p.

Neighbors Betsy Callison and Kat Ellis are as different as night and day—Betsy's a dyed-in-the wool conservative wife; where Kat's a hippie Democrat. Somehow they managed to forge a friendship that lasted decades, until Betsy's cheater of an ex-husband convinces the newly widowed Kat to marry him.

Keywords: Friendship, Humorous, Older Women.

Out of Warranty. 2013. St. Martin's. ISBN 9781250003522. 352p.

Recently widowed, Cassie Jones suffers from a rare, genetic form of arthritis, but her health insurance refuses to cover the cost of treatment, and her medical bills are about to bankrupt her. Enter Jack Wilson, a fellow patient and born curmudgeon. He proposes an unusual arrangement: a marriage—in name only—that would give Cassie the health insurance that she needs. The odd couple finds that their arrangement provides not only insurance but companionship as well.

Keywords: Humorous, Older Women.

Smith, Lee.

Smith's Southern fiction centers on everyday women and their families and friendships, with eccentric characters. They range in style, time period, and setting.

Black Mountain Breakdown. 1980. Putnam. ISBN 0399125310. 228p.

Crystal Spangler is bright, ambitious, and strikingly beautiful, but her dysfunctional family impedes her success in life. After Crystal is raped by her uncle, she drifts through life unmoored, testing out a variety of identities and homes and attempting to cope with the damage of her troubled childhood.

Keywords: Family, Self-Actualization, Southern.

The Last Girls. 2002. Algonquin Books of Chapel Hill. ISBN 1565123638. 400p.

Twelve co-eds take a river-rafting trip down in Mississippi in 1965. Nearly thirty-five years later, four of them gather together for another trip, this time on a luxury riverboat instead of a raft, and the women tell each other what's happened in their lives since the last outing. Anna is a romance author, Courtney is a society maven, Catherine is happily married, and Harriet is a repressed schoolteacher.

Keywords: Ensemble, Friendship, Older Women, Southern.

On Agate Hill: A Novel. 2006. Algonquin. ISBN 1565124529. 416p.

Grad student Tuscany discovers a young girl's diary in the attic of her family's North Carolina bed-and-breakfast. The diary chronicles the life journeys of Molly Petree, an orphan at the end of the Civil War who grows up to be a cultured lady. Escaping to the past helps Tuscany confront her present.

Keywords: Saga, Southern.

Smolinski, Jill.

Next Thing on My List. 2006. Shaye Areheart Books. ISBN 9780307351241. 304p.

June offers Marisa, a complete stranger, a ride home from their Weight Watchers meeting. They get into a car accident and Marisa dies—leaving behind a list of "20 Things to Do by My 25th Birthday," which June decides to complete for her. She discovers that following Marisa's list gives her life the purpose and direction she had been looking for.

Keywords: Self-Actualization, Thought-Provoking.

Objects of My Affection. 2012. Touchstone. ISBN 9781451660753. 320p.

Lucy's life has hit a low point: she's just been dumped, she's out of money, and her nineteen-year-old son desperately needs a trip to rehab. When opportunity presents itself in the form of a job decluttering the home of a reclusive painter, Lucy can't say no. While working with Marva to eliminate the things that have taken over her space, Lucy makes some important discoveries about herself and her family.

Keywords: Family, Friendship, Self-Actualization.

Snow, Carol.

Snow's contemporary fiction features everyday women who find themselves in humorous situations.

Been There, Done That. 2006. Berkley. ISBN 9780425210062. 336p.

Journalist Kathy finds her youthful looks benefit her when she goes undercover at a college in order to get the scoop on a prostitution ring. What she doesn't expect however is that her youthful classmates will remind her of what being eighteen was like—not all that fun—and she realizes it's time to outgrow her crush on her old college boyfriend.

Keyword: Humorous.

Just Like Me, Only Better. 2010. Berkley. ISBN 9780425232484. 306p.

Veronica is a wreck when her husband dumps her for another woman, and getting mistaken for a popular celebrity isn't helping matters. But her resemblance to Haley Rush brings a new opportunity into Veronica's life—a job as a celebrity double. Veronica's game of pretend becomes all too real when she falls for Haley's handsome boyfriend. Can she reconcile her two lives?

Keywords: Humorous, Romantic.

What Came First. 2011. Berkley. ISBN 9780425243039. 368p.

Single mother Laura, a prominent lawyer, decides to give her son a sibling, but now she must track down the sperm donor she used nine years earlier. Her search leads to Wendy, a frustrated housewife, and Vanessa, a young woman dealing with her boyfriend's fear of commitment. As the three women's lives intertwine, they rethink what they thought they knew about motherhood and the meaning of family.

Keywords: Ensemble, Friendship, Humorous.

Stewart, Leah.

*The Myth of You and Me. 2005. Shaye Areheart Books. ISBN 1400098068. 288p.

Cameron and Sonia were best friends from junior high to after college, until they had a huge falling out. After not speaking for ten years, Sonia sends Cameron a letter announcing her engagement, prompting Cameron to track her down and figure out just where they went wrong.

Keywords: Friendship, Thought-Provoking.

Husband and Wife. 2010. Harper. ISBN 0061774502. 352p.

Sarah Price went back to work so her husband could stay home and focus on his writing career. When his upcoming novel reveals that he has been unfaithful, Sarah feels betrayed, and she begins to revisit the choices that she has made that lead her to her current life. Is it too late to change her path and live the life she wants?

Keywords: Marriage, Self-Actualization, Thought-Provoking.

*The History of Us. 2013. Touchstone. ISBN 9781451672626. 384p.

When her sister and brother-in-law die in a tragic accident, Eloise Hempel gives up her promising career as a history professor at Harvard to take care of her two nieces and her nephew. Eloise didn't expect to be a mother, and she didn't expect to move back to her hometown of Cincinnati, but family duty calls. Sixteen years later, Eloise is still in Cincinnati, the children are grown, and Eloise is mourning the life she could have had. All three children have their own problems, and the bickering and fighting threatens to tear the family apart.

Keywords: Ensemble, Family, Thought-Provoking.

Sullivan, J. Courtney.

*Commencement. 2009. Vintage. ISBN 9780307454966. 432p.

Four very different women are randomly assigned to the same dorm at Smith College in the late 1990s, and what begins as a tense situation soon becomes a seemingly unbreakable bond. As the women move toward adulthood, their close friendship is tested, and they struggle with a variety of life choices while continuing to lean on one another.

Keywords: Ensemble, Friendship, Thought-Provoking.

*Maine. 2011. Knopf. ISBN 9780307595126. 388p.

The Kelleher family has spent their summers at the family cottage in Maine for three generations. Driven by family loyalty, guilt, and their desire to escape from their busy lives, matriarch Alice, her daughter Kathleen and daughter-in-law Ann Marie, and her granddaughter Maggie spend part of their summer arguing, drinking, and seeking each other's approval and forgiveness.

Keywords: Ensemble, Family, Thought-Provoking.

Taylor, Mary Ellen.

The Union Street Bakery. 2013. Berkley. ISBN 9780425259696. 344p.

Daisy McCrae has always been an outsider in her close-knit family. Adopted at a young age, she's never quite fit in, so returning home following a bad breakup and a professional setback is tougher than she expected. Daisy is ostensibly learning how to run the family's bakery business, but the business is in trouble, leaving Daisy feeling even more adrift. When a long-time customer of the bakery leaves Daisy a slave girl's journal from the 1850s, Daisy is baffled, but as she reads Susie's story, she begins to learn more about her birth family and her place in the world.

Keywords: Family, Self-Actualization.

Tessaro, Kathleen.

The Debutante. 2010. Avon. ISBN 9780061125782. 400p.
Artist Cate leaves New York after a disastrous affair to work in her aunt's London auction house. When she is paired with handsome Jack, on the run from his own demons, sparks fly but their baggage doesn't seem to be a matched set. As they work together valuing an old estate, Cate becomes obsessed with the former owners—the Blythe sisters, known as the most beautiful debutantes of the 1920s. When Cate discovers a hidden shoebox filled with seemingly random items, she goes on a quest to uncover the box's secrets and find out more about the Blythe sisters and their glamorous, tragic lives.

Keyword: Romantic.

Thayer, Nancy.

Thayer specializes in light, humorous ensemble fiction, often set on the New England coast.

Hot Flash Club series.

The Hot Flash Club—women of a variety of backgrounds and interests brought together by their shared stage of life—share humorous adventures, proving that age is nothing more than a number.

The Hot Flash Club. 2004.

The Hot Flash Club Strikes Again. 2005.

Hot Flash Holidays. 2006.

The Hot Flash Club Chills Out. 2007.

Summer House. 2009. Ballantine. ISBN 0345498208. 384p.
Charlotte's Nantucket-based organic gardening company has finally started to take off when her sprawling family returns to the island for their annual visit. Jealousies rage when Charlotte's family realizes that their beloved grandmother has gifted some of her land to Charlotte to keep her business going. Family tensions threaten to ruin the good thing that Charlotte has going—can she have both a happy family and a successful business?

Keyword: Family.

Beachcombers. 2010. Ballantine. ISBN 0345518284. 368p.
When news that their widowed father may have eyes for another woman, the three Fox sisters converge on the family home on Nantucket to confront the

situation. But all three have their own problems to run away from, and what begins as a summer escape turns into a time of healing for the sisters.

Keywords: Ensemble, Family, Sisters.

Heat Wave. 2011. Ballantine. ISBN 0345518314. 304p.

After her husband's death, Carley has to find a way to keep her family afloat financially, so she opens a bed-and-breakfast in her Nantucket home. Carley's mother-in-law is unhappy with this plan, and Carley has to juggle her relationship with her late husband's family with the demands of her new business. When a late summer heat wave hits the island, everything changes, and Carley is forced to face the truth about her new life.

Keywords: Beach, Grief, Family.

Summer Breeze. 2012. Ballantine. ISBN 9780345528719. 320p.

Stay-at-home mom Morgan, artist Natalie, and teacher Bella spend a summer finding themselves on Dragonfly Lake, an idyllic New England vacation spot. Each woman feels stuck in a personal or professional rut, and with each others' encouragement, they are able to forge new lives and make new connections with friends and family.

Keywords: Beach, Ensemble, Self-Actualization.

Trigiani, Adriana.

Trigiani writes about loving families, usually Italian, and the people in their communities. She has a strong sense of place and of society and writes vivid characters.

Big Stone Gap series.

Small-town pharmacist Ave Maria is enjoys life in the tiny town of Big Stone Gap, Virginia, but even though she was born and raised there, she is considered a foreigner simply because her mother is Italian. When her mother dies, she finds out her real father is not who she thought. Her many friends in town provide comic relief.

Big Stone Gap. 2000.

Big Cherry Holler. 2001.

Milk Glass Moon. 2002.

Home to Big Stone Gap. 2006.

Very Valentine. 2009. HarperCollins. ISBN 9780061257056. 384p.

Valentine loves her job designing custom wedding shoes at her family's shoe company. Unfortunately, the business is on the brink of financial ruin, so Valentine and her grandmother head to Italy for inspiration—and find romance. Followed by *Brava, Valentine.* 2010.

Keywords: Family, Romantic.

Trollope, Joanna.

Trollope is best known for writing realistic family stories featuring average, middle-class women, set in the modern English countryside.

Friday Nights. 2008. Bloomsbury. ISBN 9781596914070. 336p.

Retired Eleanor invites two single young moms, Paula and Lindsay, over to her house for coffee one evening, starting a Friday night tradition. Soon the circle widens to include other women from the neighborhood. When Paula finds a new boyfriend, who insinuates himself into their circle, it upsets the balance and threatens to ruin lives.

Keywords: Ensemble, Friendship.

*The Soldier's Wife. 2009. Simon & Schuster. ISBN 9781451672510. 302p.

Alexa Riley is a military wife whose husband, Dan, is in the British Army. When Dan returns home after a grueling six-month tour in Afghanistan, he finds that his family's support for his career is flagging. The constant moves and uncertainty are starting to eat away at Alexa and daughter Isabel, who are being forced to sacrifice the things that they care about to support Dan's military ambitions.

Keyword: Family.

The Other Family. 2010. Touchstone. ISBN 9781439129838. 321p.

The death of pianist Richie Rossiter is a shock to the family that he lives with, although his three daughters are shocked to find out that their parents never married. But Richie's death is also a shock to Margaret Rossiter, Richie's ex-wife, and their son, Scott, who never knew his famous father.

Keywords: Family, Marriage.

*Daughters-in-Law. 2011. Touchstone. ISBN 9781451618389. 336p.

Even though her three grown sons are all married, controlling Rachel finds it hard to not be at the center of their lives, much to the chagrin of her daughters-in-law. The first two daughters-in-laws have accepted it, but when her youngest son's wife, Charlotte, decides to stand up to her, it causes much strife across all of the households, and Rachel must decide what her role really should be.

Keywords: Ensemble, Family.

Tucker, Lisa.

Tucker's contemporary family stories feature women working through a variety of issues.

*The Promised World. 2009. Atria. ISBN 9781416575382. 319p.

Lila Cole's world is torn apart when her twin brother commits suicide. In the aftermath of Billy's death, Lila learns that her brother's life was far more troubled than she could have imagined, and sorting through Billy's secrets takes its toll on Lila's sanity.

Keywords: Ensemble, Family, Thought-Provoking.

The Winters in Bloom. 2011. Atria. ISBN 9781416575405. 288p.

Kyra Winter and her husband, David, seem to have it all, but anxiety-ridden Kyra is always waiting for the other shoe to drop. It happens when their young son, Michael, disappears from their backyard one summer day. David is convinced his unstable ex-wife is to blame, but Kyra fears it's someone from her past, instead. Family secrets and tragedies soon come to light.

Keywords: Emotional, Marriage, Thought-Provoking.

Tunnicliffe, Hannah.

The Color of Tea. 2012. Scribner. ISBN 9781451682823. 316p.

Grace Miller's marriage is already strained when she and her husband relocate to Macau for his job. Removed from her comfortable, familiar life, Grace decides to make an unexpected move, and she opens a bakery specializing in coffee, tea, and macaroons. As her bakery becomes more successful, Grace begins to find friends among the women of her new community, and she'll need their support to overcome the challenges of her personal life.

Keywords: Emotional, Marriage, Self-Actualization.

Vincenzi, Penny.

Vincenzi's glitzy novels cover the jet-setting lives of glamorous women and their high-powered families. Though less over the top than the novels published at the genre's peak during the 1980s, readers yearning for novels reminiscent of the glitz-and-glamour potboilers of the era will enjoy Vincenzi's books, especially her titles set in contemporary London.

Almost a Crime. 2006. Overlook. ISBN 1585679437. 672p.

Octavia and Tom's high-powered careers leave little time for family or marriage. When Octavia realizes that Tom is having an affair, she goes after him with a vengeance. Her anger is magnified when she discovers the identity of her husband's mistress—one of her oldest friends.

Keywords: Family, Glitzy, Marriage.

Sheer Abandon. 2007. Doubleday. ISBN 9780385519885. 640p.

Three young British women meet on a plane to Thailand in 1985. A year later, on her way home after living the high life, one of them abandons her newborn baby at Heathrow. Fast-forward to 2000, when random circumstances reunite the three women—along with teenage Kate, who longs to find her birth mother. So, which one is it? Gentle and caring Clio, a doctor trapped in a loveless marriage; high-powered and high-strung lawyer Martha, who's just been tapped to be a major political leader; or freewheeling tabloid reporter Jocasta, living glamorously in London?

Keywords: Ensemble, Glitzy.

An Absolute Scandal. 2007. Anchor. ISBN 9780767926263. 575p.

Loosely based on real-life events that shook the London financial world during the late 1980s, Vincenzi's take on corporate greed involves a scandal at insurance giant Lloyd's of London and the families affected by the crisis. From the wealthy to the ordinary, fortunes are lost and lives are destroyed by greed.

Keywords: Ensemble, Glitzy, Saga.

The Best of Times. 2010. Anchor. ISBN 9780767930857. 608p.

A devastating car crash outside of London sets the scene for a tale of drama and intrigue. The motorists involved in the accident must take stock of their lives (and, in the case of the man trapped in the car with his mistress, worry about their future), while the first responders scramble into action. Meanwhile, the driver who caused the accident has amnesia, and his passenger, a mysterious hitchhiker, has disappeared.

Keywords: Ensemble, Glitzy.

More Than You Know. 2012. Doubleday. ISBN 9780385528252. 608p.

It's the swinging 1960s, and rich girl Eliza has a glamorous career in the magazine world. When she meets a boy from the wrong side of town, she gives it all up for love and marries him. A decade later, in the midst of a nasty divorce, what more will Eliza give up in order to retain her family home and custody of her daughter?

Keywords: Glitzy, Romantic, Saga.

Wicked Pleasures. 2012. Overlook. ISBN 9781590203583. 640p.

A wealthy family is rocked by scandal when its matriarch reveals her deepest secret: all three of her children have different fathers, and none of them are her long-suffering husband.

Keywords: Ensemble, Glitzy, Saga.

Waldman, Ayelet.

Ayelet Waldman is also the author of the essay collection *Bad Mother*, as well as the Mommy-Track Mystery series, which features a stay-at-home mom/amateur sleuth. Her women's fiction novels focus on how families cope with crises.

Love and Other Impossible Pursuits. 2006. Doubleday. ISBN 0385515308. 340p.

Emilia Greenleaf is happily married to the love of her life—but along with her husband, she's inherited a stepson with special needs that may or may not be psychosomatic. When Emilia loses her newborn daughter, she is forced to confront her feelings about her stepson.

Keywords: Family, Grief, Thought-Provoking.

*Red Hook Road. 2009. Doubleday. ISBN 9780385517867. 343p.

Tragedy strikes at Becca and John's wedding—as they leave their wedding, their limousine is involved in an accident that kills them both. As their families deal with the aftermath, they are forced to reconsider their priorities and their beliefs in an attempt to rebuild their lives.

Keywords: Family, Grief, Thought-Provoking.

Wax, Wendy.

Wax got her start in chick-lit-style humorous contemporary romance but has moved on to emotionally charged ensemble fiction featuring groups of friends.

The Accidental Bestseller. 2009. Berkley. ISBN 0425227677. 432p.

> Four very different women, all aspiring writers, meet at a conference. Ten years later, they're still friends, and they're relying on each other for help as their personal and professional lives collapse. They band together to write a novel featuring a thinly veiled version of their lives, and when their book becomes a best seller, they must help each other deal with the consequences of what they've written.
>
> **Keywords:** Ensemble, Friendship.

Magnolia Wednesdays. 2010. Berkley. ISBN 9780425232354. 437p.

> Vivien has spent years building her career as an investigative journalist, only to have her life derailed by a freak injury, as well as a surprise pregnancy. Exiled to her native Georgia, she picks up a job writing a column about the lives of suburban soccer moms, only to find that she actually enjoys the company of the people she's writing about.
>
> **Keywords:** Friendship, Self-Actualization, Southern.

Ten Beach Road. 2011. Berkley. ISBN 9780425240861. 423p.

> Madeline, Avery, and Nikki find themselves broke after a corrupt financial manager steals their money. All they have left is co-ownership of an historic beachfront home in Florida—and it needs a lot of work. None of the women has any home-restoration experience, but they take on the challenge and find friendship and healing in the process. The characters return in *Ocean Beach* (2012), where they take on a second home-restoration project, this time in South Beach.
>
> **Keywords:** Beach, Ensemble, Friendship.

Weiner, Jennifer.

> Weiner is known for giving her characters real personalities and quirks, and for her sense of humor. Her first two novels, *Good in Bed* and *In Her Shoes*, were solidly chick lit and represent the best of the genre, but she has since shifted her focus to contemporary women's fiction.

Little Earthquakes. 2004. Atria. ISBN 0743470095. 432p.

> Four unlikely friends bond over motherhood. While down-to-earth Becky deals with a tough mother-in-law, glamorous Ayinde worries that her basketball-star husband is having an affair, and Kelly tries to mother both her baby and her out-of-work husband. Lia, an outsider, observes the group of friends while hiding a tragic secret that makes her keep her distance.
>
> **Keywords:** Family, Friends, Humorous, Motherhood, Thought-Provoking.

Goodnight Nobody. 2005. Atria. ISBN 9780743470117. 371p.

> Something creepy is afoot in tony Upchurch, Connecticut, an idyllic community where the mothers are hyperinvolved and the fathers seem to be absent. When a local mother is murdered, Kate Klein is compelled to investigate, and she unearths troubling secrets lurking below the shallow surface of her privileged community.
>
> **Keywords:** Humorous, Motherhood, Thought-Provoking.

Best Friends Forever. 2009. Atria. ISBN 9780743294294. 384p.

Addie has always been the good, quiet girl in comparison to her freewheeling friend Valerie. Everything changed in high school, when Valerie became one of the popular girls. When a jock sexually assaults Valerie, Addie comes to her rescue, only to be betrayed when Valerie denies everything, leaving Addie humiliated and outcast. Fifteen years later, on the night of their high school reunion, Valerie decides to try and make things right, only to end up turning their worlds upside down.

Keyword: Friendship.

Fly Away Home. 2010. Atria. ISBN 9780743294270. 401p.

The Woodruff family has its share of troubles. Mother Sylvie has transformed from freewheeling hippie to tailored politician's wife, her youngest daughter is a recovering addict struggling to keep her life together, and her older daughter's perfect-on-the-outside life hides a sad secret. When Richard Woodruff's extramarital affair is revealed, the Woodruff women must come together to heal their lives.

Keywords: Family, Mothers and Daughters.

*Then Came You. 2011. Atria. ISBN 9781451617726. 338p.

In a light take on issue-driven fiction, an egg donor, a surrogate mother, and the infertile woman who hires them all get to tell their side of the story. Another character enters the picture in an interesting twist—the grown daughter of the soon-to-be dad gets to tell her story as well.

Keywords: Ensemble, Family, Thought-Provoking.

The Next Best Thing. 2012. Atria. ISBN 9781451617757. 400p.

Ruth, a scriptwriter, navigates the shaky world of Los Angeles, from romance to celebrities, when she lands her own television comedy series. With the help of her plucky grandmother, she comes to terms with her past and with her future.

Keywords: Family, Romantic.

Wells, Rebecca.

Wells writes fully formed, strong female characters, and injects a lot of humor into her stories, while telling dramatic family stories.

Ya-Ya Sisterhood Novels.

The grand friendship of the Ya-Ya Sisterhood: four childhood best friends who grow up to be amazing, if crazy, women. Ringleader Vivi is glamorous and fearless. Teensy is the spunky one and the common sense of the group. Caro is strong and noble, while Necie is the pious, conservative one. Follow their wild adventures as girls in the 1940s through their sobering, tough times as mothers and wives.

Little Altars Everywhere. 1992.

Divine Secrets of the Ya-Ya Sisterhood. 1996.

Ya-Yas in Bloom. 2005.

West, Michael Lee.

Mermaids in the Basement. 2008. HarperCollins. ISBN 0060184051. 304p.

Screenwriter Renata comes from a true Southern family, complete with a formidable grand-dame grandmother. Mourning the death of her mother, Renata escapes to the family cottage, but instead of finding rest and relaxation, she finds more stress—she discovers that her parents led secret lives to which she was never privy, until now: grandmother Honora and pals have decided it's time to let all of the skeletons out of the family closets.

Keywords: Family, Humorous, Southern.

White, Karen.

White's Southern fiction features women dealing with family problems and other relationship issues, often with secrets at the heart of the plots.

On Folly Beach. 2010. NAL. ISBN 9780451229212. 390p.

In an attempt to heal and regroup after the death of her husband, Emmy Hamilton purchases a bookstore on Folly Beach, an idyllic barrier island on the coast of South Carolina. When Emmy finds a cache of love letters inside a box of new books, she grows closer to Lulu, an eccentric older woman who has experienced a devastating loss of her own. Together, both women learn to accept what life has brought them.

Keywords: Friendship, Grief, Southern.

Falling Home. 2010. NAL. ISBN 9780451231444. 437p.

After her sister steals her fiancé, Cassie Madison flees to New York, leaving her Georgia hometown behind. When Cassie gets a phone call with news that her father is dying, she is drawn back to her home, where she must confront her sister's betrayal.

Keywords: Family, Grief, Sisters, Southern.

The Beach Trees. 2011. NAL. ISBN 0451233077. 432p.

Julie leaves New York for the Gulf Coast when her friend dies, leaving Julie a beach house in Biloxi, Mississippi, and custody of her five-year-old son. When Julie arrives, she discovers the house has been flattened by Hurricane Katrina and the boy nearly penniless. She takes him to the only family he has left, aunts in New Orleans, who share an interesting family secret.

Keywords: Family, Grief, Southern, Thought-Provoking.

Sea Change. 2012. NAL. ISBN 9780451236760. 432p.

Ava Whalen thinks she has found her soul mate in child psychologist Matthew Frazier, but their whirlwind courtship and sudden marriage fail to reveal some troubling secrets about Matthew's past. As Ava sorts through her new husband's family history, she discovers unexpected truths about herself.

Keywords: Family, Marriage, Southern.

Wickham, Madeleine.

Also well known under her pen name, Sophie Kinsella, Wickham writes slightly less fluffy women's fiction. Many of Wickham's early novels have been reissued due to the success of her Shopaholic series.

Cocktails for Three. 2001. St. Martin's. ISBN 0312281927. 300p.

Candice, Maggie, and Roxanne are work pals who meet up in London for cocktails on the first of every month to dissect their current situations. Roxanne is having a heated affair, Maggie is a new mom with an unsympathetic mother-in-law and distant husband, and Candice has a guilty secret. When scheming Heather enters the mix, the friendships are tested.

Keywords: Ensemble, Friendship.

Sleeping Arrangements. 2008. St. Martin's Griffin. ISBN 9780312565763. 295p.

Two families book a dream vacation in Spain, but when they arrive, they realize that they've both booked the same villa and must spend a week sharing the same space. As the week progresses, it becomes apparent that the double-booking may not have been an accident, and a romance is rekindled.

Keywords: Humorous, Romantic.

The Wedding Girl. 2010. St. Martin's Griffin. ISBN 9780312628208. 327p.

Wacky Milly helps out her gay friend Rupert by agreeing to marry his partner in order to get him citizenship. Ten years later, she thinks she has left that all in the past and is now engaged to a conservative man who wouldn't understand. When the wedding photographer Milly has booked turns out to be the same one who worked her first wedding, all hell threatens to break loose.

Keyword: Humorous.

40 Love. 2011. Thomas Dunne. ISBN 9780312562755. 276p.

Four very different couples get together for a lavish tennis weekend. As the weekend progresses, the attendees soon realize that tennis is the last thing that the party is actually about.

Keyword: Humorous.

Williams, Polly.

Williams's first novel, *The Yummy Mummy*, was one of the first "mom lit" novels to break in the United States. (It's annotated in chapter 6.) Her recent novels stray from the chick lit/mom lit formula into contemporary women's fiction.

Afterwife. 2013. Berkley. ISBN 9780425259436. 308p.

Narrator Sophie Brady is no longer alive, but that doesn't stop her from being involved in the lives of her family and friends. She's got her eye on her husband Ollie and her young son, both of whom are devastated by their loss, but Sophie wants her husband to find love again. Fortunately, Sophie's friend Jenny is there to help console Ollie, but as their relationship deepens, Jenny learns that there was more to Sophie than she knew.

Keywords: Friendship, Romantic.

Wolff, Isabel.

Wolff's charming British women's fiction tends to be multilayered, and her sassy sense of humor will appeal to fans of chick lit.

🎗 *A Vintage Affair.* 2010. Bantam. ISBN 9780553807837. 368p.

Vintage clothing lover Phoebe opens her own resale boutique in London's Blackheath neighborhood. She's grateful for the hustle and bustle the shop provides, because it lets her forget the guilt she feels over the death of her best childhood friend, not to mention the fact that she just left her fiancé at the altar. When Mrs. Bell contracts with Phoebe to sell her entire wardrobe, Phoebe finds herself reeled in by the elderly woman and her stories.

Keywords: Family, Romantic.

The Very Picture of You. 2011. Bantam. ISBN 9780553807844. 336p.

Ella is a successful artist living in London and making a name for herself painting portraits. When her sister commissions Ella to paint her fiancé's portrait, Ella discovers the young man is not who he seems to be.

Keywords: Family, Romantic.

Wolitzer, Meg.

Wolitzer is a crossover author—she's literary, yet her fiction features the intimate details of ordinary women's lives and relationships. They also comment on women's roles in society.

*The Ten-Year Nap 2008. Riverhead. ISBN 978594489785. 351p.

Amy's feminist mother is constantly nagging her to go back to being a lawyer; reserved and wealthy Karen goes on multiple interviews every month but can't see the need to work; while Roberta, an artist, fears she's lost her talent. Now that their children, classmates at an exclusive New York private school, are preteens, is it time for the women to rejoin the working world—and do they even want to? A quiet, insightful meditation on women's work and what it means to be a mother.

Keywords: Ensemble, Motherhood, Thought-Provoking.

*The Uncoupling. 2011. Riverhead. ISBN 978159448788X. 288p.

In this modern take on the Greek play *Lysistrata*, where the women refuse to have sex with their mates until the men stop going to war, the women of Stellar Plains, New Jersey, all lose their sex drive at the same time.

Keywords: Ensemble, Thought-Provoking.

Humorous Women's Fiction

There are times when a tearjerker is just the thing, but there are other times when a reader just wants to laugh. In this section, we highlight novels written by consistently funny authors who write with a focus on the humor first and foremost. Many of the novels in this section are reminiscent of TV sitcoms or the screwball comedies of the 1930s and 1940s, with snappy dialogue, comic conflicts, exaggerated situations, and even the occasional pratfall. The protagonists in these books tend to be Everywomen with the sorts of ups and downs that readers will identify with, even if the character always has the right witty quip or smart comeback for every situation.

Many chick lit novels, discussed in chapter 6, will also make great read-alikes for readers interested in humorous women's fiction, but the genres are different. Most chick lit is light and humorous, but the focus of chick lit tends to involve a woman in her twenties or early thirties learning to make it on her own professionally and personally, often in a glamorous setting like a large city. Humorous women's fiction features protagonists of all ages and a wide variety of settings, from rural to suburban to urban.

Andrews, Mary Kay.

Her novels feature feisty heroines, plenty of snappy dialogue, humorous situations, Southern settings, and a spark of romance.

Hissy Fit. 2004. HarperCollins. ISBN 0060564644. 432p.

Keeley Ray throws a hissy fit (and a good one!) after catching her fiancé and the maid of honor getting it on the day before the wedding.

Keywords: Humorous, Romantic, Southern.

Deep Dish. 2008. HarperCollins. ISBN 9780060837365. 384p.

Chef Gina is up for a national show on the Cooking Channel. Her rival is the handsome but annoying host of a redneck cooking show for men. The sparks fly—as does the hilarity—when the two battle it out for their final chance at stardom, while dealing with their own families and personal issues.

Keywords: Humorous, Romantic, Southern.

The Fixer-Upper. 2009. HarperCollins. ISBN 0060837381. 432p.

When Dempsey loses her job as the result of a salacious political scandal, she's set adrift. Her father, who has just purchased a tumbledown Victorian mansion, offers her an opportunity that she's in no position to refuse: in exchange for her assistance rehabbing the place, she'll have a place to live and something to do. Comic misadventures ensue as Dempsey figures out how to apply her lobbyist skills to the madcap cast of characters living in tiny Guthrie, Georgia.

Keywords: Family, Humorous, Southern.

Summer Rental. 2011. St. Martin's. ISBN 9780312642693. 416p.

A month of fun, frolicking, romance, and self-discovery awaits three friends sharing a summer cottage, while the arrival of a fourth roommate ratchets up the drama. They each find themselves needing to confront big issues in their personal lives—from new romance to confronting a stalker ex, before the summer ends.

Keywords: Beach, Humorous, Romantic, Southern.

Spring Fever. 2012. St. Martin's. ISBN 9780312642716. 416p.

Annajane doesn't know that she's looking for a second chance with her ex-husband, Mason, but when his wedding is called off at the last minute, she finds herself wanting him back. But in the town of Passcoe, North Carolina, nothing is quite as it seems, and long-buried secrets could come back to haunt Annajane and her friends.

Keywords: Humorous, Romantic, Southern.

Caldwell, Megan.

Vanity Fare. 2012. Morrow. ISBN 9780062188366. 416p.
Molly Hagan is in the midst of an ugly divorce with her (now unemployed) husband, and the love of her six-year-old son and her best friend, Keisha, are the only things keeping her going—aside from coffee. When a friend offers her a job as a copywriter for a hunky celebrity chef's new chain of pastry shops, she jumps at the opportunity. What Molly doesn't expect is to find herself torn between a torrid fling with the celebrity chef and a chance at love with the project's business manager.

Keywords: Family, Romantic, Self-Actualization.

Center, Katherine.
Center's charming contemporary novels feature realistic characters and laugh-out-loud moments.

*The Bright Side of Disaster. 2007. Random House. ISBN 1400066379. 256p.
When her boyfriend has a panic attack and leaves her the day before she gives birth, Jenny finds herself raising a baby alone. Her feisty mother comes to help, along with her stalwart best friend and a very cute neighbor who just keeps appearing whenever she needs his help. But what will Jenny do when her contrite boyfriend appears on her doorstep months later?

Keywords: Family, Friendship, Humorous, Motherhood.

Everyone Is Beautiful. 2009. Ballantine. ISBN 9781400066433. 256p.
Lanie Coates feels like a fish out of water when her family relocates from Houston to Cambridge, Massachusetts. She's given up a lot as part of this move, including her support system; and life as a stay-at-home mom to her three rambunctious boys is starting to wear her down. When a chance encounter with a high school friend alerts Lanie to the sad state of her life, she vows to make some changes, starting out by taking some time for herself. But what begins as minor changes quickly expands to something life-changing, and Lanie must decide what's most important in her life.

Keywords: Humorous, Motherhood, Self-Actualization.

Get Lucky. 2010. Ballantine. ISBN 9780345507914. 288p.
Sarah, an ad exec, is fired from her job when she forwards an inappropriate e mail to her entire firm. She decides to leave the rat race of New York to stay with her sister in Houston for a while. Her sister, Mackie, has been trying unsuccessfully to have a baby. Sarah decides that what the heck, she's not working anyway, she'll be the surrogate!

Keywords: Family, Humorous.

Cook, Claire.

Cook's light-hearted and humorous novels often feature quirky families and romantic relationships.

Must Love Dogs. 2002. Viking. ISBN 0670031062. 242p.

Divorced preschool teacher Sarah is getting pressured by her family to jump back into the dating pool. As she goes through would-be suitors, her family sticks by her, hoping for a good match.

Keywords: Family, Humorous, Romantic.

Summer Blowout. 2008. Hyperion. ISBN 1401322417. 256p.

Bella works at her father's chain of beauty salons as a makeup artist. Problem is, so does the rest of her large extended family, including ex-wives, stepmothers, and half-siblings. It wouldn't be so bad, but they are all in each other's business, which drives Bella mad. Family tensions only get worse when Bella discovers that her ex-husband has been dating her younger half-sister and they plan to wed.

Keywords: Family, Humorous, Romantic.

Seven Year Switch. 2010. Voice: Hyperion. ISBN 1401341160. 256p.

When Jill's husband Seth upends their once-happy marriage by leaving their family to join the Peace Corps, Jill is left alone to raise their three-year-old daughter. Seven years later, Seth returns, wanting a second chance, and Jill is unsurprisingly wary. But their daughter needs her father, so Jill must reconcile the seven years spent being angry and alone.

Keywords: Family, Humorous, Marriage, Motherhood.

Best Staged Plans. 2011. Voice: Hyperion. ISBN 9781401341176. 256p.

Sandra is a professional home stager who can't seem to get her own house ready for the market, thanks to her slack-off husband and son. When she gets an offer to stage a boutique hotel down south, she leaps at the chance to run away and get some distance and perspective. She soon starts to wonder whether her whole life, not just her home, needs a makeover.

Keywords: Family, Humorous, Self-Actualization.

Wallflower in Bloom. 2012. Touchstone. ISBN 9781451672763. 272p.

Deirdre has—literally—been at her brother Tag's beck and call for years. She's always been the shy sibling, and her brother has achieved fame and notoriety as a self-styled New Age guru. When her longtime boyfriend leaves her for another woman, Deirdre drowns her sorrows, then takes control of the situation via her brother's online following in order to reinvent herself, and she soon finds herself a contestant on *Dancing with the Stars*.

Keywords: Family, Humorous.

Flagg, Fannie.

Flagg's novels are set in the South, usually in small towns full of eccentric characters. She uses folksy dialogue and gentle humor in her books, and often portrays strong women who exceed societal expectations. She is a good read-alike choice for readers in search of gentle reads, as well.

Fried Green Tomatoes at the Whistle Stop Café. 1987. Random House. ISBN 039456152X. 403p.

> Ninny Threadgoode, a spry eighty-six years old, recounts her adventures in 1930s-era Alabama to Evelyn, a visitor at Ninny's nursing home. The Whistle Stop Café, run by two outspoken women ahead of their time, forms the central setting for Ninny's funny and heartwarming stories of courage, love, and friendship.

> **Keywords:** Friendship, Gentle, Humorous, Southern.

I Still Dream About You. 2010. Random House. ISBN 9781400065936. 336p.

> Maggie, a former beauty queen, has decided it's time to end her life. While it's true she's suffered a series of recent setbacks, she's not clinically depressed or in any kind of trouble, she's just had it with the world and since her real-estate business is tanking, why not get out now? When her nemesis returns to town, the women lock horns over a particularly special property and Maggie decides maybe she'd better stick around some more, after all.

> **Keywords:** Humorous, Gentle, Self-Actualization.

Gideon, Melanie.

Wife 22. 2012. Ballantine. ISBN 9780345527950. 380p.

> Alice Buckle seems like she's going through the motions with her life. Her marriage is all right, her children are good enough, and her job is reasonably satisfying. When Alice begins participating in an anonymous online study of contemporary marriage, she's surprised at the honest responses that she gives to the researcher's questions, and the deeper she gets into the study, the more critical she gets of her marriage—leading her to a crossroads that could affect every aspect of her life.

> **Keywords:** Family, Humorous, Marriage, Self-Actualization.

Heller, Jane.

Heller's romantic comedies feature sharp dialogue, funny situations, and strong female characters.

Best Enemies. 2004. St. Martin's. ISBN 0312288492. 336p.

> Since high school, Amy has always played second fiddle to her best friend, Tara. When Amy catches her fiancé and Tara together, she cuts them both out of her life. Tara marries the lout, and Amy becomes a top PR woman. When Tara writes a book about her perfect lifestyle—a total lie—Amy is, naturally, assigned to promote it.

> **Keywords:** Friendship, Humorous.

An Ex to Grind. 2005. Morrow. ISBN 0060599251. 384p.

> Manhattan banker Melanie discovers that she is responsible for a large alimony settlement to keep her ex-husband Dan in the lifestyle he's grown accustomed to. So, she enlists a matchmaker to bring her husband up to snuff and find him a new love. The plan backfires, however, when it

works too well, and Melanie finds the new and improved Dan a lot better than the old one.

Keyword: Humorous.

Some Nerve. 2006. William Morrow. ISBN 9780060599270. 336p.

Anne loves her job as a celebrity gossip reporter in L.A.—it's exciting and she's good at it. When she can't get an interview with a hot actor, she loses her job and is forced to retreat to her small Mississippi hometown. It just so happens the actor is there too, incognito at a local hospital. So naturally, Anne's next career move is . . . candy striper.

Keywords: Humorous, Southern.

Lancaster, Jen.

Best known for her comic memoirs, Lancaster writes fiction about adults who came of age in the 1980s and are nostalgic for the popular culture of their youth.

If You Were Here. 2011. NAL. ISBN 9780451234384. 320p.

Young-adult novelist Mia, slightly obsessed with 1980s film director John Hughes, decides to spend her royalties buying the house featured in his films. It's not the house of her dreams, however, when Mia and her husband realize the laundry list of renovations the house requires will turn it in to a money pit complete with nasty neighbors, too many subdivision rules, and bathtubs that fall from the sky.

Keyword: Humorous.

Here I Go Again. 2013. NAL. ISBN 9780451236722. 320p.

Lissy Ryder's life is falling apart. She's been fired from her job, kicked out of her gym, and her husband wants a divorce. She hopes her twenty-year class reunion will cheer her up (she was the most popular girl in school, after all), but her former classmates—most of them successful—shun her. After drinking herself into oblivion, Lissy wakes up at her hippie-chick classmate Deva's apartment, and Deva offers her a fascinating proposition: a do-over. Lissy returns to 1991 and tries to change everything, but the end result isn't what she expected.

Keyword: Humorous.

Lipton, Lauren.

Mating Rituals of the North American WASP. 2009. 5 Spot. ISBN 9780446197977. 353p.

Peggy, the co-owner of a Manhattan boutique, discovers that what happens in Vegas doesn't always stay in Vegas. It was bad enough that she woke up in a stranger's hotel room, but it gets worse when said stranger calls her a few days later from rural Connecticut to explain that they are now legally wed. Luke, her new husband, is Old Money, meaning he doesn't really have any, but his doddering aunt has rewritten her will, giving an expensive house to Luke and Peggy. One catch—they need to stay married for one year in order for them to lay claim and sell it.

Keywords: Humorous, Romantic.

Riley, Jess.

*Driving Sideways. 2008. Ballantine. ISBN 0345501101. 342p.

In this laugh-out-loud road trip novel, Leigh travels cross-country to visit the family of her organ donor. Living with kidney disease since she was a teen, Leigh has always been a homebody, carefully choosing her next steps. However, since her transplant, she's been trying all kinds of new things and decides to throw caution to the wind to set out on an adventure.

Keyword: Humorous.

Ritchie, Cinthia.

Dolls Behaving Badly. 2013. Grand Central. ISBN 9780446568135. 341p.

By day, Carla is a waitress at a Mexican restaurant in Anchorage, Alaska; by night, she's an artist who turns fashion dolls into erotic art. Her life is as discordant as her two jobs—she has an ongoing sexual relationship with her late husband, her bossy older sister is pregnant thanks to an affair with a local TV broadcaster, her son is a precocious genius-in-training, and she seems to have adopted her Goth-y teenage neighbor. Figuring everything out is a challenge, but keeping a diary, with prompts from a popular TV talk-show host, seems to help.

Keywords: Family, Friendship, Humorous.

Strohmeyer, Sarah.

Strohmeyer, who also pens a series of light mysteries, writes funny contemporary women's fiction.

The Secret Lives of Fortunate Wives. 2005. Dutton. ISBN 0525949097. 349p.

This campy novel features the denizens of an exclusive Cleveland gated community, Hunting Hills. McMansions, platinum AmEx cards, and shallow trophy wives abound. When socially awkward Claire marries into the mix, she finds herself dodging odd social norms and scandals.

Keyword: Humorous.

Sweet Love. 2008. Dutton. ISBN 0525950648. 320p.

Julie, a forty-something journalist and single mom, is happy enough living in a duplex above her mother, Elizabeth. Elizabeth is not happy that her daughter has no love life, and, regretting forcing her daughter to dump her first love Michael, surreptitiously signs the ex-sweethearts up for a cooking class so they can rekindle their relationship.

Keywords: Family, Humorous, Romantic.

Kindred Spirits. 2011. Dutton. ISBN 9780525952220. 304p.

Best friends Mary Kay, Beth, and Carol mourn their friend Lynne, who has died after battling cancer. When they get together to go through her belongings, they discover a letter that reveals a shocking secret and her final wish—instructions for them to make right something that she couldn't face in life.

Keywords: Emotional, Ensemble, Friendship, Grief.

Thomas, Janis.

 Something New. 2012. Berkley. ISBN 97804257692. 369p.

Ellen Ivers is forty-two years old and bored with married life and suburban motherhood. When her "perfect" cousin Jill encourages her to enter a blog contest sponsored by a women's magazine, Ellen balks at the idea but realizes that trying something new may be the right thing to get her life back on track. When Jill's sexy neighbor Ben Campbell makes his attraction to Ellen abundantly clear, Ellen must decide how much newness her life can take.

Keywords: Marriage, Friendship, Family.

Wilde, Samantha.

I'll Take What She Has. 2013. Bantam. ISBN 9780385342674. 416p.

Annie and Nora, best friends since childhood, find their friendship challenged by the arrival of Cynthia Cypress, the glamorous new wife of Nora's ex-boyfriend and a colleague at the boarding school where Nora teaches. Annie lets her jealousy of Cynthia get the best of her, while Nora is drawn in to Cynthia's charmed inner circle. Both women begin to question the decisions that they have made about their lives, until a crisis at the school causes them to recognize the importance of their friendship.

Keywords: Friendship, Ensemble.

Chapter 4

Gentle Reads

Gentle reads are often requested by readers who are looking for something cozy to read, something with no sex, scandal, or violence. These are heart-warming stories, the "comfort food" of women's fiction. Many of them have Southern, British, or rural settings. Often family stories or sagas, gentle reads are the perfect books to curl up with and get lost in.

In addition to the basic characteristics of women's fiction that we described in the introduction, gentle reads have two distinguishing characteristics:

- no graphic sex, violence, or profanity; and

- a hopeful tone or message, often with a happy ending.

It is important to note that some authors write a mix of books, so you cannot always count on being able to recommend all of the titles from any particular author as a gentle read without checking first. The focus in this chapter is on authors who consistently write gentle reads, but do note that there are other titles suitable for fans of the genre throughout the book, noted by the keyword "Gentle."

Though gentle reads are not necessarily Christian fiction, most Christian fiction qualifies as a gentle read. Some readers who enjoy the books in this chapter may also enjoy Christian women's fiction. Authors like Karen Kingsbury, Robin Jones Gunn, Kristin Billerbeck, Susan May Warren, and Colleen Coble write novels in a variety of women's fiction genres, including chick lit, romantic fiction, and romantic suspense. Like the gentle reads annotated here, Christian women's fiction avoids sex, scandal, or violence, but it also includes a strong spiritual message. For more about Christian women's fiction, see chapter 9, or the "Contemporary Christian Life" section of *Genreflecting*, 7th ed. (2013).

Barclay, Tessa.

Ties of Affection. 2008. Severn House. ISBN 0727866540. 250p.
> Olivia Fletcher runs an eco-friendly housecleaning firm in Surrey, England. When none of her employees are willing to clean the Moorfield family's Victorian, Olivia is left to the task and discovers why — they are unlikable and demanding.

Olivia decides to help them all clean up their personal lives as well as their home and finds herself becoming emotionally attached to the family.

Keywords: Friendship, Gentle.

Battle, Lois.

The Florabama Ladies' Auxiliary and Sewing Circle. 2001. Viking. ISBN 0670894699. 358p.

Bonnie strikes out on her own after she divorces her bankrupt husband. She settles in the small town of Florabama, Alabama, where she takes a job coordinating an education program for women who have lost their sewing factory jobs.

Keywords: Gentle, Friendship, Southern.

Binchy, Maeve.

Binchy, an Irish author known for her gentle sagas of family and friendship, is one of the grand dames of women's fiction. A full list of her novels is included in chapter 2, and two of Binchy's later novels, which began to stray from the women's fiction formula, are annotated in chapter 9.

Light a Penny Candle. 1983. Viking. ISBN 0670428272. 542p.

Brought together by World War II, Elizabeth and Aisling become fast friends. This saga traces the two women's friendship through coming-of-age, marriage, and tragedy, showing how the bonds of friendship can endure any strain.

Keywords: Friendship, Saga.

*Circle of Friends. 1991. Delacorte. ISBN 0783108346. 565p.

Binchy transports readers to a 1950s Irish village for her semiautobiographical story of Benny, overweight and shy; her best friend Eve, an orphan; their deceitful friend Nan, and a host of colorful local characters. The girls grow up and endure the conservative decade, heartbreak, and betrayal.

Keywords: Friendship, Gentle, Historical.

Chiaverini, Jennifer.

Elm Creek Quilts series.

Chiaverini's gentle, heartwarming Elm Creek Quilts series revolves around the women of Elm Creek Manor, Pennsylvania, who become friends despite their different backgrounds and personalities.

The Quilter's Apprentice. 1999.

Round Robin. 2000.

The Cross Country Quilters. 2001.

The Runaway Quilt. 2002.

The Quilter's Legacy. 2003.

The Master Quilter. 2004.

The Sugar Camp Quilt. 2005.

The Christmas Quilt. 2005.

Circle of Quilters. 2006.

The Quilter's Homecoming. 2007.

The Winding Ways Quilt. 2008.

The Quilter's Kitchen. 2008.

The Lost Quilter. 2009.

A Quilter's Holiday. 2009.

The Aloha Quilt. 2010.

The Union Quilters. 2011.

The Wedding Quilt. 2011.

Sonoma Rose. 2012.

The Giving Quilt. 2012.

Herron, Rachael.

Cypress Hollow series.

Herron's Cypress Hollow series is gentle romance, featuring a cast of knitters living in a sleepy northern California town.

How to Knit a Love Song. 2010.

How to Knit a Heart Back Home. 2011.

Wishes and Stitches. 2011.

Hinton, Lynne.

Readers who enjoy Christian fiction may also like Hinton's novels, which bring spirituality into stories about small-town life.

Pie Town. 2011. Morrow. ISBN 0062045083. 352p.

Pie Town, New Mexico, was named for its delicious homemade pies, but the pies are no more. The close-knit, insular, multicultural community rallies around a sick boy named Alex, who was abandoned by his mother and lives with his grandparents. When newcomers Trina, a woman with a troubled past, and Father George, a recently ordained Catholic priest, arrive in Pie Town, the locals aren't open to accepting them. Then strange things begin to happen, and the residents of Pie Town are forced to reconsider their lives. Followed by *Welcome Back to Pie Town* (2013).

Keywords: Family, Gentle.

Hope Springs series.

The Hope Springs Community Church women's group is eclectic, at best. Beatrice is the town gossip, Louise is tough on the outside but ready to crack, young Charlotte is the new pastor. When the women get together to create a community cookbook, they realize they can be friends despite seemingly having nothing in common.

Friendship Cake. 2000.

Hope Springs. 2002

Forever Friends. 2003

Christmas Cake. 2009.

Wedding Cake. 2010.

Hoffman, Beth.

Saving CeeCee Honeycutt. 2010. Viking. ISBN 9780670021390. 320p.
Precocious teen CeeCee is sent off to Savannah to live with an elderly aunt after her eccentric mother is killed in an accident. Luckily for CeeCee, her aunt's housekeeper, Oletta, takes her under her wing. The quirky neighbors add to the charm and humor in this coming-of-age tale.

Keywords: Ensemble, Gentle, Humorous, Southern.

Looking for Me. 2013. Viking. ISBN 9780670025831. 368p.
Teddi Overman may have found her ideal path in life when she opened her antique furniture shop in Charleston, South Carolina. But family secrets still haunt her—specifically, her beloved brother Josh's mysterious disappearance. When clues to Josh's whereabouts emerge, Teddi returns to her Kentucky hometown, where she must confront her family's troubled past.

Keywords: Family, Southern.

Landvik, Lorna.
Landvik's novels feature eccentric characters, folksy stories, and charming homespun humor. She often features quirky families and strong communities—but her main characters are not always women. The featured selections below showcase strong female characters.

*Angry Housewives Eating Bon Bons. 2003. Ballantine. ISBN 0345438825. 336p.
Five housewives in small-town Minnesota meet in the turbulent late 1960s and form a book club. There's socially and politically active Slip; young widow Kari; meek and shy Merit; sexy and audacious Audrey; and transplanted Southerner Faith, who's not too thrilled with the Minnesotan tundra. The book follows the women to the present day, as they form close ties and act as sounding boards, partners in crime, and rescuers for one another.

Keywords: Ensemble, Family, Friendship.

Oh My Stars. 2005. Ballantine. ISBN 0345472314. 400p.
During the Depression, shy Violet runs away from her boring life and abusive father and ends up with a musical motley crew touring the country. She becomes the manager of the Pearltones, a racially mixed rockabilly band.

Keywords: Historical, Humorous.

'Tis the Season!: A Novel. 2008. Ballantine. ISBN 0345499751. 240p.

Young socialite Caroline Dixon (a Paris Hilton type) gets out of rehab and attempts to live a more stable life. Having alienated everyone she knows by writing a bitter letter that gets leaked to the tabloids, she goes into hiding and tries to reach out to people from her past, including her former nanny and the ranch hand who was kind to her as a teenager.

Keywords: Humorous.

Medlicott, Joan.

Ladies of Covington series.

Medlicott's gentle series follows Grace, Hannah, and Amelia, three friends living in a retirement boarding house near Philadelphia. When Amelia inherits a crumbling farmhouse in Covington, North Carolina, the women pack up and set off for a new chapter in their lives.

The Ladies of Covington Send Their Love. 2000.

The Gardens of Covington. 2001.

From the Heart of Covington. 2002.

The Spirit of Covington. 2003.

At Home in Covington. 2004.

A Covington Christmas. 2006.

Two Days after the Wedding. 2006.

An Unexpected Family. 2007.

Promises of Change. 2009.

A Blue and Gray Christmas. 2009.

Monroe, Mary Alice.

Monroe's gentle novels, set in the South, feature women dealing with everyday trials and tribulations.

Time Is a River. 2008. Pocket. ISBN 9781416544364. 369p.

After dealing with the one-two punch of breast cancer and her husband's infidelity, Mia escapes to a fishing cabin in the mountains outside of Asheville, North Carolina, to heal. When Mia finds the journal of a scandalous woman from the 1920s whose past is strongly tied to the cabin and the area, she opens a Pandora's box of secrets that may be the key to her recovery.

Keywords: Emotional, Southern, Thought-Provoking.

Last Light over Carolina. 2009. Pocket. ISBN 9781416549703. 369p.

Bud Morrison, a shrimp boat captain, is lost at sea off the coast of North Carolina. His wife, Carolina, must deal with the possibility that her husband of thirty years may never come home, and their small, close-knit community rallies behind her in the hopes that he'll return. Bud's disappearance forces Carolina to analyze her marriage and reconsider their relationship.

Keywords: Emotional, Grief, Marriage, Southern.

*The Butterfly's Daughter. 2011. Gallery. ISBN 1439170614. 400p.
Luz has been raised by her grandmother Abuela after being abandoned by her mother at a young age. Abuela's last wish is to take a trip to her home village in Mexico, but she passes away before they can go. Luz, full of regret, decides to take Abuela's ashes on the trip. Along the way she meets a cast of extraordinary women.

Keywords: Emotional, Family.

Beach House Memories. 2012. Gallery. ISBN 9781439170663. 400p.
South Carolina's Isle of Palms is a beachfront paradise, and Lovie Rutledge has longstanding memories of summers spent at her family's ramshackle beach cottage. A society marriage changes Lovie's life, but she holds on to her passion for the sea turtles who lay their eggs on the beach outside the cottage. When Lovie meets a biologist who is on the island to research the sea turtles, their shared interest soon turns into a passionate affair. But divorce is taboo among local society, and Lovie could lose everything by going against societal expectations.

Keywords: Emotional, Family, Southern.

Patton, Lisa.

Whistlin' Dixie in a Nor'easter. 2009. Thomas Dunne. ISBN 0312556608. 320p.
Spoiled Leelee is forced to leave her beloved Memphis and move with her husband to rural Vermont, where he has purchased a run-down inn. Unfortunately, as part of the contract, the former owners still get a say in how the business is run. Can she use her charms on the cranky Yankee couple and win them over with Southern hospitality? Followed by *Yankee Doodle Dixie* (2011).

Keywords: Humorous.

Pilcher, Rosamunde.

One of the grand dames of women's fiction, Pilcher writes gentle romantic sagas.

The Shell Seekers. 1988. St. Martin's. ISBN 0312010583. 530p.
After a health scare lands her in the hospital, Penelope Keeling revisits the events of her life, from her childhood spent with free-spirited parents to her first love, her grand romance with her husband, and her relationship with her children. At the heart of the story is a painting by Penelope's father, "The Shell Seekers," which gives Penelope fond memories of her youth but would also earn her family a small fortune if she chose to sell it. Characters from *The Shell Seekers* reappear in Pilcher's *September* (1990).

Keywords: Family, Romantic.

Winter Solstice. 2000. St. Martin's. ISBN 0312244266. 464p.
Elfrida Phipps retires from her stage career and moves to Scotland with her musician friend Oscar, who has recently lost his wife and daughter in a car crash.

They are soon joined by Elfrida's young cousin, Carrie, who is getting over a broken heart, and Carrie's teenage daughter. When a handsome stranger stops by for Christmas, he is of course welcomed into the motley group with open arms.

Keywords: Ensemble, Family, Romantic.

Ross, Ann B.

Miss Julia series.

Ross is best known for her "Miss Julia" series, which showcases the eccentric characters and inner workings of a gossipy small town and features the proper yet feisty Miss Julia, a strong-minded, straight-talking Southern septuagenarian.

Miss Julia Speaks Her Mind. 1999.

Miss Julia Takes Over. 2001.

Miss Julia Throws a Wedding. 2002.

Miss Julia Hits the Road. 2003.

Miss Julia Meets Her Match. 2004.

Miss Julia's School of Beauty. 2005.

Miss Julia Stands Her Ground. 2006.

Miss Julia Strikes Back. 2007.

Miss Julia Paints the Town. 2008.

Miss Julia Delivers the Goods. 2009.

Miss Julia Renews Her Vows. 2010.

Miss Julia Rocks the Cradle. 2011.

Miss Julia to the Rescue. 2012.

Miss Julia Stirs Up Trouble. 2013.

Shaw, Rebecca.

Barleybridge series.

Shaw's series features a rollicking cast of eccentric characters centered around a veterinary practice in the small English farming village of Barleybridge.

A Country Affair. 2006.

Country Wives. 2006.

Country Lovers. 2007.

Country Passions. 2007.

One Hot Country Summer. 2007.

Love in the Country. 2007.

Willett, Marcia.

Willett's novels, set in the rural West Country English countryside, feature mature women and their families. Much like her read-alike author, Maeve Binchy, Willett has been featuring more and more male protagonists in her family sagas.

A Week in Winter. 2002. St. Martin's. ISBN 0312287852. 342p.

Widow Maud wants to sell her Cornwall estate and retire to Devon. But she can't decide between the potential buyers. There's her stepdaughter Selina, who after thirty years still hasn't forgiven Maud for marrying her father; the building contractor who has lovingly restored the home to its former glory; and a mysterious young woman with a secret. Romances and family secrets come to light, complicating matters further.

Keywords: Family.

The Children's Hour. 2004. Thomas Dunne Books. ISBN 0312327773. 367p.

Nest and Mina, sisters in their seventies living on the English coast, are worried when their ailing older sister Georgie comes to live with them. Georgie is on the brink of Alzheimer's and threatens to spill long-dormant family secrets.

Keywords: Family, Thought-Provoking.

*The Summer House. 2012. Thomas Dunne. ISBN 9781250003690. 304p.

Willet's latest features a male protagonist, but his mother's story is the heart of the tale. When Matt comes across the box of his childhood memories that his mother has saved, why don't the photos make any sense? He doesn't recognize many things from his childhood photographs, and why doesn't his sister appear in any of them?

Keywords: Family, Thought-Provoking.

Chapter 5

Issue-Driven Women's Fiction

Issue-driven novels are common across many genres and are often found in general fiction. However, in the 1990s, issue-driven novels became extremely popular, thanks in part to Oprah Winfrey and her book club. The continued popularity of book clubs keeps the demand high for issue-driven fiction, particularly issue-driven women's fiction, since the controversial issues and difficult topics make for spirited discussions. This is a trend that is not going away any time soon!

The topics covered in issue-driven women's fiction vary considerably. An exciting story line is a must. Family and personal issues, including divorce, illness, and death, are common themes. Some authors, particularly Jodi Picoult, specialize in plots that focus on controversial issues or hot topics of the day, such as medical ethics, teenage pregnancy, or school violence. Authors of issue-driven women's fiction tend to pull no punches, and part of the appeal of issue-driven novels is that they make most readers' problems seem minimal, even nonexistent.

Readers looking for issue-driven women's fiction are often looking for something that packs an emotional wallop, something that they can sink into and find themselves absorbed in. As mentioned, these books tend to make good choices for book discussion groups, as they have a lot of issues for people to identify with or rail against.

In a rare exception to the criteria for identifying women's fiction that we laid out at the beginning of the book, you will note that several authors of issue-driven novels choose to use a male protagonist who either carries the story or shares equal time with a female protagonist. Because the plots deal with families and relationships, it makes sense to include them as women's fiction.

Bourret, Amy.

Mothers and Other Liars. 2010. St. Martin's. ISBN 0312586582. 320p.
> Ruby lives a fine life with her young daughter, Lark. Ruby took in Lark as an abandoned baby but never quite got around to making everything official. When she sees Lark's picture in the newspaper as a missing child, Ruby realizes she must do the right thing—but can't stand to lose her precious daughter.

Keywords: Family, Mothers and Daughters.

Chamberlain, Diane.

Chamberlain's many novels also include romances, but the titles listed here are issue-driven novels concerning families and friendships. Most involve dark, long-held secrets.

Breaking the Silence. 2009. Mira. ISBN 9780778327424. 416p.

Laura Brandon's dying father had one unusual wish: that his daughter meet with Sarah Tolley, an elderly woman living in a nursing home. Out of love for her father, Laura meets with Sarah, setting a chain of events in motion that leads to her husband's suicide and her five-year-old daughter's emotional breakdown.

Keywords: Family, Grief.

The Lies We Told. 2010. Mira. ISBN 9780778328537. 379p.

As teens, sisters Maya and Rebecca witnessed their parents' brutal murder—an event that has scarred them for life. As adults, both have successful careers as physicians, but their responses to life continue to be different. Maya is a homebody, while Rebecca loves adventure and risk-taking. When a hurricane devastates their home, both women spring into action to help in the aid effort, but Maya is lost in a helicopter crash. In the aftermath of the accident, Rebecca finds herself attracted to Maya's husband—but is Maya dead or just missing?

Keywords: Grief, Sisters.

*The Midwife's Confession. 2011. Mira. ISBN 9780778329862. 432p.

When Noelle commits suicide, her two best friends, Tara and Emerson, are shocked—they never would have guessed she would do something like that. It turns out that Noelle was hiding lots of secrets, which the two friends start to uncover. The more determined they are to get to the truth, the more disturbing facts come to light about the friend they thought they knew.

Keywords: Friendship, Grief.

Keeper of the Light. 2011. Mira. ISBN 9780778329541. 512p.

When Annie O'Neill is murdered, everyone is shocked. She was one of the lights of her small Outer Banks community and beloved by many—including the husband of Dr. Olivia Simon, an emergency room doctor who tries to save Annie's life. After Annie's death, Olivia's marriage breaks down even further, and in a last-ditch attempt to save things, Olivia begins to transform herself into the woman her husband loved. Followed by *Kiss River* (2011) and *Her Mother's Shadow* (2012).

Keywords: Family, Marriage.

The Good Father. 2012. Mira. ISBN 9780778313465. 400p.

Travis Brown tries to be the best father he can be, but times are difficult. He loves his daughter more than anything and is willing to make whatever sacrifices are needed to keep her happy and safe. When Travis is offered a construction job, he is grateful for the opportunity, but when he arrives on the site, he learns that he has been misled, and in a fit of desperation he makes a choice that will affect his family's future.

Keywords: Ensemble, Family.

Cohen, Leah Hager.

Cohen's literary issue-driven family fiction showcases fractured families dealing with extraordinary circumstances.

House Lights. 2007. Norton. ISBN 9780393064513. 320p.

Aspiring actress Beatrice contacts her estranged grandmother, Margaret, a famous stage star, in the hopes of getting career advice. When Beatrice's esteemed father is accused of sexual harassment, Beatrice runs away to Margaret, who takes the young girl under her wing. When Beatrice is cast in a summer stock production, she falls in love with a much older theater director, learns more about what strained the relationship between her mother and grandmother, and begins to come to terms with the dysfunction in her family.

Keywords: Family.

*The Grief of Others. 2011. Riverhead. ISBN 9781594488054. 384p.

When John and Ricky's newborn baby dies before they can take him home from the hospital, they do not know how to express their grief. Mindful of their two older children, they try to pretend life goes on as normal. The stress, however, is too much for all of them to bear—it leads to a painful secret coming to light and finds their children acting out at school and at home.

Keywords: Emotional, Family, Grief.

Colin, Emily.

The Memory Thief. 2012. Ballantine. ISBN 9780345530394. 420p.

Madeleine Kimble doesn't want her husband to climb Mount McKinley— she fears that he will never return. Her fears are not unfounded, and when she receives the news that Aidan has died in a climbing accident, her world collapses. Aidan's friend J. C., who delivers the tragic news, has a secret of his own—he's in love with Madeleine and has been for many years. As Madeleine and her young son grieve, Nicholas, who lives on the other side of the country, awakens from a motorcycle accident and finds that his memories are gone, replaced with mysterious glimpses of a woman and boy who he has never met.

Keywords: Emotional, Family, Grief.

Dale, Lisa.

Slow Dancing on Prince's Pier. 2011. Berkley. ISBN 0425239950. 368p.

Thea Celic and Garret Sorensen were in love—but then Thea married Garret's brother, destroying the brothers' relationship. Now Thea and her husband are divorcing, and she is having a difficult time letting go of the stability of the close-knit Sorensen clan, who have become her family after fifteen years of marriage. When Thea's feelings for Garret begin to return, both must learn to forgive one another for past betrayals before they can move on.

Keywords: Emotional, Family, Marriage.

A Promise of Safekeeping. 2012. Berkley. ISBN 9780425245149. 352p.

Attorney Lauren is filled with both fear and regret when Arlen, an innocent man she helped put in prison, is released nine years later. Desperate for forgiveness, she tracks him down, but to get to him she must go through his best friend, who isn't willing to forgive.

Keywords: Romantic.

Delinsky, Barbara.

Barbara Delinsky started out writing category romance but shifted into more character- and issue-driven novels with the publication of her 1994 novel, *For My Daughters.*

For My Daughters. 1994. HarperCollins. ISBN 0060176180. 290p.

Wealthy socialite Ginny St. Clair is estranged from her three daughters, so they are surprised when their mother summons them to her new home. But when they arrive, their mother isn't there, and the women are forced to hash out their issues and make amends for past wrongs.

Keywords: Ensemble, Mothers and Daughters, Sisters.

Lake News. 1999. Simon & Schuster. ISBN 0684864320. 380p.

When a reporter unjustly accuses Lily Blake of having had an affair with a newly appointed Catholic cardinal, the cabaret singer retreats to her rural hometown of Lake Henry, New Hampshire. Unfortunately, the town is still whispering about the youthful indiscretions from her past.

Keywords: Family.

The Summer I Dared. 2004. Scribner. ISBN 9780743246439. 368p.

A boating accident brings three strangers together, transforming their lives in unexpected ways. Julia's marriage is outwardly happy, yet she stays with her husband for the same reason she does pretty much everything in her life—a feeling of obligation to others. Julia soon finds herself drawn to Noah, the man who rescued her, and is forced to reevaluate the choices she has made.

Keywords: Family, Romantic, Self-Actualization.

Family Tree. 2006. Doubleday. ISBN 9780385518659. 368p.

Dana knew it would be difficult to transition into her husband Hugh's highbrow family. After all, she doesn't even know her real father, while the Clarkes can trace their lineage back to the *Mayflower.* When the couple's first baby has distinctly African American coloring and features, suspicions and accusations abound.

Keywords: Family.

The Secret between Us. 2007. Doubleday. ISBN 9780385518680. 352p.

One moment can have long-reaching repercussions—teenage Grace causes a car accident, injuring her history teacher. Impulsively, her mother Deborah sends Grace home and takes the blame herself. The next day, the man dies from his injuries, and the lie becomes much more serious.

Keywords: Family.

Not My Daughter. 2010. Doubleday. ISBN 9780385524988. 352p.

When three popular high school girls make a pregnancy pact, it sends their parents in to a tailspin. Since one of the pregnant teens is the daughter of the high school principal, who happened to be a teen mother herself, the local school board is up in arms. When the national press gets a hold of the story, the principal's job is in jeopardy, as is her standing in the community.

Keywords: Family.

Escape. 2011. Doubleday. ISBN 9780385532723. 320p.

Emily hates her job as a corporate lawyer—she once dreamed of representing the little guys against the big bad companies but instead finds herself working on the side of the bad guys. One day, unable to take it any more, she leaves work early, packs her bags, and takes off, leaving her apathetic husband and needy sister behind. She heads to the sleepy New Hampshire town where she last remembers being truly happy, back in college one summer.

Keywords: Self-Actualization.

Diffenbaugh, Vanessa.

The Language of Flowers. 2011. Ballantine. ISBN 9780345525543. 336p.

Victoria is emancipated from the foster care system on her 18th birthday. Abandoned at birth, she has grown up in a string of bad foster homes, except for the one year she spent on a vineyard with Elizabeth who taught her the meaning of flowers. As she moves through life as an independent adult, she starts to question what's been missing in her life and is forced to confront a painful secret from her past.

Keywords: Self-Actualization.

Dilloway, Margaret.

The Care and Handling of Roses with Thorns. 2012. Putnam. ISBN 9780399157752. 356p.

Gal Garner's life is governed by three things: her rose-breeding hobby, her job as a high school biology teacher, and her kidney disease, which has plagued her since childhood. When her teenage niece Riley appears on her doorstep, Gal's life is shaken up. Riley's life has been unstable, thanks to her mother's frequent absences and disregard for others' needs, and Gal provides some much-needed stability. As the two women learn to navigate life with each other, they wonder how they ever managed to go it alone.

Keywords: Family, Thought-Provoking.

Doughty, Louise.

Whatever You Love. 2011. Faber & Faber. ISBN 9780571254767. 320p.

When Laura's nine-year-old daughter is killed in a car accident, she wants take revenge and begins to track down the man responsible. Haunted by not only this loss but also her failed marriage, she slips into near obsession.

Keywords: Family, Grief, Self-Actualization.

Ferriss, Lucy.

The Lost Daughter. 2012. Berkley. ISBN 9780425245569. 384p.

Brooke O'Connor is hiding a devastating secret from her family: at age seventeen, after hiding her pregnancy from her friends and family, she gave birth to a stillborn child in a motel room. Fifteen years later, she's happily married and has a daughter, but she is reluctant to have a second child and she's afraid to reveal her secret to her husband. When Brooke's high school boyfriend returns, her husband suspects that Brooke is having an affair—but the truth is even more heartbreaking.

Keywords: Family, Marriage.

Fielding, Joy.

Fielding actually writes in a variety of styles, from romantic suspense to tearjerker issue-driven novels. Her women's fiction listed here—though many of them have suspense elements—centers around ordinary women dealing with extraordinary circumstances and focuses on complex issues such as divorce, child abductions, abusive relationships, and fatal illnesses.

The First Time. 2000. Pocket. ISBN 9780743407052. 352p.

The facade of Mattie Hart's seemingly perfect life crumbles around her when her husband leaves her for another woman. She's not too surprised, as she's been ignoring his infidelities for a long time. But this couldn't have come at a worse time—Mattie's just been diagnosed with ALS (Lou Gehrig's disease), so her guilt-ridden husband comes back to care for her.

Keywords: Family, Emotional.

Grand Avenue. 2001. Pocket. ISBN 0743407075. 392p.

Four women meet at their children's playground in the 1970s and remain friends for the next twenty-odd years. Each woman's life holds a story—abusive husbands, fading beauty queens, sexual harassment at work, and workaholic moms. A saga of four lives worthy of any daytime Emmy.

Keywords: Family, Friendship.

Now You See Her. 2011. Atria. ISBN 9781416585312. 368p.

Marcy is in Ireland celebrating her twenty-fifth wedding anniversary—but her husband is not, having recently left her for his mistress. Their daughter, Devon, disappeared under mysterious circumstances two years prior, and everyone wants to convince Marcy that the girl, suffering from bipolar disorder, committed suicide. But Marcy believes Devon ran away to start a new life and wishes she could, too. When Marcy thinks she spots Devon in Ireland, she is given hope and vows to track her down.

Keywords: Family, Self-Actualization.

Fitch, Janet.

*White Oleander. 1999. Little, Brown. ISBN 0316569321. 390p.

Astrid is bounced around through the foster care system after her flighty and disturbed mother, Iris, is sent to prison. When she finally lands with a "dream" family, there is trouble in that home as well, manipulated by Iris. How Astrid gets through her ordeals and grows up into a mature young woman makes for an absorbing read.

Keyword: Family.

Fowler, Therese.

Souvenir. 2008. Ballantine. ISBN 9780345499684. 384p.
> When Meg discovers she has ALS (Lou Gehrig's disease), she decides it's time to make peace with the past, and seeks out the boy she left behind—who might just be the father of her teenage daughter. A juicy subplot involving her daughter's online romance with an older boy provides just enough spark to keep this from descending into tearjerker territory.

Keyword: Family.

Genova, Lisa.

Still Alice. 2009. Gallery. ISBN 9781439102817. 292p.
> Alice Howland is a professor of psychology at an Ivy League university, and her brilliant mind has been the centerpiece of her storied career. When Alice begins to forget simple things, she first blames it on menopause but quickly realizes that there is something more serious going on. The diagnosis is early-onset Alzheimer's, and Alice's life rapidly begins to break down, putting a tremendous strain on those who love her.

Keywords: Emotional, Older Women.

Love Anthony. 2012. Gallery. ISBN 9781439164686. 309p.
> Two women—Beth, a stay-at-home mom whose husband has left her, and Olivia, still grieving the death of her autistic son Anthony—meet one another on Nantucket. They become close friends and help each other heal the wounds of their troubled pasts.

Keywords: Emotional, Friendship, Grief.

Hanauer, Cathi.

Gone. 2012. Atria. ISBN 9781451626414. 350p.
> Eve and Eric's marriage is far from equitable—her private nutritionist practice is thriving, and his career as a sculptor has hit the skids. One night, Eric leaves on a routine errand and does not return, causing Eve to re-evaluate her marriage and her priorities in life.

Keywords: Marriage, Thought-Provoking.

Hatvany, Amy.

*Best Kept Secret. 2011. Washington Square Press. ISBN 9781439193310. 352p.
> Cadence, a writer and single mom, is struggling to keep up and to take care of her preschool son, Charlie. She turns to alcohol to help her get to sleep

and soon finds she can't function without it. One fateful night, she leaves Charlie alone to make a wine run, and her ex-husband shows up at her door.

Keywords: Family, Self-Actualization.

Outside the Lines. 2012. Washington Square Press. ISBN 1451640544. 384p.
Eden West is haunted by her father's suicide attempt and her parents' subsequent divorce. Her father hasn't been a part of her life for years, but when her mother is diagnosed with cancer, Eden wants to find her father and bring him back into her life. The problem is that David has been alternating between psychiatric hospitals and homelessness for years, and he may not want to be found.

Keywords: Family, Thought-Provoking.

*The Language of Sisters. 2012. Washington Square Press. ISBN 9781451688139. 320p.
Nicole Hunter's younger sister, Jenny, is severely developmentally disabled, and she is institutionalized because her family cannot care for her. When Jenny is raped by a nurse's aide, a series of events transpires that brings out Nicole's guilt for abandoning her sister—and allows her to become the person she wanted to be for Jenny.

Keywords: Family, Thought-Provoking.

Heart Like Mine. 2013. Washington Square Press. ISBN 9781451640564. 368p.
Thirty-seven-year-old Grace has finally found love with Victor, a Seattle-based chef who owns his own restaurant and accepts her decision to not have children. When Victor's ex-wife Kelli dies suddenly, Grace finds herself helping Victor's two children, teenage Ava and her younger brother Max, cope with their grief and figure out what happened to their mother.

Keywords: Family, Motherhood.

Hegland, Jean.

*Windfalls. 2004. Pocket. ISBN 0743470079. 339p.
Two different young women in the late 1970s have the same choice to make: each finds herself pregnant and unmarried. Anna, a college student with career ambitions, chooses an abortion, while Cerise, a lonely high-schooler, chooses to have her child. Anna becomes a successful photographer who marries and has two daughters, and Cerise ends up in a series of bad situations that eventually cause her to lose her home and her second child. Their paths cross when Anna hires Cerise as a daycare provider and the women forge an unexpected friendship.

Keyword: Emotional.

Johnson, Rebecca.

*And Sometimes Why. 2008. Putnam. ISBN 9780399154522. 320p.
Sixteen-year-old Helen lies in a coma after a car accident, and everyone involved gets a story here. Her father Darius refuses to believe she won't recover; while her mother Sophia becomes obsessed with Helen's secret boyfriend, Bobby, who also died in the crash. Their other daughter, Miranda, withdraws from the family;

and Harry, the driver of the other vehicle, allows his life to be consumed by guilt, even though he was not at fault.

Keywords: Emotional, Family.

McCreight, Kimberly.

Reconstructing Ameila. 2013. Harper. ISBN 9780062225436. 384p.

Attorney Kate Baron is the single mother of a fifteen-year-old daughter who attends Grace Hall, a prestigious private school. When Kate gets a frantic call telling her that her daughter has cheated on an English paper, she's shocked—and when she arrives at Grace Hall to find that her daughter has committed suicide by jumping off the school's roof, she can't believe that it happened. Then a mysterious text arrives: "She didn't jump." Kate starts to investigate on her own, and what she finds implicates everyone from the school administrators to Kate's colleagues to Amelia's best friend.

Keywords: Family, Mothers and Daughters.

Meyers, Randy Susan.

The Comfort of Lies. 2013. Atria. ISBN 9781451673012. 336p.

Tia is involved in a passionate affair with a married man. When she gets pregnant, Nathan abandons her and she gives her daughter up for adoption. Nathan confesses his affair to his wife, Juliette, but he doesn't tell her about Tia's pregnancy. When Juliette discovers photographs of Tia and Nathan's daughter, now named Savannah, she becomes obsessed with the idea of being part of the girl's life. Savannah's mother, Caroline, is ambivalent about parenthood and worries that she isn't a good parent. The three women's lives converge in a dramatic fashion as they explore the meaning of motherhood.

Keywords: Family, Friendship, Motherhood.

Miller, Sue.

Miller's fiction tackles serious subjects that people never think will happen to them, and families in crisis. Her emotionally complex characters are often on a search for identity.

The Good Mother. 1986. Harper & Row. ISBN 9780060155513. 310p.

After an ugly divorce, Anna Dunlap has been granted custody of her three-year-old daughter, Molly. When Anna meets Leo Cutter, she experiences a sexual awakening, and when her husband finds out what's going on, he sues for custody, accusing Anna of being an unfit mother. Psychologists are called in, lawyers do their work, and a harrowing trial ensues.

Keywords: Family, Motherhood.

Lost in the Forest. 2005. Knopf. ISBN 1400042267. 256p.

After leaving her first husband, Mark, for cheating on her, Eva is happily remarried. When her second husband dies in a tragic accident, she is devastated and finds she can't cope with her three children, two daughters from her first marriage and a son from her second. Mark reappears in her life to help out and finds that he's still in love with her. Meanwhile, their younger and emotionally unsure daughter finds herself lured into a dangerous relationship with an older man.

Keywords: Family, Grief, Marriage, Mothers and Daughters.

The Lake Shore Limited. 2010. Knopf. ISBN 9780307264213. 288p.
Two women are brought together by the tragedy of 9/11. When Gus dies in one of the planes used in the attack, his sister Leslie needs to know if he ever found true love with his girlfriend, Billy. Billy, a playwright, has created a play exploring the tragedy and her feelings toward Gus's death.

Keywords: Emotional, Grief.

Mitchard, Jacquelyn.

Mitchard's emotionally absorbing novels are characterized by seemingly improbable situations happening to everyday families. She focuses on the connections between women and their families and friends.

The Deep End of the Ocean. 1996. Viking. ISBN 9780670865796. 434p.
Beth's son Ben was abducted as a toddler, and she spends nine years searching for him. Endless guilt leads her to neglect her other two children, and the family tension increases as older son Vincent becomes more and more aggressive at school and at home. When Ben finally returns, it causes more pressure than relief for the beleaguered family. This novel is especially notable for being the first-ever selection of Oprah's Book Club.

Keywords: Emotional, Family.

The Breakdown Lane. 2005. HarperCollins. ISBN 0060587245. 400p.
Leo abandons Julianne, his wife of twenty years, to live on a commune. Added to her woes is a diagnosis of multiple sclerosis. This could have easily become a weepy disease-of-the-month novel, but Mitchard tackles illness, abandonment, and family issues with grace.

Keywords: Emotional, Family.

Second Nature. 2011. Random House. ISBN 9781400067756. 384p.
Young Sicily has had a very hard life—she loses her father in a tragic fire that leaves her entire face terribly disfigured. Two years later her mother passes away. Still, she manages to grow up into a resilient young woman. Nearly a decade later, she is offered the chance at a total face transplant but decides against it until a startling revelation causes her to end her engagement and decide to take a new chance at life.

Keyword: Emotional.

Moriarty, Laura.

The Rest of Her Life. 2007. Hyperion. ISBN 9781401302719. 320p.
Leigh's teenage daughter, Kara, is responsible for killing a classmate in a car accident. As Leigh tries to cope with the aftermath and reach out to her daughter,

Kara withdraws. Meanwhile, Leigh's son, Justin, feels ignored and unimportant. A smartly woven tale of a mother trying to connect to her teenage children in the wake of a tragedy.

Keywords: Family, Mothers and Daughters.

While I'm Falling. 2009. Hyperion. ISBN 1401302726. 320p.
College student Veronica is having a difficult time coping with her parents' messy divorce. When a series of events bring Veronica and her mother closer together, she must find a way to help them both cope with their changing family.

Keywords: Emotional, Mothers and Daughters.

Packer, Ann.

*Songs without Words. 2007. Knopf. ISBN 9780375412813. 352p.
Liz and Sarabeth, both in their forties, have been friends since childhood. Liz is a down-to earth, responsible mother of two teenagers while Sarabeth is a free-spirited artist. When Liz's daughter attempts suicide, the bonds of their friendship are tested as Sarabeth withdraws just when Liz needs her most.

Keywords: Family, Friendship.

Pagan, Camille Noe.

The Art of Forgetting. 2011. Dutton. ISBN 9780525952190. 291p.
Shy and timid Marissa and self-centered, charismatic Julia have been friends since they were fourteen. When Julia is hit by a cab, she suffers brain damage, losing some of her memory and altering her personality, leaving Marissa in charge of helping her regain her life.

Keyword: Friendship.

Picoult, Jodi.
Picoult's issue-driven fiction revolves around contemporary women and their families, dealing with a tragedy or some unforeseen, improbable situation. There is always something that seems "ripped from the headlines" in her plots, often featuring "what would you do"-type situations. It would be remiss of me to not mention that, in truth, Picoult's books *do* break one of the criteria that we stated at the beginning of this book: several of her novels have a male protagonist. For example, *The Tenth Circle* (2011) is about a man whose daughter is date raped, *Salem Falls* (2007) is about a male teacher who is falsely accused of sexually abusing a student, and *Change of Heart* (2002) is about a man on death row who wants to donate his organs. However, since readers identify her so closely as the top issue-driven fiction author, and her novels focus on edgy family issues, we think it's reasonable to make her an exception to the rules.

Harvesting the Heart. 1993. Penguin. ISBN 9780140230277. 464p.

Abandoned by her mother at a young age, Paige struggles with self-confidence. Working in a diner after dropping out of art school, she meets and marries Nicholas, whose upper-crust parents promptly disown him. Often left alone due to Nicholas's demanding schedule as a surgeon, Paige is soon overwhelmed after the birth of their son, becoming emotionally and physically exhausted. She leaves her husband and their baby behind to try and find her mother—and herself.

Keywords: Emotional, Motherhood, Mothers and Daughters.

The Pact. 1998. Morrow. ISBN 9780688158125. 384p.

Nobody is surprised when teens Chris Harte and Em Gold become romantically involved—they've been friends since they were babies, and their families are very close. But there's more to their relationship than meets the eye, and when both are found dead in an apparent suicide pact, it sends shock waves through their close-knit families. As both sets of parents work through the aftermath of Chris and Em's suicide, secrets are revealed that transform their lives.

Keywords: Emotional, Grief.

Perfect Match. 2002. Atria. ISBN 978074341827. 368p.

Nina, a district attorney, knows how hard it is to prosecute sex crimes when the victims are juvenile. When her young son Nathaniel is molested and identifies their priest as the perpetrator, Nina becomes frustrated by the threat of an unsatisfactory outcome and takes the law into her own hands, shooting the priest at his arraignment. During her own trial, DNA evidence shows a shocking fact—the priest may have been innocent.

Keyword: Family.

My Sister's Keeper. 2004. Atria. ISBN 9780743454529. 423p.

Thirteen-year-old Anna has spent her life keeping her older sister, Kate, alive via a series of surgeries and transplants. Kate has leukemia, and Anna was conceived specifically to be a bone marrow match for her sister. Now that she is older, Anna starts to question her role in the family, and the consequences for Kate's survival could be serious.

Keywords: Emotional, Family.

House Rules. 2010. Washington Square. 9780743296441. 560p.

Jacob Hunt has Asperger's, and he's fascinated with forensic science—to the point where he follows a police scanner from his bedroom at home. When a grisly murder tears Jacob's hometown apart, his parents are shocked to find that their son is the prime suspect.

Keywords: Emotional, Family.

Sing You Home. 2011. Washington Square. ISBN 9781439102732. 496p.

Zoe and her husband, Max, desperately want a baby, and thanks to in vitro fertilization, they have finally conceived. When Zoe's pregnancy ends in a stillbirth, Max can't handle his grief and their marriage crumbles. As she rebuilds her life, Zoe falls in love with a woman, and Zoe and Vanessa want to become parents using the frozen embryos from her IVF cycle, but her husband disagrees and sues for custody.

Keywords: Emotional, Thought-Provoking.

Lone Wolf. 2012. Atria. ISBN 9781439102749. 432p.

When Cara and her father, Luke, are gravely injured in a car accident, Cara's brother, Edward, reluctantly returns home after being out of the country for many years. Cara recovers, but their father is left comatose. Edward wants to pull the life support, but Cara is convinced that a medical miracle is possible. Complicating matters is the fact that Luke is a perfect candidate to have nearly all of his organs donated to waiting matches.

Keyword: Family.

Quindlen, Anna.

Journalist Quindlen's issue-driven fiction explores families and tragedies.

One True Thing. 1994. Random House. ISBN 067940712X. 289p.

Ellen abandons a promising career in journalism to return home and care for her mother, Kate, who is dying of cancer. Through long hours as her mother's companion, Ellen must deal with Kate's pain and suffering, her father's coldness, and family secrets.

Keywords: Emotional, Family, Mothers and Daughters.

Every Last One. 2010. Random House. ISBN 9781400065745. 299p.

When Mary Beth's teenage daughter, Ruby, casually announces that she's breaking up with her boyfriend, the family has no idea what's in store for them. Ruby's boyfriend, Kirenan, a neighbor boy, is practically family but hides an unstable personality under boyish charm. Distracted by issues with her twin boys, Mary Beth and her family are blindsided by Kirenan's violent reaction to the breakup.

Keyword: Family.

Schwarz, Christina.

All Is Vanity. 2002. Doubleday. ISBN 0385499728. 400p.

Margaret, a struggling author, begins to manipulate her best friend's life in order to get a good story out of her troubles. Letty has moved with her husband and children to an exclusive neighborhood in Los Angeles and is finding it hard to keep up with the wealthy neighbors. When she starts calling Margaret for advice, Margaret begins to egg Letty on to buy more, spend more, be more, even though Letty is plunging into debt and personal destruction, all so that Margaret can turn around and write about it.

Keyword: Friendship.

Sebold, Alice.

The Almost Moon. 2007. Little, Brown. ISBN 0316003611. 304p.

Helen resents her duty as caretaker for her senile mother, Clair. One evening, unable to cope further with the stress and tediousness, she suffocates Clair and then doesn't quite know how to cope with the aftermath. The relationship between Helen and her mother unravels at a slow pace but gives the reader much insight into how it turned Helen into the person she has become.

Keywords: Family, Grief, Mothers and Daughters.

Shreve, Anita.

Shreve's novels feature strong women characters and explore stories of loss and violence. Decidedly literary in tone, she fits into the "issue-driven" camp thanks to her tragic themes, yet her focus is on the characters and their feelings and not as much on the dramatic plots. It is also valid to note that her novels do feature male protagonists, as well.

The Pilot's Wife. 1998. Little, Brown. ISBN 0316789089. 293p.

As a pilot's wife, Kathryn Lyons is used to worrying about the fate of her husband. When his plane explodes, she is forced to confront the truth about his life, and learning his secrets is the only way she can heal.

Keywords: Emotional, Grief, Marriage.

Sea Glass. 2002. Little, Brown. ISBN 0316780812. 378p.

Newlyweds Honora and Sexton rent a house on a picturesque beach, with hopes of fixing it up and turning it into a home. When the couple finds the money to buy the house, their fortunes change, leaving their marriage in shards and forcing Honora to confront the truth about her husband.

Keywords: Emotional, Marriage.

Body Surfing: A Novel. 2007. Little, Brown. ISBN 9780316059855. 304p.

Sydney has had a hard romantic life. Only twenty-nine, she's endured both divorce and widowhood. When she retreats to New Hampshire to tutor a teenage girl, Julie, she hopes it will be a noneventful summer escape. Unfortunately, the family she works for draws her into their drama. Julie's anti-Semitic mother can't hide her dislike for half-Jewish Sydney, Julie's older brothers appear on the scene and both fall for Sydney, and Julie runs away with a secret.

Keywords: Family, Grief.

Rescue. 2010. Little, Brown. ISBN 9780316020725. 304p.

Pete fears that his teenage daughter, Rowan, suddenly moody and caught drinking, is heading down the same path as her mother, his alcoholic ex-wife Shelia. To try and save Rowan, he reluctantly contacts the estranged Shelia, and they need to figure out what they can do to save their child. Will Shelia's return be helpful or damaging to Pete and his daughter?

Keyword: Family.

Winston, Lolly.

Good Grief. 2005. Grand Central. ISBN 0446694843. 368p.

Sophie Stanton never expected to be a young widow, and the death of her husband has thrown her for a loop. Unable to cope with her new life, she decides to start over in a different town and finds that reinvention brings its own challenges—and its own rewards.

Keywords: Emotional, Grief, Humorous.

*Happiness Sold Separately. 2006. Warner. ISBN 0446533068. 304p.

Elinor and Ted's once-perfect marriage is rocked by infertility. Elinor's hormone treatments make her unhappy and withdrawn, and Ted finds solace in another woman. They decide to separate, not really sure if they want their marriage to end but not sure if they are strong enough to weather infertility and infidelity. Everyone's got a decision to make, and how it all ends may surprise you.

Keyword: Family.

Woodruff, Lee.

*Those We Love Most. 2012. Hyperion. ISBN 9781401341787. 305p.

The lives of Maura and Pete Corrigan change in a split second when their nine-year-old son, James, is hit by a car and killed. Their grief is overwhelming, and Maura blames herself—she was texting instead of watching her son. The disintegration of Maura and Pete's marriage is compared with the disintegration of Maura's parents' marriage—both relationships forever changed by secrets and shame.

Keywords: Family, Grief, Marriage, Thought-Provoking.

Chapter **6**

Trend: Chick Lit and Beyond

The scene: any bookstore, circa the turn of the millennium. What do you see? Pink. Fuchsia. Mauve. Hot Pink. And legs, oh the legs! High-heeled shoes dangling from legs. Legs with bare feet and daisies tucked in the toes. Every swirly font ever imagined . . . what's happening? It's the attack of . . . CHICK LIT! Distinguished by its humor—wisecracking characters or ridiculous situations, usually involving work or dating—chick lit offers fun, entertaining reading. This type of book's aim of eliciting a response of "I'm exactly like that" or "That just happened to me!" has really struck a chord with women in their twenties and thirties who want to be reassured that they are not alone in screwing up their lives—or that screwing up doesn't preclude a happy ending.

Chick lit took the world by storm in the late 1990s, mainly thanks to the huge response to Helen Fielding's modern Everywoman, Bridget Jones (the protagonist of the best-selling *Bridget Jones's Diary*). These funny, light, romantic novels appealed to women readers of all ages and life stages, even though they tended to feature young working women making their way in a big city.

Partially due to oversaturation, and partly due to a maturing readership, the trend started to fade a bit by the mid-2000s, but it's not over yet. In some ways, it has really simply matured. The materialism and brand awareness that seemed so in trend in the 1990s were out of step with the more austere climate of post–9/11 America. Also, the natural progression of being single in the big city is to be married in the suburbs, then trying your best as a working mom and wife, and so on. Publishers are still putting light, fun women's reads out—they just may have decided to subdue the covers a bit. Chick lit has, for better or for worse, become a catch-all term for much of women's fiction. Unfortunately, in some literary circles, it's taken on a rather negative connotation. (See "Articles of Interest" in appendix D for many interesting online discussions relating to the rise and fall of chick lit.) Throughout this volume (particularly in chapter 3), chick lit has been used in a general sense to mean lighter fiction that often skews younger.

Meg Cabot, Jennifer Weiner, Marion Keyes, and Jane Green all have early novels with a chick lit flavor to them and are good read-alikes for readers who like chick lit. Many of the humorous women's fiction novels are also good bets for chick lit fans (see chapter 3). This chapter showcases titles that are "classic chick lit"—the Manolos and martinis that everyone thinks of first when they hear the term. Some of chick lit's successors make an appearance in this chapter, as well, as do more recent titles that hearken back to the best of the chick lit days but are decidedly of this decade.

Bagshawe, Louise.

The Go-To Girl. 2005. St. Martin's Griffin. ISBN 0312339917. 372p.
> London script reader Anna desperately wants to make it big in the film industry, but she's just too mousy to get ahead. When a hot new director uncovers her screenwriting talent, she may be on the way to bigger and better things.

> **Keywords:** Humorous, Workplace.

Ballis, Stacey.

Ballis's charming and funny chick lit features modern, relatable women.

Room for Improvement. 2006. Berkley: Penguin. ISBN 0425209822. 304p.
> Chicago interior designer Lily takes a job designing for a reality makeover TV show that pairs up singles looking for a new room and a new love interest. She thinks it's going to be simple and fun, but a half-wit host, a cranky but cute carpenter, and a diva designer make things difficult. When a playboy producer gets into the mix (and into Lily's bed), life becomes a lot more complicated.

> **Keywords:** Humorous, Romantic, Workplace.

Good Enough to Eat. 2010. Berkley. ISBN 0425229637. 320p.
> When Melanie opens a good-for-you cafe and loses almost 150 pounds, she thinks life can't get any better. Then her husband announces he's been cheating on her—with a woman the size Melanie used to be—and she discovers her business is not bringing in the income she had expected. When her condo association levies a huge special assessment, she must get a roommate to help pay the bills. Enter the enigmatic Nadia, who slowly becomes Melanie's friend and starts working in the café.

> **Keywords:** Self-Actualization.

Off the Menu. 2012. Berkley. ISBN 9780425247662. 416p.
> Alana's career as the culinary assistant to a celebrity chef is keeping her so busy that she has little time for life outside of work. After some comic attempts at online dating, Alana stumbles across RJ, a Southern man who recently relocated to her area. The two hit it off, and Alana has to figure out how to balance her blossoming love life with her increasingly busy professional life.

> **Keyword:** Humorous, Romantic, Workplace.

Bate, Dana.

The Girls' Guide to Love and Supper Clubs. 2013. Hyperion. ISBN 9781401311001. 394p.
> Hannah Sugarman has an enviable life—a high-powered job, a handsome boyfriend, and a gorgeous apartment. Unfortunately, none of this satisfies her as much as cooking a good meal does. When her relationship ends, Hannah turns to cooking for solace, founding an underground supper club. When her fledgling

club begins to attract attention, Hannah is both thrilled and terrified. What she's doing is technically illegal, but it could lead to the culinary career she's always wanted.

Keywords: Humorous, Self-Actualization.

Bosnak, Karyn.

20 Times a Lady. 2006. HarperCollins. ISBN 0060828358. 352p.
Delilah wakes up in bed with her boss. Why is that a problem, besides her having been fired just yesterday and her boss being kind of disgusting? Because it means she has now hit her self-imposed limit of sleeping with twenty men. Refusing to up her number, Delilah tracks down her previous nineteen conquests, convinced that she has to make it work with one of them.

Keywords: Humorous, Romantic.

Browne, Hester.
Brown's charming British chick lit is light and quite humorous.

The Finishing Touches. 2010. Gallery. ISBN 1416540083. 411p.
Betsy was abandoned as an infant on the steps of the Phillimore Academy, a London finishing school for well-bred young ladies. She was raised by the proprietors, Lord and Lady Phillimore, and as an adult, she returns to find that the academy's legacy is in jeopardy. She goes to work updating the curriculum with all of the things that modern young ladies need to know, like cell phone etiquette and choosing the right little black dress. But while rescuing the legacy of her adoptive parents, she learns more about her own history—and falls in love, too.

Keywords: Humorous, Romantic.

Swept Off Her Feet. 2011. Gallery. ISBN 9781439168844. 352p.
Fanciful Evie, an antiques appraiser in London shop, is in love with anything from the past. Her sister, Alice, a professional organizer, is infatuated with Fraser, a dashing Scotsman. When family friends of Fraser's need help appraising the contents of their crumbling Scottish castle, Alice pulls strings to get Evie the job. There Evie meets the estate's handsome heir and the sparks fly.

Keyword: Romantic.

🎗 *The Runaway Princess.* 2012. Gallery. ISBN 9781439168851. 448p.
Amy Wilde's new boyfriend, Leo, is quite the catch—he's attentive, handsome, and sweet. He also has a secret—he's the heir to an obscure throne, so he's not just a figurative prince—he's a real prince. But royal life soon begins to exhaust Amy, who's more comfortable with low-key living than life in the spotlight, and her reluctance to become tabloid fodder could destroy her relationship.

Keywords: Humorous, Romantic.

The Little Lady Series.

When serious and stable Melissa finds herself out of work and bored, she decides to start her own business, lending her skills to single men in need of those tasks only a woman can perform—picking out clothing, buying gifts, going to company parties.

The Little Lady Agency. 2006.

The Little Lady Agency and the Prince. 2008.

The Little Lady, Big Apple. 2009.

Bushnell, Candace.

Bushnell's *Sex and the City*—both the essay collection and the TV show that it spawned—was an integral part of the late 1990s chick lit boom and an era-defining pop-cultural landmark. Her novels focus on characters similar to Carrie, Miranda, Samantha, and Charlotte—successful New Yorkers with expensive tastes and an eye for style.

Trading Up. 2003. Hyperion. ISBN 078686818X. 404p.

Janey Wilcox is gorgeous, and her attempts to sleep her way to wealth and security aren't going as well as she would like. During a sun-soaked Hamptons summer, Janey befriends an equally superficial socialite, who plays matchmaker by hooking Janey up with cable-channel CEO Selden Rose. Money can't make their relationship work, and Janey finds herself enmeshed in the kind of scandal the tabloids and gossip columns love to cover.

Keyword: Glitzy.

Lipstick Jungle. 2005. Hyperion. ISBN 0786868198. 353p.

Nico, Wendy, and Victory seem to have it all—success in their glitzy careers, glamorous lives, and relationships with equally successful and wealthy men. But beneath the veneer of success lie personal and professional problems, and the three must decide whether they really can "have it all" or if that idea is just a myth.

Keywords: Ensemble, Glitzy, Workplace.

One Fifth Avenue. 2008. Hyperion. ISBN 9781401301613. 433p.

One Fifth Avenue is one of the most prestigious addresses in Manhattan, and an apartment at this tony address is one of the most sought-after status symbols a social climber could want. When a society doyenne dies, her penthouse apartment becomes available, and a cadre of strivers seeks admittance to the exclusive address.

Keywords: Ensemble, Glitzy.

Cabot, Meg.

Cabot's writing spans many genres—preteen series, teen novels, adult romances (under the name Patricia Cabot), chick lit, a paranormal series, and a series of light mysteries. Her chick lit-esque novels noted here feature snappy dialogue, laugh-out-loud situations, and a touch of romance.

Boy Meets Girl. 2004. Avon. ISBN 0060085452. 387p.

> Kate is an HR person at a New York City newspaper. When she has to fire someone, all hell breaks loose—she loses her job, gets sued, and ends up falling for the handsome lawyer representing her in the case. Told as a series of e-mails, memos, and voice mails, this format works as a fast read that's a lot of fun.

Keywords: Humorous, Workplace.

Queen of Babble series.

> Lizzie, who can't keep a secret to save her life, finds herself in a series of wacky adventures that always end up with her shooting off her big mouth.

Queen of Babble. 2006.

Queen of Babble in the Big City. 2007.

Queen of Babble Gets Hitched. 2008.

Close, Jennifer.

Girls in White Dresses. 2011. Knopf. ISBN 9780307596857. 304p.

> New York friends Isabella and Mary feel like everyone they know is getting married as they deal with relationships, careers, and finding their way in the world. Isabella hates her boring job, while Mary fears she'll never find Mr. Right. In a series of interlinked short stories, we meet several of their friends who have similar tales to tell. Not frothy in the least—in fact, at times quite serious—this is a refreshingly contemporary take on chick lit.

Keywords: Ensemble, Friendship.

Donohue, Meg.

How to Eat a Cupcake. 2012. William Morrow. ISBN 9780062069283. 320p.

> Annie and Julia, childhood friends who have been estranged since a long-ago falling out decide to open a cupcake bakery together in San Francisco. Annie's got the baking skills while Julia has a head for business—it should be a winning combination. Unfortunately, their past threatens to come between them—Annie's mother used to be a maid for Julia's wealthy parents, and each young woman has secrets she'd prefer to keep in the past.

Keywords: Ensemble, Friendship.

Duffy, Erin.

Bond Girl. 2012. Morrow. ISBN 9780062065896. 304p.

> Fresh out of college, Alex lands a job on Wall Street training in bond sales. While it's difficult to break into the boys' club of a trading firm (she is given a folding metal chair inscribed "Girlie" instead of a desk, she's the office

gofer, and practical jokes abound), Alex makes the best of it and tries to work as hard as she can, even managing to find time to date a cute coworker.

Keywords: Humorous, Workplace.

Evanovich, Stephanie.

Big Girl Panties. 2013. Morrow. ISBN 9780062224842. 352p.

Holly is in a rut. After the death of her husband, her self-esteem is at an all-time low, and she's been self-medicating with food. When she meets hotshot personal trainer Logan on a flight from Toronto to New Jersey, he challenges her to join his gym, where he will take her on as a client. As Holly and Logan get to know each other, romance blossoms, and both are forced to overcome their personal demons.

Keywords: Grief, Romantic, Self-Actualization.

Fielding, Helen.

Fielding's 1997 novel *Bridget Jones's Diary* was her breakout work and kicked off the chick lit phenomenon.

Bridget Jones's Diary: A Novel. 1997. Viking. ISBN 0670880728. 271p.

Fielding's first novel was one of the books that started the chick lit craze. Insecure Bridget smokes too much, eats too much, worries too much, and chronicles it all in her diary. Somehow, she finds herself in the most embarrassing predicaments, from a mix-up at a costume party to exposing her bum on national TV. She also looks for true love. Followed by *Bridget Jones: The Edge of Reason* (2000), *Bridget Jones: Mad about the Boy* (2013).

Keywords: Humorous, Romantic.

Frankel, Valerie.

Frankel, a prolific essayist and magazine writer, crafts light and very funny chick lit.

Smart vs. Pretty. 2000. Avon. ISBN 0380805421. 304p.

Francesca and Amanda are sisters who run a neighborhood coffee shop in Brooklyn Heights. When a chain coffee shop moves into the neighborhood, Francesca (the smart one) and Amanda (the pretty one) must put aside their sibling rivalry and team up with a wacky marketing student to revitalize the family business.

Keywords: Family, Humorous.

Girlfriend Curse. 2005. Avon. ISBN 0060725540. 320p.

Peg is gaining a reputation as the girl you date before you find the girl you marry. Tired of the New York dating scene and determined to change her fate, she moves from Manhattan to rural Vermont, where she attends Inward Bound, a dating boot camp.

Keywords: Humorous, Romantic.

Four of a Kind. 2012. Ballantine. ISBN 9780345525406. 352p.

Four women have very little in common aside from the fact that their kids all attend the same exclusive prep school in New York City. Thrown together on a school committee, they start to turn the meetings into poker games, but instead of betting with money, they use secrets as currency. Housewife Bess tells stories about her surly teenage daughter and judgmental mother. Single mom Robin struggles with the truth about her child's father. Carla, a doctor, reveals her dream of owning her own private practice, and shy Alicia fantasizes about a coworker.

Keywords: Ensemble, Friendship, Humorous, Motherhood.

French, Wendy.

sMothering. 2003. Forge. ISBN 0765307936. 301p.

What do you do when your overbearing, critical beast of a mother drops by . . . and stays? Claire is not happy when her domineering mother comes by for an unexpected and open-ended visit. Between trying to find a boyfriend, work pressures, and unreliable friends, the arrival of her mother causes Claire to have a breakdown. Of course, Mom has problems of her own, and mother and daughter come to realize they can help each other through life's little crises. A fun, chick lit take on mothers and daughters.

Keywords: Family, Humorous, Mothers and Daughters.

Gaskell, Whitney.

Gaskell's early chick lit showcases a fine comedic talent and an ear for funny dialogue.

Pushing 30. 2003. Bantam. ISBN 0553382241. 326p.

Good girl Ellie seems to have a great life—she's an attorney, has a sassy best friend, and a great boyfriend. But as she approaches thirty, her life starts to take a distinct downturn. She loses her job, breaks up with her boyfriend, and her mother is about to drive her absolutely crazy. Things start to look up when a potential new beau comes on the scene, but then she discovers he's almost twice her age—and she's already feeling "old" herself.

Keywords: Humorous, Romantic.

Good Luck. 2008. Bantam. ISBN 9780553591514. 400p.

Lucy loses her teaching job after unfairly being accused of sexual misconduct with a student. That same day her car breaks down, and she finally returns home in time to catch her boyfriend in bed with another woman. Her luck turns around however when she buys a winning lottery ticket, to the tune of $34 million. Can money buy girl happiness?

Keyword: Humorous.

When You Least Expect It. 2011. Bantam. ISBN 9780553386271. 320p.

The Halloways have the perfect artsy-boho life, but they're missing one thing that they desperately desire—a baby. With two years of failed fertility treatments behind them, the couple decides to adopt. They are matched with Lainey Walker, a wannabe reality TV star whose unplanned pregnancy threatens to derail her fledgling career. When Lainey moves into the Halloways' guest house, the trio forges an unexpected friendship.

Keywords: Friendship, Humorous, Motherhood.

Gold, Robin.

Perfectly True Tales of a Perfect Size 12. 2007. Plume. ISBN 9780452288126. 272p.
Delilah White, an aspiring Martha Stewart, is up for a promotion that could make her a star. She's confident she'll get it—she's got personality, experience, and skills—but she finds herself thwarted at every turn by a rival determined to get the promotion at any cost.

Keywords: Humorous, Workplace.

Goldstein, Meredith.

The Singles. 2012. Plume. ISBN 9780452298057. 256p.
Bee's perfect wedding includes all of her female guests bringing dates. When that doesn't happen, the frustrated bride-to-be dubs them "The Singles." The stories of these five women intersect and each chapter is told from a different friend's point of view, culminating in the big event.

Keywords: Ensemble, Friendship.

Graff, Laurie.

You Have to Kiss a Lot of Frogs. 2004. Red Dress Ink. ISBN 0373250460. 443p.
Forty-five and tired of attending bridal showers, New Yorker Karrie chronicles her dating life from the early 1990s to the present day. She's had a lot of dates, but why didn't she ever find true love? And is true love really necessary for a good life?

Keyword: Humorous.

Green, Jane.

Green is an author who started out in chick lit during the peak of the chick lit boom but moved toward contemporary women's fiction as the trend cooled.

Jemima J: A Novel about Ugly Ducklings and Swans. 1999. Broadway. ISBN 0767905180. 373p.
Overweight Jemima is the Cinderella to her slim roommates—they treat her like dirt, which drives her further into emotional overeating. Her crush on an unattainable coworker isn't helping matters, either. When she meets sexy Brad online, she reinvents herself a model type and he falls hard. But when Brad wants to meet in person, Jemima has to figure out a way to either become the woman she pretended to be or confess what she has done.

Keywords: Humorous, Self-Actualization.

Straight Talking. 2003. Broadway. ISBN 0767915593. 310p.

Television producer Tasha and her best friends are all looking for love, and they're not having a whole lot of luck. Everyone they meet is either self-absorbed, commitment-phobic, or too nice to be sexy. Can these London ladies find their perfect man, or will they be forced to settle for second best?

Keywords: Friendship, Humorous.

Grose, Jessica.

Sad Desk Salad. 2012. Morrow. ISBN 9780062188342. 304p.

Alex Lyons is a professional blogger for Chick Habit, a women's interest Web site known for its coverage of celebrity gossip. Though she works from home, her boss is a slave driver, so Alex barely has time to shower and change her clothes; and her relationship with her boyfriend is starting to suffer. Then Alex gets the scoop of a lifetime: a video of the daughter of a well-known parenting expert snorting cocaine. Does she post the video, knowing that doing so could stir things up with the anonymous hate blogger who seems set on taking Chick Habit (and its writers) down? And who is the hate blogger, who seems to have a serious grudge against Alex?

Keywords: Friendship, Humorous, Workplace.

Gruenenfelder, Kim.

A Total Waste of Makeup. 2005. St. Martin's. ISBN 031234872X. 384p.

Charlize enjoys her job as a personal assistant to a hot male movie star, but as her thirtieth birthday approaches, she wonders what she's missing. Convinced that she'll never have children of her own, she writes advice in a journal to pass on to a future grandniece and realizes she knows a lot more than she gives herself credit for—and that thirty isn't so bad after all.

Keywords: Humorous, Workplace.

There's Cake in My Future. 2010. St. Martin's. ISBN 0312614594. 368p.

Nic has a unique plan for her bridal shower: a cake pull, featuring charms specifically chosen for herself and her two closest friends. Each charm represents something that one of the women needs to get her life back on track. But when the women draw different charms than Nic anticipated, the results are surprising—and Nic wonders if fate had a hand in the draw.

Keywords: Friendship, Humorous.

Harbison, Beth.

Harbison's frothy and fun chick lit features contemporary situations and plenty of humor.

Shoe Addicts Anonymous. 2007. St. Martin's. ISBN 9780312364687. 327p.

Lorna Rafferty can't stop buying shoes, but her habit is destroying her financial stability. Her creative solution: gather a group of like-minded women to swap shoes, allowing them fresh footwear without the price tag.

Though Lorna, Helene, Sandra, and Jocelyn bond over their shared love of shoes, as their friendship develops, they come to rely on each other for much more than shoe swapping.

Keywords: Ensemble, Friendship, Humorous.

Secrets of a Shoe Addict. 2008. St. Martin's. ISBN 9780312348267. 340p.

Abbey, Tiffany, and Loreen are in a variety of predicaments, all of which require money for escape. Fortunately, Tiffany's sister Sandra has a suggestion: working as phone sex operators. The three women bumble through their new job with hilarious results, while discovering a few new things about themselves and the people in their lives.

Keywords: Ensemble, Friendship, Humorous.

Hope in a Jar. 2009. St. Martin's. ISBN 9780312381967. 340p.

Allie and Olivia were best friends in high school, until their friendship was destroyed by malicious gossip. Twenty years later, neither woman has any interest in attending her high school reunion, but circumstances bring them to the party—and help them mend their broken friendship.

Keywords: Friendship, Humorous.

Thin, Rich, Pretty. 2010. St. Martin's. ISBN 9780312381981. 256p.

Holly and Nicola became fast friends at summer camp twenty years ago, united in their hatred of rich, spoiled Lexi, who loved making fun of the shy Nicola and the overweight Holly. Now in their late thirties, Holly is an art gallery owner, Nicola is a Hollywood star, and Lexi, well, she's just been tossed out of her home when her father dies and her stepmother seizes everything. When the three meet up again, secrets from summer camp come to the surface, and they realize it's time to grow up, each in her own way.

Keywords: Ensemble, Humorous.

Always Something There to Remind Me. 2011. St. Martin's. ISBN 9780312599102. 368p.

Erin has spent the last twenty years unable to forget her first love, Nate. Despite having a successful career, a teenage daughter, and a great new boyfriend, she still gets lost in memories of Nate and their turbulent teen romance. When he appears back on the scene, Erin obsesses over what could have been.

Keyword: Romantic.

When in Doubt, Add Butter. 2012. St. Martin's. ISBN 978312599096. 338p.

Gemma Craig is a personal chef with a successful business and an unsuccessful love life. Her favorite client is Mr. Tuesday, a workaholic attorney with a taste for comfort food. They've never met, but their flirtation (via notes to each other) gives Gemma a feeling that he's her kind of guy. When a night out to unwind leads to a one-night stand with unexpected consequences, Gemma has a lot of decisions to make about her future. Will Gemma find her mystery man again, and can her career recover from a bitter client who's spreading lies that are ruining her business?

Keywords: Self-Actualization, Romantic.

Harding, Robyn.

The Journal of Mortifying Moments. 2004. ISBN 034547628X. 304p.
> Kerry's therapist forces her to start keeping a journal of all of her bad dates, in order to help her overcome her self-defeating dating habits. She starts in the past, chronicling laugh-out-loud funny moments from her dating history. These entries pop up against what's happening in her life now—she hates her ad agency job, her boyfriend's using her; and to try and gain some perspective, she begins mentoring an at-risk teen.

Keywords: Humorous, Self-Actualization.

Harmel, Kristin.

The Blonde Theory. 2007. 5 Spot. ISBN 0446697590. 304p.
> Overachieving lawyer Harper is finding it hard to keep a steady boyfriend. She outearns most of the men she meets and intimidates the rest with her intellect. When her friends urge her to spend two weeks undercover as a ditzy blonde, she gives it a try, wearing skimpy outfits and playing down her intelligence. It's not easy, and she ends up with disastrous results. Her social calendar quickly fills up, but all of the men she attracts are simply interested in casual sex. Who says blondes have more fun?

Keywords: Humorous, Romantic.

Holden, Wendy.
> Holden's wacky British chick lit often revolves around young women in odd jobs or who find themselves in outlandish situations. Her novels are witty and fast-paced.

Gossip Hound. 2003. Plume. ISBN 0452283930. 352p.
> London book publicist Grace finds herself trapped in a job with a failing publisher. When a major U.S. star hires her to promote his new book, she thinks her life is ready for a turnaround—until she reads the novel, that is.

Keyword: Humorous.

The Wives of Bath. 2005. Plume. ISBN 0452285895. 292p.
> Two very different expectant couples become friends when they attend a prenatal class in Bath, England. Alice, a lawyer, has married hippie environmentalist Jake after a one-night stand left them parents-to-be. Amanda, a celebrity journalist, is married to Hugo, a real estate agent, and they've left their high-powered careers in the city to move to the country life. Will these mismatched couples remain unlikely friends once the babies arrive?

Keywords: Friendship, Humorous.

Jewell, Lisa.
> Jewell's early novels were published during the chick lit boom of the late 1990s, and though she has disavowed the term as "insulting to women writers," her light stories focusing on the romantic entanglements of young, single Brits place her firmly in the category.

Ralph's Party. 1999. Penguin. ISBN 0452281636. 308p.

Jem rents a room at 31 Almanac Road, where she shares a flat with Smith, a shameless flirt and the owner of the building, and Ralph, a starving artist. A love triangle develops, and the other residents of the building, including sexy femme fatale Cheri and bored couple Karl and Siobhan, become caught up in various romantic entanglements. Followed by *After the Party* (2011), which follows Ralph and Jem eleven years into their relationship.

Keywords: Humorous, Friendship, Romantic.

Kendrick, Beth.

Nearlyweds. 2006. Downtown Press. ISBN 0743499603. 352p.

A different take on typical bridal chick lit, this is the story of three women who discover that their marriage paperwork was never filed—so they aren't really married. Would they do it again, or is this the perfect time to run out?

Keywords: Humorous, Romantic.

Kinsella, Sophie.

Kinsella writes the frothy and funny Shopaholic series as well as several stand-alone breezy chick lit novels. Her novels are fast paced and feature humorous dialogue and over-the-top situations, with young female characters. In 2013, Kinsella received the Outstanding Achievement Award from the U.K.-based Romantic Novelists' Association.

Shopaholic series.

Meet Becky Bloomwood, the world's best shopper and worst decision maker. In this series of comic novels, Becky attempts to give money advice while her financial house is in ruins, falls in love, manages not one but two weddings booked on the same day in different countries, and has a daughter, her own little Mini Shopaholic.

Confessions of a Shopaholic. 2001.

Shopaholic Takes Manhattan. 2002.

Shopaholic Ties the Knot. 2003.

Shopaholic and Sister. 2005.

Shopaholic and Baby. 2007.

Mini Shopaholic. 2009.

Can You Keep A Secret? 2005. Dial. ISBN 9780385338080. 384p.

Emma has a seemingly perfect boyfriend and is up for a promotion at her seemingly perfect job. On a turbulent plane ride back from a terrible client meeting, Emma fears for her life and she spills her most intimate secrets, including the fact that she hates her job, to the handsome man sitting next to her. After a safe landing and back at work, she discovers he's her new boss.

Keyword: Humorous.

Remember Me? 2008. Dial. ISBN 9780385338721. 384p.

> After a nasty bump to the head, Lexi wakes up in a hospital room, unable to remember the past three years of her life. She can't recall a single thing about her glamorous life—not her rich husband, mind-boggling home, or new set of friends. She has to decide which life she really wants—her new ultra-glam one or her old comfortable one from three years earlier.

> **Keyword:** Humorous.

Twenties Girl. 2010. Dial. ISBN 9780385342039. 448p.

> In a quirky shift from her standard fare, Kinsella tells a ghost story with a chick lit twist. Lara's being haunted by her great-aunt Sadie—a feisty flapper. Before Sadie can rest eternal, she sends Lara on the hunt for a missing necklace.

> **Keywords:** Humorous.

🎗 *I've Got Your Number.* 2012. Dial. ISBN 9780385342063. 448p.

> Flighty Poppy's life suddenly becomes a series of disasters. She loses her engagement ring in a hotel fire drill, and in the panic that follows, her phone is stolen. In turn, she keeps a phone she finds abandoned in a trash can. She can't help herself and starts replying to the text messages the phone gets, even though they are clearly not for her. When the phone's owner, a stuffy businessman named Sam discovers this, he wants his phone back and doesn't appreciate Poppy invading his personal life.

> **Keywords:** Humorous.

Wedding Night. 2013. Dial. ISBN 9780812993844. 480p.

> Lottie is certain that her stodgy nice-guy boyfriend is about to propose—so sure, in fact, that she buys him an engagement ring. When she finds out that Roger's big news is that he's moving from London to San Francisco, she's devastated enough to end their relationship immediately. Unfortunately, Lottie has a habit of making bad decisions after breakups, and her rebound from this breakup involves marrying her gap-year fling, who reenters her life on a whim. Determined to keep Lottie from consummating her new and unexpected marriage, her sister Fliss orchestrates a series of comic mishaps that not only keep Ben and Lottie from having sex but also help them figure out whether they are truly right for each other.

> **Keywords:** Humorous, Romantic.

Larkin, Allie.

Why Can't I Be You? 2013. Plume. ISBN 9780452298378. 304p.

> Jenny Shaw is headed to Seattle for her first-ever business trip when her boyfriend dumps her on the way to the airport. Upon arrival at her hotel, a woman mistakes Jenny for one of her former classmates, Jessie Morgan, and invites her to attend a class reunion. Jenny quickly realizes that life as Jessie is more exciting than life as Jenny and that Jessie's friends are the family that she never had—making her want to keep her new found (mistaken) identity.

> **Keywords:** Friendship, Self-Actualization.

Lebenthal, Alexandra.

The Recessionistas. 2010. Grand Central. ISBN 9780446563673. 307p.
Socialite Grigsby Somerset is unaware of her husband's business activities—
she's too busy entertaining and enjoying her lavish lifestyle—so she is taken
by surprise when the economic collapse hits and she is forced to cut back.
Meanwhile, executive assistant Renee Parker and her friend Sasha Silver, a bond
manager, investigate the shady dealings of Renee's boss, and they discover that
he's up to something nefarious with Grigsby's husband.

Keywords: Friendship, Glitzy.

Lee, Cavanaugh.

Save as Draft. 2011. Simon & Schuster. ISBN 9781439190692. 336p.
Told in a series of very funny e-mails—some wisely unsent, hence saved as
drafts—and text messages, Izabell recounts her disastrous attempts at online
dating and ultimately has to decide between two men she likes. Her friends egg
her on (via e-mail) and try and help, to no avail.

Keywords: Humorous, Romantic.

Lorello, Elisa.

Faking It. 2010. Amazon Encore. ISBN 9781935597353. 270p.
Writing professor Andi Cutrone is ashamed of her body, and this shame has kept
her from physical relationships—even with her ex-fiancé. Enter Devin, an escort
who comes highly recommended by a number of Andi's friends. The two enter
into an agreement: Andi will teach Devin to write, and Devin will help Andi gain
the confidence she needs. Followed by *Ordinary World* (2011).

Keywords: Humorous, Romantic, Self-Actualization.

Lorello, Elisa, and Sarah Girrell.

Why I Love Singlehood. 2010. Amazon Encore. ISBN 9781935597575. 356p.
Eva Petrino writes a popular blog about being unmarried and proud, but is her
"single pride" just a facade? Worried about betraying her audience, she secretly
embarks on a search for love, encountering comic misadventures every step of
the way.

Keywords: Humorous, Romantic, Self-Actualization.

Lyles, Whitney.

Here Comes the Bride. 2006. Berkley. ISBN 0425211304. 304p.
Cate was always the bridesmaid—four times in fact. Now that it's finally her
turn, problems abound. Moving in together turns into a construction nightmare,
her fiancé's ex-girlfriend is hanging around way too much, and mom won't stay
out of the planning. Followed by *First Comes Love* (2007).

Keywords: Humorous, Romantic.

MacDowell, Heather, and Rose MacDowell.

Turning Tables. 2008. Dial. ISBN 9780385338561. 336p.

When Erin loses her high-powered marketing position, she pulls some strings to get a job as a waitress for Roulette, a top New York restaurant. Problem is, she's got no experience and this shows loud and clear—she can't manage to cope with demanding customers, she has problems getting orders straight and she even makes the faux pas of getting drunk during the restaurant's wine seminar. Trying to date two men at the same time isn't helping her concentrate on work. Written by industry-insider sisters, this is a fun and fast-paced look at the upscale restaurant scene.

Keywords: Humorous, Workplace.

Manby, Chrissie.

Getting Over Mr. Right. 2012. Bantam. ISBN 9780345529022. 290p.

Londoner Ashleigh is dumped (via Facebook) by her Mr. Perfect boyfriend, and she's angry—very angry. Her over-the-top reaction to the breakup includes psychic intervention, a fling with a much younger man, and an extremely pricey voodoo curse.

Keyword: Humorous.

Margolis, Sue.

British chick lit author Margolis writes sassy and funny comic novels, featuring sexy romance and quirky characters.

Apocalipstick. 2005. Bantam. ISBN 9780440242963. 352p.

What could be worse than having your widowed father marry the blond bombshell from your high school class who used to bully you? This is only one of the bad things that happen to beauty magazine columnist Rebecca Fine. Along the way she falls in and out of love, deals with a prying grandmother, and scoops a major beauty news scandal.

Keyword: Humorous.

A Catered Affair. 2011. NAL Trade. ISBN 9780451233356. 384p.

Tally, jilted at the altar, ends up getting very drunk at the reception and spends the night with the caterer—having him hold her hair back as she gets sick, that is. The two become fast friends—and maybe more? If Tally's bordering-on-ridiculous family would only leave her time to explore her new romance, who knows what could happen?

Keywords: Humorous, Romantic.

Markham, Wendy.

Slightly Single. 2002. Red Dress Ink. ISBN 0373250134. 288p.

Insecure New Yorker Tracey decides to perform a makeover on all aspects of her life once her boyfriend, an actor, leaves town for summer stock. She gets a new job, loses weight, finds a better apartment, and meets a new man—but she's just interested in being friends. Tracey's witty, sarcastic sense of humor makes her a fun heroine. Tracey's story continues in *Slightly Settled* (2004), *Slightly Engaged* (2006), *Slightly Married* (2007), and *Slightly Suburban* (2008).

Keywords: Humorous, Romantic.

Maxted, Anna.

British author Maxted's take on chick lit has a bit of a harsh edge—less about shoes, more about betrayal, revenge, and family issues.

A Tale of Two Sisters. 2007. Plume. ISBN 0452288517. 368p.

London sisters Lizbet and Cassie are different as night and day—Lizbet is scatterbrained but has a nice stable life, while glossy and high-powered Cassie leads a strained and stressful life. When Lizbet discovers she's unexpectedly pregnant, she is overjoyed, but Cassie, trapped in a loveless marriage, is less than happy for her sister.

Keyword: Family.

McElhatton, Heather.

Jennifer Johnson Is Sick of Being Single. 2009. Morrow. ISBN 0061461369. 292p.

Jennifer Johnson has an unfulfilling job as a marketing copywriter for a department store, no romantic prospects, a Cinnabon addiction, and a bratty younger sister who is about to marry a man who calls himself the King of Ham. Then a chance encounter with the black-sheep son of the department store's owner leads to a whirlwind relationship. Brad Keller might be "the one," but he's not what Jennifer expected.

Keyword: Humorous.

Jennifer Johnson Is Sick of Being Married. 2012. Morrow. ISBN 9780062064394. 352p.

Jennifer Johnson's marriage to Brad Keller is off to an inauspicious start. Their honeymoon at a Christian resort results in a horrific bout of food poisoning, and Brad's mother seems to be taking over the newlyweds' life. When Jennifer discovers that her mother-in-law is purposely sabotaging everything from an important dinner with Japanese business executives to a charity party, she knows it's time to retaliate.

Keyword: Humorous.

McKean, Erin.

The Secret Lives of Dresses. 2011. 5 Spot. ISBN 9780446555722. 304p.

Aimless Dora can't decide what she wants to do in life. When her grandmother suffers a stroke, Dora rushes to her side and takes over her grandmother's vintage clothing store. Dora discovers her grandmother has been keeping a memoir of sorts—random notes tucked into the pockets of the store's inventory that recount her adventures as a young woman.

Keyword: Romantic.

McKenzie, Catherine.

Spin: A Novel. 2012. Morrow. ISBN 9780062115355. 448p.

Kate lands an interview for her dream job at a music magazine. She goes out the night before to celebrate, and unfortunately, shows up still drunk the next morning. Needless to say, she doesn't get the job, but, in a strange twist of events, it does cause the magazine's publishers to help get her into rehab—so that she can get them an interview with a famous starlet who will also be at the facility.

Keywords: Humorous, Self-Actualization, Workplace.

Arranged. 2012. Morrow. 9780062115393. 416p.

After another bad breakup, Anne Blythe has had it with relationships. Then her best friend announces her engagement, and Anne calls a dating service—only to find that it's an arranged marriage service. Given her bad luck, she throws caution to the wind and goes for it, finding herself married to Jack, a nice guy who may or may not be the man for her.

Keywords: Humorous, Romantic.

Forgotten. 2012. Morrow. 9780062115416. 448p.

Emma, an up-and-coming lawyer, is thrown for a loop when her mother dies. She's thrown for another loop when she receives her inheritance: an airplane ticket to Africa, a place she has always dreamed of visiting. Though she worries about her future, she makes the trip—only to get sick in a remote village and then get stuck in an earthquake. Six months later, her friends and family assume she's dead, and when she returns, she finds her assets frozen, her belongings gone, and her apartment rented to another person. Now that her perfectly organized life is in complete turmoil, can she get back on track?

Keywords: Humorous, Self-Actualization.

McLaughlin, Emma, and Nicola Kraus.

The Nanny Diaries. 2002. St. Martin's. ISBN 9780312278588. 306p.

The aptly named Nan works for a wealthy Manhattan couple, Mr. and Mrs. X. She's responsible for four-year-old Grayer, who is merely another status symbol for his uncaring mother and workaholic father. Nan finds herself stuck at this low-wage, high-stress job, mainly out of loyalty to the little boy. Followed by *Nanny Returns* (2009).

Keywords: Humorous, Workplace.

Between You and Me. 2012. Atria. ISBN 9781439188187. 272p.

Logan Wade barely knows her pop-star cousin Kelsey, other than what she can glean from tabloids and magazines. But when Kelsey needs an assistant, Logan rushes to her side—just in time for Kelsey to experience a spectacular public breakdown (à la Britney Spears). Can Logan help her cousin escape from the spotlight so she can pick up the pieces of her broken life?

Keyword: Family.

Mlynowski, Sarah.

Mlynowski's fun and flirty chick lit features young women trying to make something out of life in the big city. Her novels are humorous and realistic, with romantic overtones.

Milkrun. 2001. Red Dress Ink. ISBN 0778327094. 352p.

When Jackie's boyfriend dumps her via e-mail, her life is turned upside down. While he's in Thailand "finding himself," she throws herself headfirst into the dating pool, with disastrous results. As soon as Jackie finds a man worth dating, her ex returns, and she has to figure out which man is right for her.

Keywords: Humorous, Romantic.

As Seen on TV. 2003. Red Dress Ink. ISBN 9780373250363. 384p.

Sunny moves to New York City to be with her boyfriend, but she quickly realizes that she won't be able to stay very long without a job. When a family collection lands her an audition for a reality show, she gets the part—and a makeover, too. As Sunny becomes a minor celebrity, her life changes, and she begins to have a tough time distinguishing real life from TV life.

Keyword: Humorous.

Me vs. Me. 2006. Red Dress Ink. ISBN 9780373895885. 311p.

Gabby has to make an important choice: should she leave her stable but slightly boring boyfriend behind in Phoenix for her dream job in Manhattan? When her boyfriend proposes, it only complicates matters. She wishes she could have both—the husband and home and the flashy career in an exciting city. She makes a wish that she could have it all, which suddenly comes true—she wakes up one morning and realizes she's living two lives. Whenever she falls asleep in one, she wakes up in the other.

Keywords: Humorous, Self-Actualization.

Mulry, Megan.

A Royal Pain. 2012. Sourcebooks Landmark. ISBN 9781402269974. 338p.

American Bronte Talbott is obsessed with British royalty. When she meets Max, a British doctoral student, Bronte sees him as a temporary fling. But Max is serious about Bronte, and when he reveals his secret—he's the Duke of Northrop—Bronte quickly learns that being a duchess isn't as glamorous and fun as the tabloids make it seem.

Keywords: Humorous, Romantic.

Murnane, Maria.

Waverly Bryson series.

Waverly Bryson, newly single after a broken engagement, has comic misadventures in both work and love.

Perfect on Paper: The (Mis)Adventures of Waverly Bryson. 2010.

It's a Waverly Life. 2011.

Honey on Your Mind. 2012.

Chocolate for Two. 2013.

Pekkanen, Sarah.

Pekkanen's heroines usually find themselves starting over in life, in new situations and relationships. Chick lit, yet not frothy—Pekkanen tackles serious subjects with a light touch.

Skipping a Beat. 2010. Washington Square Press. ISBN 9781451609820. 327p.
Party planner Julia Dunhill lives a glamorous life filled with parties, benefits, and black-tie events, but her relationship with her husband, Michael, has suffered because they are both so busy with their companies. When Michael has an unexpected heart attack, it changes his perspective on life and their marriage, but Julia isn't sure about Michael's newfound passion for life.

Keywords: Marriage, Relationships.

The Opposite of Me. 2010. Washington Square Press. ISBN 9781439121986. 377p.
Lindsey and Alex are fraternal twins with different goals in life. Lindsey is the successful, hardworking twin, and her years of diligence and effort are about to pay off with a major promotion. Alex, meanwhile, is planning a lavish wedding to the man of her dreams. When Lindsey's professional life implodes, she returns home to her family, where she and Alex discover a long-hidden family secret.

Keywords: Family, Sisters.

These Girls. 2012. Washington Square Press. ISBN 9781451612547. 376p.
Three friends navigate life in New York City. Cate has just landed a successful publishing job, but it's harder than she ever imagined. Her roommate Renee would die for such a job, and thanks to the dangerous diet pills she's been taking in order to lose weight, she just might. Rounding out the drama, their friend Abby holds a powerful secret.

Keywords: Ensemble, Friendship.

The Best of Us. 2013. Washington Square Press. ISBN 9781451673517. 352p.
Four friends from college reunite for a dream vacation/thirty-fifth birthday party at a private villa in Jamaica. Tina, the mother of four young children, is overwhelmed with the responsibilities of being a parent and a wife; her best friend, Allie, has just learned of a family secret that could topple her perfect world. Savannah's husband left her for a younger woman, and Dwight is a multimillionaire who escaped the dot-com bubble with his fortune intact, but his marriage is a mess. Over the course of a week in paradise, old flames are reignited, secrets are revealed, and friendships are threatened.

Keywords: Beach, Friendship, Romantic.

Rice, Zoë.

Pick Me Up. 2006. NAL: Penguin. ISBN 0451218442. 288p.

Isabel loves her job at a New York art gallery and can't wait for her promotion, but when the wealthy owner of the gallery dies suddenly, Isabel's life goes into a tailspin. She manages to make a horrible first impression on both her gorgeous new boss and the gallery's latest hot-shot artist. Meanwhile, her best guy friend is turning into a newspaper sensation—a male Carrie Bradshaw—with his article on using pickup lines, and her cousin, who once stole Izzy's boyfriend, is now stealing her dream wedding.

Keywords: Humorous, Workplace.

Rockland, Kate.

Falling Is Like This. 2010. St. Martin's Griffin. 9780312576004. 304p.

Harper Rostov hooks up with punk musician Nick Cavallaro on the rebound from a long-term relationship, and she's astonished at how quickly and how deeply she falls for him. But after their sexual chemistry fades, is Nick really a long-term prospect?

Keywords: Romantic, Self-Actualization.

150 Pounds: A Novel of Waists and Measures. 2011. St. Martin's. ISBN 9780312576011. 332p.

Two bloggers—proudly plus-sized Shoshana and diet junkie Alexis—find themselves the unlikeliest of allies after their joint appearance on a television talk show. As Shoshana loses weight and Alexis gains weight, they begin to realize that life—and happiness—are more than numbers on a scale.

Keywords: Humorous, Friendship, Self-Actualization.

Rose, Melanie.

Life as I Know It. 2010. Bantam. ISBN 9780385343992. 368p.

In this quirky, charming story, Jessica is struck by lightning and wakes up in the hospital—in the body of Lauren, who was also struck at the same time across town. Jessica fakes amnesia until she can figure out what the heck is going on and realizes she has the chance to live parallel lives. Which one is the better one remains the question—Jessica's boring single life or Lauren's perfect (on the outside) married life with kids?

Keyword: Romantic.

Ross, Jennifer.

The Icing on the Cupcake. 2010. Ballantine. ISBN 9780345492968. 320p.

Texas Southern belle Ansley is on the brink of getting engaged when her boyfriend reveals that he just doesn't like her very much. Her general cattiness and downright meanness have gotten the best of her, and she finds herself fiancé-less as well as friendless. When she runs off to New York City to live with her estranged grandmother, she realizes it's time to find a purpose for her life and turn things around. Cooking and baking skills run in the family, and she soon decides to open a cupcake bakery all on her own.

Keywords: Family, Humorous.

Senate, Melissa.

Senate's brand of funny chick lit has New York flavor and more than a touch of romance.

See Jane Date. 2001. Red Dress Ink. ISBN 0373250118. 283p.

After lying to her family about having a steady boyfriend, Jane has two months to find a date for her cousin's wedding, and that's the least of her woes. She lives in a typically cramped and expensive New York City apartment and has an unfulfilling job as an assistant publishing editor—classic chick lit elements.

Keyword: Humorous.

Whose Wedding Is It Anyway? 2004. Red Dress Ink. ISBN 0373250770. 304p.

At first, Eloise is thrilled that working at *Wow Weddings* magazine means she'll get the whole shebang paid for, and it will be featured in an upcoming issue. But when her conniving boss starts to take over every last detail—including choosing a hideous yellow bridal gown—she's not sure how her dream wedding turned into such a nightmare. Soon she starts to wonder if she even wants to get married at all.

Keywords: Humorous, Workplace.

The Love Goddesses' Cooking School. 2010. Gallery. ISBN 1439107238. 352p.

Holly inherits her grandmother Camilla's cooking school but is unsure if she also has her grandmother's cooking skills or her fortune-telling ability. Determined to revive the business, Holly brings in four new students and becomes able to give them recipes for happiness. Single father Simon wishes for his daughter's love; Holly's childhood pal, Juliet, hides a painful secret; Tamara can't settle down and find love; and young Mia hopes that learning to cook will stop her dad, Liam, from marrying his girlfriend.

Keyword: Ensemble.

Shumway, Charity.

Ten Girls to Watch. 2012. Atria. ISBN 9781451673418. 368p.

Dawn's not sure what happened—she meant to move to New York and make it big as a writer. Instead, she lives with a roommate who skips on the rent, loses her boyfriend, and has no job prospects beyond ghostwriting a lawn care blog. When a magazine job finally comes her way (thanks to the old boyfriend's new girlfriend, wouldn't you know) she is determined to make her mark—much like the women she is profiling, from decades of past winners of the magazine's "Ten Girls to Watch" annual feature.

Keywords: Self-Actualization, Workplace.

Van der Kwast, Jennifer.

Pounding the Pavement. 2005. Broadway Books. ISBN 9780767919531. 288p.
   After the film company she works for goes bust, Sarah begins to search for the perfect job—if only she could figure out what that is, exactly. Her parents are bribing her to go to law school, her unemployment is about to run out, and she really wants to hold out for that "perfect" job. What's a single-in-the-city gal to do? When she meets a "perfect" boyfriend, maybe that's good enough?

   Keywords: Romantic, Workplace.

Weiner, Jennifer.
   Jennifer Weiner's first two novels are widely considered some of the best of the chick lit boom. Though a deft sense of humor and well-formed characters are still her hallmarks, Weiner has shifted her focus to contemporary women's fiction. Her most recent novels are annotated in chapter 3.

Good in Bed. 2001. Washington Square. ISBN 9780743418171. 400p.
   Cannie Shapiro is confident, intelligent, and comfortable in her own skin—but not so comfortable that she's willing to accept that her ex-boyfriend published a magazine article about her titled "Loving a Larger Woman." Getting over the humiliation fuels a renaissance for Cannie, who spends the next year trying her best to realize her dreams. Followed by **Certain Girls** (2008), which picks up Cannie and her daughter Joy's life thirteen years after the events of *Good in Bed.*

   Keywords: Humorous, Self-Actualization.

In Her Shoes. 2002. Atria. ISBN 0743418190. 432p.
   Slightly frumpy and very dependable Rose allows her extremely pretty and very flighty sister, Maggie, to move in with her when Maggie loses yet another job. But Rose finally hits her limit when Maggie steals her shoes, her credit cards, and her boyfriend. The sisters are finally brought back together when the grandmother they never knew tracks them down and wants them all to be family.

   Keywords: Family, Humorous, Sisters.

Weisberger, Lauren.

The Devil Wears Prada. 2003. Doubleday. ISBN 9780385509268. 368p.
   Wanting to break into the world of journalism, unfashionable Andrea somehow manages to land a plum job as assistant to Miranda Priestly, the celebrated (and hated) editor of *Runway* magazine, but it's not all it's cracked up to be. Miranda is a bitch on wheels and makes Andrea's life a living hell. For example, when Miranda's out of the office, Andrea is not allowed to leave her desk—even to use the bathroom—in case Miranda calls. Andrea finds herself playing personal shopper, errand girl, and all-around slave girl, but she's desperate for a good recommendation so she can get a "real" job at the *New Yorker*. Followed by **Revenge Wears Prada** (2013), which picks up eight years after Miranda leaves *Runway.*

   Keywords: Humorous, Workplace.

Everyone Worth Knowing. 2005. Simon & Schuster. ISBN 9780743262293. 367p.

> Bette impulsively quits her staid, stable banking job but soon finds herself with no employment prospects. Enter Kelly, a PR maven, who hires Bette for a job that seems like an aspiring socialite's dream: see and be seen at New York's hottest nightspots. Soon, Bette is rubbing elbows with celebrities—and seeing her name in the city's most vicious gossip columns.
>
> **Keywords:** Humorous, Self-Actualization.

Last Night at Chateau Marmont. 2010. Atria. ISBN 9781439136614. 370p.

> Brooke is used to her life as the wife of a struggling musician. She works two jobs to allow her husband to pursue his dreams, while setting her own aside. When Julian makes it big, her nice-guy husband starts to change, and Brooke finds that her marriage is becoming tabloid fodder.
>
> **Keywords:** Humorous, Marriage.

Zigman, Laura.

> Zigman's novels are categorized as chick lit because they feature young women on the cusp of something big—a career, a relationship, or a life choice. However, they are not as fluffy as some in this category.

Piece of Work. 2006. Warner. ISBN 044657838X. 304p.

> Julie's husband, Peter, loses his job, so she goes back to work as a celebrity publicist after three years as a stay-at-home mom. When she lands a difficult client, she quickly remembers that dealing with some adults is the same as dealing with toddlers. A warm and witty look at the struggle between raising a family and having a career.
>
> **Keywords:** Family, Humorous.

Mommy Lit

Motherhood is a common topic in women's fiction, and what distinguishes "mommy lit"—a subgenre of chick lit that enjoyed a brief burst of popularity in the mid-2000s—from women's fiction about motherhood is the tone. Mommy lit tends to be lighthearted in its treatment of motherhood, though it often touches on tensions typical of women's lives. Looking past the jokes about postpartum body changes, dirty diapers, and recalcitrant toddlers, readers will find thoughtful commentary on the various professional and personal choices mothers make.

If chick lit is about women in their twenties finding themselves personally and professionally, mommy lit is about women in their thirties revisiting the choices that they've made—and often wondering if their life would be better if they'd made different choices. The focus here is on the way women's lives change after they've had children and on changing relationships with spouses, friends, and professional colleagues.

Bilston, Sarah.

Bed Rest. 2006. HarperCollins. ISBN 9780060889937. 224p.

Quinn is a young British lawyer married to an American, living in New York City. When she gets pregnant, she is overjoyed until she is put on bed rest for the last three months of her pregnancy. Her formerly busy, organized life comes to a screeching halt. When she makes friends with the neighbors in her building, she finds a new purpose doing some pro bono work for the residents next door. This element of the story lends a more serious tone to the book, making it stand out from other chick lit fare.

Keyword: Humorous.

Sleepless Nights. 2009. HarperCollins. ISBN 0060889942. 304p.

Once baby Samuel arrives, Quinn thinks she can go back to normal and balance motherhood and corporate law. Unfortunately, that's not the case, and things only get worse when her husband's firm starts talking of downsizing. On a vacation in Connecticut, the couple consider taking over a local law practice—but will that be as exciting as life in the big city?

Keywords: Humorous, Motherhood.

Brown, Josie.

The Baby Planner. 2011. Gallery. ISBN 9781439197127. 337p.

"Baby planner" Katie Johnson guides San Francisco's wealthy women through pregnancy, childbirth, and early childhood, providing guidance, information, and the inside scoop on everything a baby needs to fit in with the haute crowd. But Katie longs for a child of her own, and her husband is disinterested in fatherhood. Can she reconcile her desire for a baby with her high-pressure job?

Keyword: Humorous.

Green, Risa.

Notes from the Underbelly. 2004. New American Library. ISBN 0451214161. 304p.

Lara, a counselor at a Bel-Air prep school, decides that working with kids is the best form of birth control. But her husband has other ideas. When they realize it's time to start a family, she finds herself completely unprepared for the changes she goes through, from those in her body to those in her life. Followed by *Tales from the Crib* (2006).

Keywords: Humorous, Motherhood, Self-Actualization.

Neill, Fiona.

Slummy Mummy. 2007. Riverhead. ISBN 9781594489440. 337p.

The opposite of the "yummy mummy"—that mother who always looks good, whether she's dropping her child off at preschool or attending a cocktail party with her equally well-put-together spouse—is the "slummy mummy," who can't seem to pull herself together no matter the circumstance. Lucy Sweeney is definitely the latter. Her life with her three children and her super-organized husband is messy, to say the least. What begins as an innocent flirtation with the father of one of her children's friends takes a turn toward a fling, and Lucy wonders if the answer to her disastrous life is a quick escape.

Keywords: Humorous, Motherhood.

Scheibe, Amy.

What Do You Do All Day? 2005. St. Martin's. ISBN 0312343035. 320p.
Jennifer, a former antiques expert for Christie's, now spends her days raising five-year-old Georgia and baby Max. She's having a hard time preserving her identity, and when her husband leaves for a three-month trip to Singapore, she decides to seek out other stay-at-home moms—and possibly an ex-boyfriend—to boost her spirits. This is a mashup of *Sex and the City* with *Parents* magazine.

Keywords: Humorous, Motherhood.

Star, Nancy.

Carpool Diem. 2008. 5 Spot. ISBN 9780446581820. 326p.
Annie Fleming is a type A corporate executive who finds herself out of work thanks to a meddling coworker. As she tries to apply her executive management skills to stay-at-home motherhood, she realizes that the two have more in common than she could have expected.

Keywords: Humorous, Motherhood.

Wilde, Samantha.

This Little Mommy Stayed Home. 2009. Bantam. ISBN 9780385342667. 388p.
Joy McGuire loves her infant son, but she's not so sure about the sleep deprivation and isolation that new motherhood has introduced to her life. When her college sweetheart reappears in her life, Joy wonders if she married the wrong man—and lost herself when she became a mother.

Keywords: Humorous, Motherhood.

Williams, Polly.

The Yummy Mummy. 2007. Hyperion. ISBN 1401302319. 384p.
New mom Amy is torn between two groups of friends—the frumpier pals she made in her childbirth classes and the new friends she's dying to fit in with, the "Yummy Mummies." She feels lost without her high-powered job at a prestigious British PR firm, yet she's not sure where to fit in now that she has a six-month-old in tow. When new "yummy" friend Alice takes over her life in a massive makeover she calls "Project Amy," Amy comes to realize this might not be the place she belongs in after all.

Keywords: Humorous, Motherhood, Self-Actualization.

Chapter 7

Multicultural Women's Fiction

Multicultural women's fiction is a subgenre that will endure and deserves to be showcased. Characters that readers of a particular ethnicity can relate to always hold appeal, and right now, multicultural fiction is really popular among readers of all ethnic and cultural backgrounds. Whether or not to separate these out in library collections can be a difficult call to make, however, because these books all have stories that appeal to women of any race. Readers enjoy stories of women of other cultures experiencing similar daily challenges. Multicultural women's fiction novels can demonstrate that we all have common ground no matter where in the world we come from or what our history may be.

As author Virginia deBerry eloquently stated in a letter to *Library Journal*, "What we write is women's fiction with Af-Am characters—stories of struggle and triumph, loss, coping, love, life, and learning. But we are labeled—handicapped—before we're out of the gate. Those who are expecting urban lit are disappointed, and those (white folks) who might enjoy our work because the theme might be relevant to their life don't ever see it because it's in 'that' section and they aren't going 'there'."[1]

As our ever-changing world grows and diversifies, that diversification is naturally reflected in fiction. This section includes books from African American, Asian American, East Indian American, and Latina authors, and the titles often reflect situations of interest to those ethnic groups while still containing the overarching themes of women's lives and relationships.

African American

Bandele, Asha.

Daughter: A Novel. 2003. Scribner. ISBN 0743211847. 266p.
Miriam's world is rocked when her college-age daughter, Aya, is shot by a police officer in a case of mistaken identity. Having already lost her husband to police violence, she now loses her daughter just as they were trying to connect. As Miriam waits by Aya's bedside, she is overcome by recollections of love and regret.

Keywords: Emotional, Self-Actualization.

Briscoe, Connie.

Briscoe's books center on the personal struggles of contemporary middle-class African American women, covering romantic relationships, work issues, and family.

P.G. County. 2002. Doubleday. ISBN 0385501617. 336p.

Barbara and Bradford Bentley reside in one of the country's most affluent African American neighborhoods, Prince George's County, Maryland. In this soapy novel, Barbara reigns over a group of neighbors including the adulteress Jolene, white hippie Candice, and hairdresser Pearl. When a runaway teenager, looking for her unknown father, enters the scene, drama ensues.

Keywords: Ensemble, Family, Friendship.

Money Can't Buy Love. 2011. Grand Central. ISBN 9780446534840. 304p.

Photographer Lenora is dealing with dwindling funds and a man who won't commit. When she wins the lottery, she decides her life is always going to be perfect—until she's caught having an affair. Money can't buy happiness and apparently can't buy class, either.

Keyword: Romantic.

Campbell, Bebe Moore.

Campbell's women's fiction features strong female characters dealing with love and loss and personal hardships.

Singing in the Comeback Choir. 1998. Putnam. ISBN 0399142983. 372p.

No one can deny that Maxine, the executive producer for a successful TV talk show, has a stressful life. Her Hollywood career ebbs and flows with the ratings, her husband has cheated on her, and she worries about her grandmother, Lindy, a woman who refuses to leave her dangerous Philadelphia neighborhood. When Lindy has a small stroke, Maxine must leave Los Angeles to assist her.

Keyword: Family.

*What You Owe Me. 2001. Putnam. ISBN 9780399147845. 400p.

Shortly after World War II, two hotel maids become friends at work and decide to go into business together. Hosana, who is black, meets Gilda, a white Polish immigrant, and immediately knows that the hand lotion Gilda makes is something special. They team up to produce it together and sell it locally, and become famous. Shortly after, Gilda embezzles all of their money, and years later, Hosana's daughter infiltrates the now-global cosmetics company bent on revenge.

Keywords: Friendship, Thought-Provoking.

*72-Hour Hold. 2006. Anchor. ISBN 9781400033614. 336p.

Keri, a successful businesswoman, struggles to care for her teenage daughter, Trina, who has bipolar disorder. Keri's ex-husband refuses to believe their daughter is really ill, and her friends start to shun her, as if worried it's catching. Since Trina is legally an adult, Keri can't even get assistance from authorities, so she signs Trina up for the Program, an underground intervention.

Keywords: Family, Thought-Provoking.

Carter, Ernessa T.

32 Candles. 2010. Amistad. ISBN 0061957844. 352p.
> Davie is a black teen growing up in the 1980s who finds herself obsessed with Molly Ringwald and the perfect life depicted in the John Huges movies that the actress is famous for. Davie's life is pretty much the complete opposite—she's skinny, not particularly attractive, and lives in a trailer with her abusive parents. After a cruel prank at school, Davie runs away to L.A. and soon becomes a semi-famous lounge singer. When the golden boy she had a crush on back in the 1980s comes into the club one night, Davie is torn between staying far away from him, trying to deceive him, or revealing their shared past.
>
> **Keywords:** Self-Actualization, Romantic.

Cleage, Pearl.

> An acclaimed playwright and poet, Cleage also writes women's fiction featuring strong African American women, social issues, and family/community relationships.

Babylon Sisters. 2005. Ballantine. ISBN 0345456092. 304p.
> Cat Sanderson has good life: a successful consulting business, a lovely home in Atlanta, and a wonderful teenage daughter, Phoebe. Things go sour, however, when Phoebe, in a fit of rebellion, contacts her mother's ex-boyfriends and demands DNA tests in order to find her real father, whom Cat has been lying about for seventeen years.
>
> **Keyword:** Family.

Till You Hear from Me. 2010. Ballantine. ISBN 9780345506375. 288p.
> After her work on the presidential campaign, Ida awaits a job offer in the White House. Unfortunately, her father, civil rights legend Rev. Horace Dunbar, is caught on tape making a racially charged rant and Ida finds herself blackballed in Washington. Concerned that her father's mental state may be in decline, she heads home to Atlanta to find out what's going on.
>
> **Keywords:** Family, Thought-Provoking.

deBerry, Virginia, and Donna Grant.

> Writing partners deBerry and Grant produce stories of family, relationships, and society that transcend race.

Tryin' to Sleep in the Bed You Made. 1996. St. Martin's. ISBN 9780312152338. 384p.
> Gayle and Pat were best friends as children, but they've grown apart as adults, mainly because of Gayle's gambling-addicted husband, Ramsey. Then Ramsey commits suicide, and Gayle's carefully constructed life collapses. Pat has gone from being an unwanted child to an unrivaled success in business, but can she help her old friend get back on her feet?
>
> **Keywords:** Friendship, Thought-Provoking.

Far from the Tree. 2000. St. Martin's. ISBN 9780312202910. 335p.

Disparate sisters Celeste and Ronnie discover that their late father has left them a house. Their mother, Della, has nothing but bad memories of the place and tries to keep the sisters from even visiting the place. Family secrets unfold, including the fact that Celeste worries that her marriage is falling apart, while Ronnie tries to hide the fact that she's not quite making it as an actress and is nearly homeless.

Keywords: Family, Self-Actualization.

Uptown. 2010. Touchstone. ISBN 1439137765. 352p.

Avery returns to her native Harlem to take care of her dying mother after twenty years abroad. When her mother passes, she leaves Avery a building, which is very hot property—in the new era of gentrification, this property is the only thing impeding a massive and pricey development to the area. Avery intends to sell, until she meets the tenants who stand to lose their homes.

Keywords: Family, Grief, Thought-Provoking.

Griffin, Bettye.

Griffin began her career as a contemporary romance author but branched out into women's fiction in the mid-2000s.

Nothing but Trouble. 2006. Dafina. ISBN 9780758207395. 304p.

Three best friends find their relationships tested when one of their sisters enters the picture. Widowed Dana is on the verge of bankruptcy, Norelle desperately longs for a baby, and Cecile is already feeling the pinch raising a stepfamily when she discovers she's pregnant again. When Cecile's sexy younger sister Michline moves to town and starts hitting on everyone's men, Cecile needs to decide between her sister and her friends. Michline returns in *Trouble Down the Road* (2010).

Keywords: Ensemble, Family, Friendship.

Jones, Tayari.

Silver Sparrow. 2011. Algonquin. ISBN 9781565129900. 352p.

Dana and Chaurisse are born just a few months apart in Atlanta. They share the same father, James, but have different mothers. James is a secret bigamist, living a dual life with two families—one part time, one full time. When the girls grow up and cross paths as teenagers, only Dana knows the truth about their dad.

Keywords: Ensemble, Family, Thought-Provoking.

Koomson, Dorothy.

British author Koomson's novels feature everyday women in extraordinary situations, dealing with family issues and romantic upheavals.

My Best Friend's Girl. 2008. Bantam. ISBN 9780553591415. 480p.

Kamryn and Adele were best friends in college, despite their radically different backgrounds. The pair are estranged when Adele has an affair with Kamryn's fiancé, but when Adele is dying of cancer, she asks her old friend for one last favor—to adopt the child that resulted from that affair.

Keywords: Friendship, Thought-Provoking.

Goodnight, Beautiful. 2010. Bantam. ISBN 9780385344265. 464p.

Nova and Mal have been best friends since childhood, so when Mal and his wife, Stephanie, ask Nova to be a surrogate mother for them, she agrees. Stephanie, already somewhat anxious about the situation, discovers a text message from Mal to Nova that suggests they were more than friends, so she calls off the agreement and cuts all ties to the pregnant Nova. Eight years later, Nova is raising her son by herself, but when he becomes critically ill, she needs Mal back in their lives.

Keywords: Family, Thought-Provoking.

McFadden, Bernice.

Nowhere Is a Place. 2006. Dutton. ISBN 9780525948759. 416p.

In this multigenerational saga, thirty-eight-year-old Sherry is always looking for a place to belong. She sets off with her estranged mother, Dumpling, on a days-long road trip to a family reunion in Georgia. Along the way, Sherry gets Dumpling to tell her family stories, from slavery to the present, and uncovers family secrets.

Keywords: Family, Saga.

McMillan, Terry.

McMillan's character-driven novels feature successful and dynamic African American women searching for fulfillment, be it in their love relationships, their friendships, or their work.

Waiting to Exhale. 1992. Viking. ISBN 9780670839803. 409p.

Four thirty-something women living in Phoenix help one another find the one good black man who will make their dreams come true. Savannah is new in town, having arrived to help her best friend Bernadine recover from a painful divorce. Flighty Robin needs to rely less on astrology and more on her gut feelings, while matronly Georgia worries her teenage son might grow up to be just like all of the rogues the women encounter. Characters return in *Getting to Happy* (2010).

Keyword: Friendship.

How Stella Got Her Groove Back. 1996. Viking. ISBN 9780670869909. 368p.

McMillan's best seller brought the idea of a woman "getting her groove back" into common parlance. Stella Payne is a forty-two-year-old divorcee with a high-powered job and a preteen son, and she seems to have it all—except romance. On a trip to Jamaica, she meets a sexy young man who is half her age and finds herself falling unexpectedly, passionately in love.

Keywords: Beach, Romantic.

A Day Late and a Dollar Short. 2001. Viking. ISBN 9780670896769. 432p.

Viola and Cecil's contentious relationship has dragged on for almost forty years, and when Viola's asthma lands her in the ICU, he's right by her bedside, much to Viola's chagrin. The couple's four adult children bring their own personal issues, too, and they range from failed relationships to a general refusal to grow up. There's no shortage of drama as this dysfunctional family does their best to help each other sort through their problems.

Keywords: Family, Humorous, Marriage.

The Interruption of Everything. 2005. Viking. ISBN 0670031445. 384p.
Marilyn Grimes spends so much time taking care of everyone else around her that she barely has any time to realize her own dreams. Her marriage isn't the greatest, and her husband seems to be going through a midlife crisis—and then she finds out that she's unexpectedly pregnant. As much as Marilyn would love to lean on her family, they all have troubles of their own, so she depends on her friends to help get her through life's trials.

Keywords: Family, Humorous, Marriage.

McKinney-Whetstone, Diane.

McKinney-Whetstone's novels, set in Philadelphia in the middle of the twentieth century, feature strong African American women and generations of close-knit families.

Trading Dreams at Midnight. 2008. HarperCollins. ISBN 9780688163860. 320p.
Neena has spent most of her adult years trying to track down her mentally ill mother, who abandoned Neena and her sister when they were young. Sadly, she has been financing her search by blackmailing married men, but her last victim turned the tables on her. Broke and exhausted, she returns to her hometown, where she has to deal with her sister, who is ill, and their strict grandmother.

Keywords: Family, Mothers and Daughters, Thought-Provoking.

Murray, Victoria Christopher.

Murray's glitzy tales feature divas, rich folk, and all the trouble that befalls them. They also explore issues of faith.

Sins of the Mother. 2010. Touchstone. ISBN 141658918x. 400p.
Jasmine has given up her drama-filled past and settled into her life as the wife of a prominent pastor and mother to two beautiful girls. Then her eldest daughter is kidnapped, and Jasmine wonders if the crime is revenge for the trouble she caused in her stripper days.

Keywords: Family, Glitzy.

The Deal, the Dance, and the Devil. 2011. Touchstone. ISBN 9781439194256. 416p.
Having come from humble beginnings, Evia and Adam have worked their way up and now live in a fancy house and have the finer things in life. When the recession hits, Adam loses his job and they stand to lose everything until Evia's boss approaches them with a multimillion dollar proposal—she wants to spend the weekend, alone, with Adam.

Keyword: Thought-Provoking.

Destiny's Divas. 2012. Touchstone. 9781451654064. 400p.
Destiny's Divas are a popular gospel music trio with some seriously unholy secrets. Their behind-the-scenes behavior is far from godly, and though they go

to great lengths to hide their true selves, the truth comes out, setting a chain of events in motion that will change the divas' lives forever.

Keywords: Friendship, Glitzy.

Ray, Francis.

Best known as an author of contemporary romance (especially her popular "Grayson Friends" series), Ray has branched out into contemporary women's fiction as well.

When Morning Comes. 2012. St. Martin's Griffin. ISBN 9780312681623. 340p.
It's not a secret that neurosurgeon Cade Mathis was adopted as a child, but the identity of his birth mother is shrouded in mystery. His troubled childhood has made him into a cold, detached adult, and his desire to find his real family leads him to patient advocate Sabrina Thomas, whose tenacity and drive helps Cade carry on in his quest for answers.

Keyword: Romantic.

Roby, Kimberla Lawson.

Roby's contemporary, soapy African American women's fiction features strong characters, romance, sex, and hard issues.

A Taste of Reality. 2003. William Morrow. ISBN 0060505656. 292p.
Anise has a great life—an MBA, a successful husband, a dream home. But underneath the surface, she's unhappy—her company won't give her the projects she wants (because she's black and female) and she discovers her husband is cheating on her with a white woman. She decides she's had enough and musters up the courage to fight back.

Keyword: Thought-Provoking.

Secret Obsession. 2011. Grand Central. ISBN 9780446572422. 192p.
Paige has always felt cold in the shadow of her sister, Camille—always the smart one, the pretty one, the popular one. As adults, Camille has the handsome husband and perfect children and expensive home, while Paige is single and can't even pay her bills. Paige hatches a plan to steal her brother-in-law. When her plain fails, Paige moves from jealousy to madness.

Keywords: Family, Sisters, Thought-Provoking.

*The Perfect Marriage. 2013. Grand Central. ISBN 9780446572507. 192p.
From the outside, Denise and Derrek Shaw look like the perfect family— successful in business and in love, with good jobs and a showplace for a home. Beneath the perfect veneer lies a dark secret: both are addicted to drugs and they are unable to kick their habit.

Keywords: Family, Marriage, Thought-Provoking.

Reverend Curtis Black series.

Roby's sudsy series follows the life and loves of Curtis Black, a Baptist preacher, and his family and friends.

Casting the First Stone. 2000.

Too Much of a Good Thing. 2004.

The Best Kept Secret. 2005.

Love and Lies. 2007.

Sin No More. 2008.

The Best of Everything. 2009.

Be Careful What You Pray For. 2010.

Love, Honor, and Betray. 2011.

Skerrett, Joanne.

Sugar vs. Spice. 2006. Kensington Strapless. ISBN 9780758211538. 322p.
> Tari, a newspaper journalist by day and an aspiring jazz singer by night, enjoys her carefree life. Her older sister, Melinda, is a wife, mother, and career woman who would like to see Tari follow in her more sensible footsteps. When Tari discovers she has breast cancer, she decides to conceal her illness from her coworkers and fellow musicians, with disastrous results. Luckily her family rallies around her when she needs them most.

> **Keywords:** Family, Sisters, Thought-Provoking.

Williams, Tia.

The Accidental Diva. 2004. Putnam. ISBN 0399152016. 245p.
> Uptown girl meets downtown boy. Billie Burke is the beauty editor of a leading national magazine. She loves her glamorous, upscale life in New York City and is on the brink of a promotion when she meets Jay, a performance artist with a shady past. Can their worlds ever combine, or are they just too different to make it work?

> **Keywords:** Glitzy, Romantic.

Asian American

Hwang, Caroline.

In Full Bloom. 2003. Dutton. ISBN 0525947116. 304p.
> Ginger Lee, a young assistant at a fashion magazine, is fine with her life the way it is. Her mother, however, is not—and shows up on Ginger's Manhattan doorstep determined to find a nice Korean husband for her daughter. Ginger, whose interest in her Korean heritage is limited to food, is appalled by this notion, but Mom helps pay the bills, so what's a girl to do?

> **Keywords:** Family, Mothers and Daughters.

Keltner, Kim Wong.

The Dim Sum of All Things. 2003. Avon Trade. ISBN 0060560754. 344p.
Third-generation Chinese American Lindsey Owyang has very little in common with her heritage. She lives with her grandmother, Pau Pau, who keeps a traditional way of life. When the two women travel from San Francisco to China to visit long-lost family, Lindsey gains a new appreciation for her background and history as she is immersed in Chinese culture.

Keyword: Family.

Lee, Min Jin.

Free Food for Millionaires. 2007. Warner. ISBN 9780446581080. 512p.
Casey Han is a first-generation Korean American dealing with the conflict between her new expensive lifestyle and her conservative immigrant family. Even though she's graduated magna cum laude from Princeton, her father kicks her out when she doesn't land a "real" job. She bunks up with a wealthy classmate and navigates the big city, from boyfriends to jobs, and works to understand her family.

Keyword: Family.

Lockwood, Cara.

Dixieland Sushi: A Novel. 2005. Downtown Press. ISBN 0743499425. 283p.
Japanese American Jen Nakamara Taylor hated growing up in a small southern town, where she constantly felt like a fish out of water. She's much more secure now as an adult, living in Chicago. But all those childhood memories come back when she is summoned home to Dixieland, Arkansas, for her cousin's wedding.

Keywords: Family, Southern.

Tan, Amy.

Tan is known for her evocative, well-drawn characters; it is important to note that Tan's literary fiction does not all fit the under the umbrella of women's fiction, despite the popularity of *The Joy Luck Club.*

The Joy Luck Club. 1989. Putnam. ISBN 9780399134203. 288p.
In the 1940s, four Chinese-born women start a mah-jongg group in San Francisco for fun. Nearly forty years later, their daughters continue to meet as the Joy Luck Club. The women all get to tell tales from their lives, revealing hopes, fears, triumphs, and heartbreaks.

Keywords: Emotional, Ensemble, Family.

The Bonesetter's Daughter. 2001. Putnam. ISBN 0399146431. 333p.
The relationship between a Chinese mother and her American-born daughter are at the heart of this literary novel. Ruth finds two bundles of writing: one titled "Things I Know Are True"; the other, "Things I Must Not Forget." They are the memoirs of her mother, who is now suffering

from Alzheimer's. As Ruth reads, she realizes that although she and her mother have lived very different lives, their struggles to find their own identities make them more alike than they would have guessed.

Keyword: Family.

Yu, Michelle, and Blossom Kan.

China Dolls. 2007. Thomas Dunne. 9780312362805. 288p.
Three Chinese American young women try to make it in New York City. M .J. is a successful sportswriter, Alex is a lawyer, and Lin is a stockbroker. All three are feeling pressure from their immigrant families to find love and career success. M. J. is locked out of promotions because of her gender. Alex and Lin are financially successful but treated like "dumb girls" in their professions.

Keywords: Ensemble, Family, Friendship.

Young, Restless and Broke. 2010. Thomas Dunne. ISBN 0312374208. 256p.
Sarah wants to become a soap-opera actress, but her family is very critical of this choice. When she meets television producer Daniel, she falls head over heels, and not just because he could possibly get her a gig. Impulsively, she moves from New York to L.A. but finds that reality doesn't quite live up to her Hollywood dreams.

Keyword: Self-Actualization.

East Indian American

Banerjee, Anjali.

Imaginary Men. 2005. Downtown Press. ISBN 1416509437. 256p.
Professional matchmaker Lina's Bengali family wants to see her quickly married off. She finds herself trapped by a lie at her sister's wedding in India, where she blurts out that she is already engaged. When everyone clamors to meet her imaginary fiancé at the next family gathering, Lina must finally get a grip on reality. Chick lit with an authentic ethnic twist.

Keywords: Family, Romantic.

Haunting Jasmine. 2011. Berkley. ISBN 0425238717. 304p.
Jasmine's ugly divorce has made her mistrustful and bitter. When she returns home to take over her aunt's bookshop, she's confronted by her family, her friends, and the spirits who purportedly haunt the bookstore—and they're all trying to get her to move on and get over her loss.

Keyword: Family.

Bantwal, Shobhan.

The Sari Shop Window. 2009. Kensington. ISBN 0758232020. 352p.
Anjali was widowed at a tragically young age, but at least she has her family to lean on. After her husband dies, she takes over the family's boutique, transforming

it into an eclectic shop featuring a beautifully curated selection of clothing and accessories. Everything seems to be going well, until Anjali finds out that the shop is about to go bankrupt. Enter Anjali's uncle and his business partner, Rishi, who has the means to save the store—and he may capture Anjali's heart in the process.

Keywords: Family, Romantic.

The Full Moon Bride. 2011. Kensington. ISBN 9780758258847. 352p.
Soorya has made a name for herself as an attorney, but she's unlucky in love. As a modern Indian American woman, she eschews the idea of arranged marriage, but the older she gets, the more appealing it seems. But just as Soorya decides to take her chances with arranged marriage, a most unacceptable man comes along, and he might change everything.

Keyword: Romantic.

The Reluctant Matchmaker. 2012. Kensington. ISBN 9780758258854. 352p.
Meena is proud of her career in technology, but her mother just wants her to meet the right man and get married. Meena's got no shortage of suitors, but none of them are holding her interest the way her new boss Prajay does. But Prajay sees Meena as little more than a friend, and that becomes clear when he enlists Meena's help writing a personal ad so he can meet the woman of his dreams.

Keyword: Romantic.

Daswani, Kavita.

The Village Bride of Beverly Hills. 2004. Putnam. ISBN 0399152148. 271p.
Priya is very unhappy that she had to leave her family in India and move to Los Angeles with her new husband, Sanjay, mainly because Sanjay's demanding and conservative parents boss Priya around. Wanting a forbidden career, she takes a job as a receptionist at a gossipy Hollywood magazine, but she must keep her new job hidden from her new family.

Keyword: Family.

Divakaruni, Chitra Banerjee.
Divakaruni's literary women's fiction featuring Indian American women has hints of mysticism and myth.

Sister of My Heart. 2000. Doubleday. ISBN 0385489501. 322p.
Cousins Anju and Sudha are born on the same day in Calcutta. They couldn't be more different—Anju's family is from a wealthy caste; Sudha is the daughter of the black sheep of the family. Sudha is extraordinarily beautiful; Anju is not. Yet the girls grow up as close as sisters. Family secrets and arranged marriages threaten to force them apart, but even Anju's move to California doesn't weaken their bond. The women narrate in alternate chapters in this moving story. Followed by *The Vine of Desire* (2003).

Keyword: Emotional, Family.

Queen of Dreams. 2004. Doubleday. ISBN 9780385506823. 352p.

Rakhi is a single mother and struggling artist who wishes she had her mother's talent to interpret dreams. She also yearns to know more about her mother's life growing up in India and her heritage. When her mother passes away unexpectedly, Rakhi becomes determined to learn more by reading her mother's dream journals.

Keywords: Family, Grief, Mothers and Daughters, Self-Actualization.

Gowda, Shilpi Somaya.

 *Secret Daughter.* 2010. William Morrow. ISBN 9780061922312. 352p.

In rural India, girl children are often unwanted and abandoned. Kavita secretly carries her newborn daughter Asha to an orphanage, knowing her husband would kill the child just as he did their first. On the other side of the world, in San Francisco, infertile Somer is persuaded by her Indian husband to adopt a child from India. They find Asha and bring her to America, and her life is chronicled here.

Keywords: Family, Motherhood, Thought-Provoking.

Malladi, Amulya.

The Mango Season. 2003. Ballantine. ISBN 0345450302. 229p.

Priya goes home to India to visit her Brahmin family, who, unaware that she is engaged to an American man back in California, have chosen a "nice Indian boy" for her to marry. Scared that they will disown her, Priya goes through the elaborate charade of meeting the prospective groom and his parents.

Keyword: Family.

Mukherjee, Bharati.

Mukherjee's literary fiction often features strong Indian and Indian American women with one foot in the past and one in the future. Not all of her titles can be considered women's fiction, but the three below have memorable characters working through emotions and relationships.

Jasmine. 1989. Grove Press. Reprint, 1999. ISBN 0802136303. 256p.

Jyoti, a poor Punjabi girl, is widowed by age seventeen and leaves India for the United States. Her life is filled with adventure, danger, sorrow, and love. Along her journey, she changes her name (several times), works for a time as a nanny in New York, ends up with children of different backgrounds, and finally settles on a farm in Iowa. An absorbing story of identity, courage, and hope.

Keyword: Self-Actualization.

Miss New India. 2011. Harcourt. ISBN 9780618646531. 336p.

Anjali is born into a lower caste in India to very traditional parents who wish to see her in an arranged marriage. But her teacher, an American, thinks she's destined for more. With his assistance she moves to the Bangalore, the big city, where she is able to reinvent herself.

Keyword: Self-Actualization.

Pradhan, Monica.

The Hindi-Bindi Club. 2007. Bantam. ISBN 055338452X. 488p.
First-generation Americans Kiran, Preity, and Rani like to mock their Indian mothers for their old-fashioned notions. The mothers simply want what they think is best for the girls—marriage to a nice Indian young man. Two cultures collide as the women find their own romances and career paths. Indian recipes, shared by the mothers, are dotted throughout the breezy narrative.

Keywords: Ensemble, Family, Friendship, Humorous.

Sreenivasan, Jyotsna.

And Laughter Fell from the Sky. 2012. Morrow. ISBN 9780062105769. 336p.
Dutiful daughter Rasika still lives at home and knows that an arranged marriage is expected of her. When she meets Abhay, the sparks fly, but they know Rasika's family will never approve, even though he is at least of the same background.

Keywords: Family, Romantic.

Umrigar, Thrity.

Umrigar writes literary women's fiction featuring characters of Indian descent.

*The World We Found. 2012. HarperCollins. ISBN 9780061938344. 320p.
Four women—Armaiti, Laleh, Kavita, and Nishta—meet as university students in the 1970s. Their feminist spirit has been tempered through the years, as they followed different paths and drifted apart. The women reunite and share their stories as they come together when one of them is gravely ill.

Keywords: Ensemble, Friendship, Thought-Provoking.

Latina

Latina women's fiction is diverse, and the novels in this section include stories of first- and second-generation immigrants to the United States from a variety of Latin American countries.

Candela, Margo.

Life Over Easy. 2007. Kensington. ISBN 075821572X. 320p.
When her boyfriend tells her it's over, Natalya doesn't quite know what to do with herself—she thought he was going to propose. She gets a makeover, joins a gym, starts volunteering, and even starts going to church, all in an effort to get her mind off of her ex and get herself out there.

Keyword: Self-Actualization.

Cano-Murillo. Kathy.

Cano-Murillo, an artist and entrepreneur, writes humorous fiction about Latina women who enjoy crafts and sewing.

Crafty Chica novels.

Waking Up in the Land of Glitter. 2010.

Miss Scarlet's School of Patternless Sewing. 2011.

Carlson, Lori M.

The Sunday Tertulia. 2000. HarperCollins. ISBN 0060195363. 208p.

Lonely New Yorker Claire strikes up a friendship with retired pharmacist Isabela and is invited to Isabela's monthly "tertulia"—an informal gathering of women. She's the youngest and the only white woman in the group, but they welcome her just the same. Lots of girl talk and an exploration of identity are the hallmarks of this novel, with poetry, recipes, and herbal remedies interspersed.

Keywords: Ensemble, Friendship.

Castillo, Mary.

In Between Men. 2006. Avon Trade. ISBN 0060766824. 304p.

When ESL teacher and single mom Isa is voted "Unsexiest Woman Alive" by her students, she thinks things can't get worse. But they do, when her ex-husband Carlos tells a shock-jock radio DJ how bad she was in bed. Determined to be a red-hot mama, she embarks on a huge makeover. Unfortunately, she discovers that juggling a job, a young son, and her new sex-symbol status is harder than it looks.

Keyword: Humorous.

Medina, C. C.

A Little Love. 2000. Warner. ISBN 0446524484. 357p.

Four Miami Latinas rely on each other in this entertaining novel. There's Isabel, a Cuban American single mom; her ambitious cousin Mercy, a high-end real estate agent; elegant Lucinda, a Dominican American socialite; and Julia, a Mexican American professor who falls in love with another woman.

Keywords: Friendship, Humorous.

Platas, Berta.

Cinderella Lopez. 2006. St. Martin's Griffin. ISBN 0312341725. 277p.

Cynthia Lopez is overworked and has two evil stepsisters. Sound familiar? When Cyn meets a cute guy, she keeps it a secret, fearing that her stepsisters will steal him away. Unfortunately, he's not who she thinks (and hopes) he is.

Keywords: Family, Humorous.

Valdes-Rodriguez, Alisa.

Valdez-Rodriguez writes sassy Latina chick lit.

The Dirty Girls Social Club. 2003. St. Martin's. ISBN 0312313810. 304p.

Six Latina college friends from different backgrounds meet every six months to catch up and offer advice to one another. Outspoken Lauren isn't as confident as she appears, Rebecca is the founder of a popular Latina magazine, Amber is a rock musician, Elizabeth is a news anchor who's in the closet, Cuban Sara is a full-time mom, and Usnavys is a high-powered executive. A nice balance of chick lit froth and serious issues. Followed by *Dirty Girls on Top* (2008).

Keywords: Friendship, Humorous, Workplace.

The Husband Habit. 2009. St. Martin's. ISBN 0312537042. 384p.

Vanessa has a bad habit of falling for married men. Her sister makes her promise that she will stop dating until she can figure out why she is only attracted to guys who are attached. When a handsome Iraq vet appears on the scene, he seems perfect, but Vanessa suspects he has a secret—and she hopes it's not a secret wife.

Keywords: Humorous, Romantic.

Zepeda, Gwendolyn.

Zepeda, who got her start as a blogger, writes humorous novels about women's lives.

Houston, We Have a Problema. 2009. Grand Central. ISBN 0446698520. 392p.

Jessica has all the typical problems—man problems, mother problems, work problems. Getting advice from the local psychic, Madame Hortensia, is not the best way to get through your issues, even though the woman seems to be eerily spot-on. When her sister sets her up with a handsome but non-Latino man, she doesn't know what to do but wants to try and finally make some decisions about her life on her own.

Keywords: Humorous, Romantic.

Lone Star Legend. 2010. Grand Central. ISBN 9780446539609. 352p.

Sandy loves her job as an investigative journalist, but when the Web site she writes for is bought out and turned into an entertainment portal, she's unhappy, but she takes on the challenge with aplomb. She vents on her anonymous blog, but when she's outed, feathers are ruffled—to say the least.

Keywords: Humorous, Workplace.

Note

1. Virginia deBerry, Letter to the Editor, *Library Journal*, April 1, 2010.

Chapter 8

Romantic Women's Fiction

As mentioned in the introduction, determining where to draw the line between romance and women's fiction can be challenging. There are often (but not always) elements of love and romance in women's fiction novels. Complicating matters is the fact that many authors cross over easily from one genre to another, and in some cases you have to consider them almost on a book-by-book basis. As stated previously, while women's fiction often incorporates romantic elements, there is more to the story than the love interest or sexual relationship.

It's safe to say that it's not much of a big deal to cast the net widely with some crossover between the genres. Some romance fiction purists may disagree with that statement and assert that it's quite a big deal, but most fans of general women's fiction will be happy having recommendations for contemporary romance titles. The authors and books listed in this chapter would make fine suggestions for women's fiction readers. Don't forget authors listed elsewhere in this book, such as Mary Kay Andrews, Eileen Goudge, Kristin Hannah, Jill Mansell, Danielle Steel, and Nora Roberts. You will also find many other novels scattered throughout the chapters in this book with the keyword Romantic—but the titles showcased here really pack in the romance and have the emotional wallop that romance fiction fans enjoy.

Ahern, Cecilia.
Ahern's recent novels have moved decidedly into magical realism territory, with fairy-tale and paranormal qualities. Her first two books, however, are charming romantic women's fiction.

P.S. I Love You. 2004. Hyperion. ISBN 1401300901. 375p.
Holly discovers a year's worth of letters that her late husband Gerry left for her to read after his untimely death. Feeling that he is still close by keeping watch, she embarks on reclaiming her life. Holly's family and friends also play a large part in her growth.
Keywords: Friendship, Grief, Romantic.

Rosie Dunne. 2005. Hyperion. ISBN 140130091X. 256p.
A delightful chronicle of the lives of Rosie and her childhood sweetheart, Alex, told through notes, letters, e-mails, and phone calls. Fated to be together, the pair

becomes separated when Alex's family moves from Ireland to America during high school. Over the next decade, a series of miscommunications and missed opportunities keep the two on the brink.

Keywords: Humorous, Romantic.

Brockway, Connie.

Best known for her historical romances, Brockway has also dabbled in women's fiction.

Skinny Dipping. 2008. Onyx. ISBN 0451412443. 432p.

Mimi's family wants to sell their summer retreat, and although she doesn't really want to take it over, she certainly doesn't want to see some developer get the site. When she takes a job caring for a neighbor boy, she finds herself falling in love with his wealthy and successful father, much to her surprise. Zany, eccentric characters and fun family dynamics set this apart from the average romance.

Keywords: Humorous, Romantic.

Chiofalo, Rosanna.

Bella Fortuna. 2012. Kensington. ISBN 9780758266538. 357p.

The DeLuca women own a popular boutique in Astoria, Queens, where they design and sew bridal gowns for a variety of women. Now it's time for Valentina DeLuca to have her dream wedding to a man she's loved for most of her life. The family decamps to Venice for the wedding, only to have everything called off at the last minute, forcing Valentina to re-evaluate her priorities and try to figure out what will make her happy in life.

Keywords: Family, Romantic, Self-Actualization.

Crusie, Jennifer.

Crusie's contemporary romances are classics of the genre and feature plenty of dysfunctionally funny families along with spicy romance.

Crazy for You. 1999. St. Martin's. ISBN 9780312198497. 325p.

Quinn leads a boring, predictable life in small-town Ohio. Then she decides to do something uncharacteristically impulsive, and she adopts a stray dog. The dog hates her nice-guy boyfriend, and that provides the impetus for Quinn to upend her entire life—falling in love with a bad-boy mechanic in the process.

Keywords: Humorous, Romantic.

Welcome to Temptation. 2000. St. Martin's. ISBN 9780312252946. 352p.

The small Ohio town of Temptation has never seen anything like sisters Sophie and Amy Dempsey, who show up to film a video featuring a has-been actress and can't manage to leave. The Dempseys become entangled with the locals, who don't know how to react to their freewheeling ways—and then the mayor enters the picture, first as an authority figure, then as Sophie's lover.

Keywords: Humorous, Romantic.

Fast Women. 2001. St. Martin's. ISBN 9780312252618. 352p.

Divorcee Nell Dysart needs a job, and she finds one as a secretary for Gabe, a private detective who is sick of his job and all the hassles that go along with it. Nell and Gabe clash over matters both professional and personal, and their bickering quickly leads to an unexpected romance.

Keywords: Humorous, Romantic, Workplace.

Faking It. 2002. St. Martin's. ISBN 9780312284688. 352p.

Tilda Goodnight is an art forger and Davy Dempsey is a con man. What could go wrong with this relationship? Plenty, especially when the Goodnight family has an overabundance of quirky characters, hit men are involved, and cons run rampant.

Keywords: Humorous, Romantic.

Bet Me. 2004. St. Martin's. ISBN 0312303467. 352p.

Minerva Dobbs, who enjoys stability and things that make sense, is about to have her world tossed upside down when charming and handsome gambler Calvin pursues her. However, Min knows that the only reason he's around is because he's made a bet with her ex-boyfriend that he can get her into bed within a month. Min strings him along but eventually realizes she's falling for him. Min's crazy family adds to the fun.

Keywords: Humorous, Romantic.

Maybe This Time. 2010. St. Martin's. ISBN 0312303785. 252p.

Andromeda is finally ready to get over her ex-husband and marry again, when he asks her for one last favor. He's been appointed guardian to two children and can't seem to keep a nanny—the house the children inherited is supposedly haunted, and the children odd, causing nannies to flee. She agrees to live with the children and tutor them for one month to get them back on track to move in with North and return to school, and discovers that the children aren't really all that strange, but the house may indeed be inhabited by several ghosts.

Keywords: Humorous, Romantic.

Fforde, Katie.

Fforde is sometimes grouped in with chick lit writers, because she's British and writes light, contemporary novels, but her plotlines and characters could not be further from chick lit—she writes about average women, of varied ages, and their families and relationships. There is typically a gentle romance in her novels—so could make a good read-alike choice as a gentle read, as well.

Stately Pursuits. 1997. St. Martin's. ISBN 9780312206765. 288p.

Having recently lost both her boyfriend and her job, Hetty agrees to house-sit a relative's stately home. To her surprise, she finds the house is due to open to the public in the spring, but a host of debts and her uncle's heir stand in her way. Helped by supportive town residents who don't want the property sold and turned into a theme park, Hetty readies the house for the opening while gaining confidence and falling in love.

Keyword: Romantic.

Restoring Grace. 2006. St. Martin's. ISBN 9780312358778. 352p.

Grace lives on a lovely but crumbling English estate. Newly divorced, she has no prospects for getting the money it will take to repair the dry rot that's threatening to ruin the house. Ellie, a newly single and pregnant artist, has nowhere to live. When Ellie tries to sell Grace a painting of the house, the women form a fast friendship and quickly realize they can help each other out if Ellie were to move in.

Keyword: Romantic.

Love Letters. 2011. St. Martin's. ISBN 9780312674533. 400p.

Bookstore manager Laura, distraught when her employer closes, takes a job with a literary agent booking authors for signings and festivals. When she meets handsome and reclusive author Dermot, she falls head over heels and is willing to give him anything—*anything*—to attend one of her events.

Keyword: Romantic.

Gibson, Rachel.

Gibson's fast-paced and fun contemporary romances would be good read-alikes for chick lit fans.

True Confessions. 2001. Avon. ISBN 0380814382. 384p.

Tabloid reporter Hope Spencer is sent to a tiny Idaho town to drum up some alien adventure stories for her editor. The local sheriff is immediately attracted to her but needs to keep his distance for the sake of his reputation and his young son. Snappy dialogue and thorough backstories for the characters round out this sweet yet sexy romance.

Keyword: Romantic.

Not Another Bad Date. 2008. Avon. ISBN 9780061178047. 384p.

Adele is tired of dating jerks and is about to give up dating forever. When she comes home to deal with a family emergency, she runs in to her old flame, Zach, who broke her heart years ago and started her down the path of bad dates. Adele's family and friends are as important to the story as the hottie football player is—an interesting side plot involving Adele's sister's family helps to make this a more engrossing read.

Keywords: Humorous, Romantic.

Jio, Sarah.

The Bungalow. 2011. Plume: Penguin. ISBN 9780452297678. 320p.

It's 1942, and best friends Kitty and Anne, questioning their staid suburban lives, decide to join the Army Nurse Corps for a nine-month tour in the South Pacific. Anne leaves behind a mystified fiancé, she but feels a strong need to taste adventure before settling down. Free spirit Kitty finds that flirting with soldiers is much more fun than nursing the wounded, while Anne falls in love with Westry, a serious-minded soldier.

Keywords: Gentle, Romantic.

The Violets of March. 2011. Penguin. ISBN 9780452297036. 304p.

> After a heartbreaking divorce, one-hit-wonder author Emily is staying on Bainbridge Island, Washington, with her elderly aunt when she comes across a diary from the 1940s. Drawn into the details of a mysterious stranger's life, Emily begins to see parallels to her own situation and senses a mystical connection with the anonymous writer.
>
> **Keywords:** Gentle, Romantic.

Blackberry Winter. 2012. Penguin. ISBN 9780452298385. 320p.

> After a late-season snowstorm blankets Seattle with snow in May, journalist Claire Aldrige gets a new assignment: write a story about the Blackberry Winter snowstorm in 1933, a similar event that brought the city to a standstill. In the course of her research, Claire discovers the tragic story of a young mother who left her son home alone during the storm so she could go to work as a night maid at a ritzy hotel, only to find him missing when she returned. The two narratives are intertwined as Claire struggles to solve the mystery of the boy's disappearance.
>
> **Keywords:** Historical, Motherhood, Romantic, Thought-Provoking.

Kleypas, Lisa.

Sugar Daddy. 2007. St. Martin's. ISBN 9780312351625. 384p.

> Liberty Jones takes a job as a personal assistant to a wealthy businessman, Churchill, a kindly older man who takes a paternal shine to Liberty and the younger sister she's raising alone. Churchill's son thinks Liberty's a gold digger, and naturally the sparks fly as they get to know one another. Liberty's family story and the dynamics between all of the characters are the real heart of this romance novel.
>
> **Keywords:** Family, Romantic, Workplace.

Friday Harbor series.

> Friday Harbor, a small town in Washington State, is the kind of place where everyone knows each other—for better or for worse. Each novel in the series centers around the romantic entanglements of a local woman.
>
> *Christmas Eve at Friday Harbor.* 2010.
>
> *Rainshadow Road.* 2012.
>
> *Dream Lake.* 2012.
>
> *Crystal Cove.* 2013.

Macomber, Debbie.

> Macomber's prolific output includes many gentle, contemporary romances that let the stories of families and friendships shine. Below are two series of Macomber's that will delight women's fiction fans who enjoy following a large cast of characters. In 2010, Macomber received the Romance Writers of America's Lifetime Achievement Award.

Cedar Cove series.

Macomber's fictional small town is filled with endearing characters, and their romantic lives and personal struggles are highlighted in the books in this series.

16 Lighthouse Road. 2001.

204 Rosewood Lane. 2002.

311 Pelican Court. 2003.

44 Cranberry Point. 2004.

50 Harbor Street. 2005.

6 Rainier Drive. 2006.

74 Seaside Avenue. 2007.

8 Sandpiper Way. 2008.

92 Pacific Boulevard. 2009.

1022 Evergreen Place. 2010.

1105 Yakima Street. 2011.

1225 Christmas Tree Lane. 2011.

Blossom Street series.

In this gentle series, Macomber explores women's friendships. Cancer survivor Lydia owns a yarn shop, A Good Yarn. When she starts a knitting class, she forms special friendships and bonds with other local women.

The Shop on Blossom Street. 2004.

A Good Yarn. 2005.

Christmas Letters. 2006.

Susannah's Garden. 2006.

Back on Blossom Street. 2007.

Twenty Wishes. 2008.

Summer on Blossom Street. 2009.

Hannah's List. 2001.

A Turn in the Road. 2001.

Starting Now. 2013.

Mallery, Susan.

Mallery is a romance writer, but recently she has started to write women's fiction.

Best of Friends. 2010. Pocket. ISBN 9781416567189. 368p.

Jayne and Rebecca have been unlikely best friends since childhood, when Jayne was abandoned at a young age and Rebecca's wealthy family took her in. Now adults, the women come to realize they may not be well suited—Jayne is serious and Rebecca is a drama queen. When the past threatens to come between them, the meaning of family and the bonds of friendship are tested.

Keywords: Family, Friendship, Romantic.

Already Home. 2011. Mira. ISBN 9780778329510. 368p.

Chef Jenna is tired of supporting her ex-husband and realizes she needs to pursue her own dreams. When an empty storefront becomes available in her old hometown, she envisions opening her own cooking store and starts working hard toward that goal. Suddenly, her life turns upside down when the birth parents she never knew show up in town.

Keywords: Family, Romantic.

Barefoot Season. 2012. Mira. ISBN 9780778313380. 368p.

Michelle, an Army veteran, seeks a new civilian life back home on Blackberry Island. When she discovers her old friend (and current enemy) Carly running into the ground the inn that should be Michelle's inheritance. Can these two women put aside old differences to bring back the glory days of Blackberry Island Inn?

Keywords: Friendship, Romantic.

Montefiore, Santa.

U.K.-based Montefiore writes romantic women's fiction, often featuring wealthy families, rich description, and exotic locales.

The Perfect Happiness. 2010. Touchstone. ISBN 9781439183465. 378p.

Angelica, a children's book author, strikes up an e-mail flirtation with Jack, a South African vineyard owner. She doesn't expect the flirtation to go anywhere—she's married, after all, and London is nowhere near Cape Town. Then a book tour takes her to South Africa, and she finds that temptation is impossible to resist.

Keywords: Marriage, Romantic, Thought-Provoking.

The Mermaid Garden. 2012. Touchstone. ISBN 9781451628937. 432p.

The life stories of two different women are juxtaposed in this romantic novel, set in England and Italy. As a child, Floriana is enchanted by her wealthy neighbor's garden, and an invitation to see the garden up close and personal sets an epic love story in motion. Years later, a young artist changes the life of Marina, the owner of a tumbledown country house in Devonshire. Both women's stories are related, but how?

Keywords: Romantic, Saga.

The Woman from Paris. 2013. Simon & Schuster. ISBN 9781451676686. 400p.

The wealthy, titled Frampton family is shocked when patriarch Lord Frampton dies in a skiing accident—and even more shocked when a mysterious woman named Phaedra appears at his funeral, claiming to be his illegitimate daughter. A bequest in Frampton's will seems to support her claim: he's left a priceless set of sapphires to her—jewelry that his family was expecting to inherit. Soon Phaedra becomes a part of the Frampton family, and companionship soon leads to a forbidden attraction between Phaedra and the eldest Frampton son.

Keywords: Glitzy, Romantic.

Moyes, Jojo.

Moyes, a best-selling author in her native England, writes emotionally charged novels with strong romantic elements. Her first three novels are excellent read-alikes for Maeve Binchy and Rosamunde Pilcher.

Sheltering Rain. 2002. Morrow. ISBN 0060012889. 358p.

In the 1950s, rebellious teenager Joy flees the stifling confines of her parental home in pursuit of love with the man of her dreams. Forty years later, Joy's granddaughter arrives at the family home—a home that her mother, Kate, fled, seeking independence. Long-hidden secrets are brought to the forefront when all three generations reunite in an attempt to heal old wounds.

Keywords: Family, Romantic.

Windfallen. 2003. Morrow. ISBN 0060012900. 382p.

The sleepy British seaside town of Merham is a quiet, unextraordinary place, but when a group of artists take over Arcadia, a landmark home on the shore, the community is shaken up by their bohemian ways. Pulled into the artists' circle are Lottie, evacuated to Merham during World War II, and her friend Celia, a Merham native. Years later, a woman involved in a renovation of Arcadia discovers a mural that depicts scenes from the home's past, and her discovery stirs up old memories and long-hidden secrets.

Keywords: Friendship, Romantic.

 The Last Letter from Your Lover. 2010. Viking. ISBN 9780670022809. 390p.

Ellie Haworth is looking for a career-making story, and she finds one in the archives of the newspaper where she works: a forty-year-old tale of star-crossed lovers tinged with tragedy. As Ellie sorts through the details of her story, she looks for guidance regarding her own tricky romantic situation.

Keyword: Romantic.

*Me before You. 2012. Touchstone. ISBN 9780670026609. 369p.

Louisa has never left the small town where she grew up, and her employment opportunities are minimal. The only job she can find is taking care of Will, a wealthy young man who is wheelchair-bound after being struck by a motorcycle. Will is frustrated with the indignities of life as a quadriplegic, and Louisa's job—trying to make Will enjoy life again—is more difficult than she could have imagined. As Will begins to warm up to Louisa, she finds herself falling in love with him—and torn over Will's decision to end his own life.

Keywords: Romantic, Thought-Provoking.

Phillips, Susan Elizabeth.

Philips adamantly calls herself a romance writer, but some of her charming and sexy contemporary romances feature such a great supporting cast of family and friends that it's hard to not consider her in the women's fiction camp as well. Trademarks of Phillips's novels are snappy dialogue, comic situations, and an overarching love story, often between two people who seem mismatched. Aside from her various stand-alone novels, Phillips also writes two ongoing series. As a testament to her longstanding popularity with romance readers, Phillips won the Romance Writers of America's Lifetime Achievement Award in 2006. Phillips is also a member of the Romance Writers of America Hall of Fame for winning multiple RITA awards in the contemporary single title category.

Wynette, Texas, series.

These loosely connected novels follow the residents (and the exiles) of the quirky small town of Wynette, Texas, which is home to everyone from former child stars to golf professionals to everyday men and women. Though some of the novels don't take place in Wynette, there's always a main character in each book with ties to the town.

Glitter Baby. 1987.

Fancy Pants. 1989.

Lady Be Good. 1999.

First Lady. 2000.

What I Did for Love. 2009.

Call Me Irresistible. 2011.

The Great Escape. 2012.

Chicago Stars/Bonner Brothers series.

This series, composed of stand-alone novels with shared characters, follows the adventures of the players, agents, and owners of the Chicago Stars football team, as well as the men of the Bonner family, who are related to one of the Stars' hottest players.

It Had to Be You. 1994.

Heaven, Texas. 1995.

Nobody's Baby but Mine. 1997.

Dream a Little Dream. 1998.

This Heart of Mine. 2001.

Match Me If You Can. 2006.

Natural Born Charmer. 2008.

Porter, Jane.

A prolific author, Porter's novels include contemporary romance, category romance, and both humorous and romantic women's fiction.

Odd Mom Out. 2007. 5 Spot. ISBN 9780446699235. 410p.

Single mom Marta Zinsser is a New York transplant to the Seattle suburbs, and she doesn't fit in among the Stepford-esque wives in her new hometown. But beneath her tough, urban exterior lies a woman who wants to make her beloved daughter happy, and Marta must find a way to reconcile her need to be an individual with her daughter's need for her to fit in.

Keywords: Motherhood, Romantic, Self-Actualization.

Mrs. Perfect. 2008. 5 Spot. ISBN 9780446699242. 419p.

On the outside, Taylor Young looks like the perfect suburban wife and mother, but beneath the surface lurks self-doubt and secrets. When one of her secrets is revealed to her neighborhood, she must rely on her former nemesis to help her find herself again. A companion to **Odd Mom Out**.

Keywords: Family, Friendship, Motherhood, Romantic.

She's Gone Country. 2010. 5 Spot. ISBN 9780446509411. 382p.

After her husband leaves her, ex-model Shey Darcy takes her teenage sons back to her Texas hometown. She quickly learns that returning home isn't easy, and conflict with her mother and brothers makes adapting to her new life difficult. When a man from her past is added to the mix, life gets even more confusing, and Shey learns to let the past go in order to find her happiness.

Keywords: Mothers and Daughters, Romantic.

The Good Woman. 2012. Berkley. ISBN 9780425253007. 357p.

Meg Brennan Roberts is the eldest of the Brennan sisters, and she's used to being the mature, careful one. Her conscientious nature has lead her to a successful career in the wine business, but her marriage is faltering, and she wonders if there's more to life than what she has. When her boss confesses his attraction to her, Meg begins to question the choices she has made and wonders if being the "good woman" is holding her back from realizing her true potential.

Keywords: Family, Romantic, Self-Actualization, Sisters.

The Good Daughter. 2013. Berkley. ISBN 9780425253427. 372p.

Kit, the middle Brennan sister, is about to turn forty, and her desire to be a mother is overwhelming. Unmarried, and without a long-term relationship, she begins to wonder if raising a child as a single mother might be an option for her. When she meets a man who might be right for her, she is surprised by the way he challenges her to rethink her life and reconsider her options.

Keywords: Family, Romantic, Self-Actualization, Sisters.

Richards, Emilie.

Happiness Key novels.

Five women meet on Happiness Key, a Florida island filled with quaint cottages. Each woman brings her own problems, and they become friends and help change each others' lives.

Happiness Key. 2009.

Fortunate Harbor. 2010.

Sunset Bridge. 2011.

One Mountain Away. 2012. Mira. ISBN 9780778313557. 467p.

Charlotte Hale has distanced herself from her troubled childhood to become a successful real-estate developer, but success has come at a tremendous price. She has few friends and has alienated most of her family. After a devastating medical diagnosis, Charlotte realizes that she needs to make amends, both to the people she loves and to the world as a whole.

Keywords: Family, Romantic, Self-Actualization.

Roberts, Nora.

Roberts began her publishing career in romance fiction in the early 1980s, and she continues to publish widely in a variety of genres, including romantic suspense and romantic women's fiction.

Bride Quartet.

Four longtime friends own and operate a wedding planning business that caters to brides seeking an exceptional wedding—but none of the women have been able to find their own perfect match. Friendship, mutual support, and love are the overarching themes of this feel-good series.

Vision in White. 2009.

Bed of Roses. 2009.

Savor the Moment. 2010.

Happy Ever After. 2010.

Inn BoonsBoro trilogy.

As the three Montgomery brothers renovate a historic hotel in a picturesque Maryland town, they find companionship and true love.

The Next Always. 2011.

The Last Boyfriend. 2012.

The Perfect Hope. 2012.

Steel, Danielle.

One of the most prominent authors of women's fiction, Steel has been publishing since the early 1970s. Her romantic stories are perennial bestsellers. For a complete list of Steel's novels, see chapter 2, "Grand Dames of Women's Fiction."

Southern Lights. 2010. Delacorte. ISBN 9780385344357. 336p.
Alexa Hamilton moved from Charleston, South Carolina, to Manhattan to pursue her career as an attorney and to escape a broken marriage. Years later, she is an assistant district attorney prosecuting notorious serial killer Luke Quentin. When her seventeen-year-old daughter begins receiving threatening letters, all signs point to Quentin—and protecting her daughter may mean sending her home to Charleston.

Keywords: Family, Mothers and Daughters, Romantic.

44 Charles Street. 2011. Delacorte. ISBN 9780385343145. 336p.
The titular house—a West Village townhouse that has seen better days—serves as the backdrop for a story of friendship, female bonding, and

healing from the wounds of the past. When Francesca realizes that she can no longer afford to pay the mortgage on her home, she puts out an advertisement for boarders—and the women who answer the ad become fast friends.

Keywords: Friendship, Romantic.

Big Girl. 2011. Delacorte. ISBN 0385343183. 336p.
Victoria and Grace Dawson play different roles in their family. Victoria spends her childhood being harassed by her parents, mainly about her weight, while Grace is the perfect daughter who takes after her parents—slim and beautiful. Not surprisingly, Victoria leaves home as soon as she can, only to find that the scars of her past continue to hurt her.

Keywords: Family, Romantic, Sisters.

Five Days in Paris. 2011. Delacorte. ISBN 9780345528193. 304p.
When Olivia Thatcher's son died, she lost her will to live. A chance occurrence in Paris offers Olivia the chance to start over, and she takes it—meeting Peter Haskell in the process. Both Olivia and Peter were secure in their lives and their marriages before they met. Will their Paris encounter change them forever?

Keywords: Marriage, Romantic.

Happy Birthday. 2011. Delacorte. ISBN 9780385340303. 352p.
Valerie Wyatt, a Martha Stewart-esque arbiter of taste, is turning sixty, and her daughter April is turning thirty. Both women face these milestone birthdays with a combination of concern and dread. Their lives aren't what they hoped for them to be, and perhaps a little romance is what it will take for things to be set right.

Keywords: Mothers and Daughters, Older Women, Romantic.

Hotel Vendome. 2011. Delacorte. ISBN 9780385343176. 336p.
Hugues Martin has thrown his life into bringing the run-down Hotel Vendome back from the dead, turning it into one of New York's great hotels. When his wife leaves him for a rock star, Hugues is left with sole custody of their daughter, Heloise—and the hotel that may have driven his wife away. When his daughter grows up and hopes to enter the family business, Hugues encourages her to fulfill her dreams, no matter the cost.

Keywords: Marriage, Romantic.

Betrayal. 2012. Delacorte. ISBN 9780385343190. 336p.
Tallie Jones seems to have it all—a spectacular career as a movie producer, a wonderful romantic relationship with a supportive collaborator, and a best friend who has been through it all with her. When a routine audit uncovers accounting discrepancies in the books of Tallie's production company, it's obvious that someone close to her is at fault, but who?

Keywords: Glitzy, Friendship, Romantic.

Friends Forever. 2012. Delacorte. ISBN 9780385343213. 320p.
Five women, friends since kindergarten, make a pact when they graduate: they will always remain friends. But as adulthood brings them further apart, can they continue to lean on each other against the odds?

Keywords: Friendship, Romantic.

Sins of the Mother. 2012. Delacorte. ISBN 9780385343206. 368p.

Olivia Grayson spent most of her childrens' youth building her furniture company—a fact that she regrets now that her children are grown. In an attempt to remedy her inattention, she invites her family to join her on the vacation of a lifetime, only to find that rebuilding a family isn't quite so easy.

Keywords: Glitzy, Family, Motherhood, Romantic.

Until the End of Time. 2013. Delacorte. ISBN 9780345530882. 336p.

Two love stories—Bill and Jenny, who leave their glamorous New York life to follow Bill's calling to serve God as a minister in Wyoming, and Bob and Lillibet, a New York publisher and his Amish protégé who meet via Lillibet's manuscript—are juxtaposed in this tale of star-crossed love and romantic destiny.

Keyword: Romantic.

Sumners, Shelle.

Grace Grows. 2012. St. Martin's Griffin. ISBN 9781250003508. 325p.

Grace Barnum prides herself on being steady and stable in every aspect of her life, even when it's uncomfortable. Her professional life and her romantic life are overwhelmingly sensible—in direct contrast with her free-spirited parents. When a handsome country music singer shows up and professes his attraction to her in a not-so-sensible way, Grace wonders if it's time for her to let her hair down and make some changes to her life, even if it means not being sensible and steady.

Keywords: Romantic, Self-Actualization.

Wiggs, Susan.

Wiggs's gentle contemporary romances also feature families and friends, making them a good choice for women's fiction readers.

Summer at Willow Lake. 2006. Mira. ISBN 0778323250. 500p.

Olivia will do anything to save the summer camp that's been in her family for decades, even if it means being nice to Connor, the handyman hired to renovate the camp for her grandparents' fiftieth wedding anniversary. Turns out Olivia and Connor knew each other at camp, and he broke her heart. Will he do the same years later? Peppered with humorous flashbacks to their summer camp days, this is both a charming romance and lovely family story. This is the first book of the Lakeshore Chronicles, loosely connected novels.

Keywords: Family, Romantic.

Just Breathe. 2008. Mira. ISBN 9780778325772. 400p.

When cartoonist Sarah discovers her husband is cheating on her—in the midst of her fertility treatments—she leaves him to return to her hometown and start over. That means starting over as a single mom because, as she soon discovers, those treatments were successful.

Keywords: Motherhood, Romantic.

The Goodbye Quilt. 2011. Mira. ISBN 9780778329961. 201p.

Linda takes her only child, Molly, on a cross-country trip to drop Molly off at her new college. Along the way, she works on a quilt, filled with fabric scraps representing many memories, leading both mother and daughter to remember the past and look forward to the future.

Keywords: Family, Gentle, Mothers and Daughters, Romantic.

Return to Willow Lake. 2012. Mira. ISBN 9780778313847. 311p.

Sonnet has a charmed life—a wonderful boyfriend, a great job, and more opportunities on the horizon. But when her mother reveals a surprising secret— she's pregnant—Sonnet's plans change instantly. The pregnancy is high risk, and Sonnet returns to her small-town roots to take care of her mom. At first, the arrangement is only temporary, but a serious turn of events may keep Sonnet in Willow Lake for good.

Keywords: Family, Gentle, Romantic.

Chapter 9

Genreblends and Outliers

As noted in the introduction, a great number of authors that may or may not belong on these lists, and we had to make the call. The nebulous nature of women's fiction means that there will always be arguments for calling one book a romance but a similar title not, and fans of any given author will fight for their beloved's honor. Again, we applied the rule that if you could replace the main female character with a man and not lose the story, it's general fiction.

This chapter focuses on some of those books and authors that some may consider to be women's fiction, and others may not. Some of these books are genreblends—books that contain some, if not all, of the elements of women's fiction, but they also contain elements of other genres. Romantic suspense is an example of a genreblend, because it contains elements of women's fiction, suspense, thrillers, and romance. We also consider Christian women's fiction to be a genreblend, because it combines elements of both genres into something entirely different. We've chosen to narrow our focus to three specific genreblends: Christian women's fiction, historical women's fiction, and romantic suspense, but books in many other genres contain enough similarities to women's fiction to make good read-alikes.

Outliers are authors and books that some might consider to be women's fiction, mainly because they were written by a woman and their primary audience is female. Though we feel that these authors or books fall outside the scope that we've set for this book, we list them here because readers of women's fiction often do enjoy them, and they could be considered good read-alikes for some of the authors in the earlier chapters of this guide. If the decision to include or not to include an author was particularly difficult, we also included the rationale behind our decision.

Genreblends

Christian Women's Fiction

Novels about women's lives and relationships are popular with readers of Christian fiction. Authors like Karen Kingsbury, Kristin Billerbeck, Robin Jones Gunn, and Susan May Warren are perennial best sellers among readers, Christian women's fiction is as varied in tone and content as mainstream women's fiction, and the novels covered in this brief sampling include chick lit, issue-driven fiction, romantic suspense, family stories, and character-driven romance. The characteristics all of these novels have in common are a strong belief in Christian values and a renewal of faith as a main plot point of the story.

There is significant crossover potential from mainstream women's fiction to Christian women's fiction, and vice versa. The novels in this section may appeal to readers who enjoy gentle reads, or any reader of women's fiction who doesn't mind a plot where the characters' faith is at the forefront of the story. Likewise, readers of Christian women's fiction may enjoy many of the novels listed in the earlier chapters of this book. Readers who prefer to avoid sex, violence, and profanity will find further suggestions in chapter 4, "Gentle Reads."

Billerbeck, Kristin.

The tagline on Billerbeck's Web site reads "faith, froth, and a designer handbag," which gives readers a good idea of her books, which are Christian chick lit written for adults and teens.

Swimming to the Surface. 2012. CreateSpace. ISBN 9781481175670. 358p.
Kelsey Mitchell's faith has been challenged multiple times—first when her husband left her and now, several years later, when her daughter's life is in danger. When she meets local pastor Alex Bechtel, she may have met her match. The two must turn to faith and compassion to overcome the obstacles in their way.
Keyword: Romantic.

The Scent of Rain. 2012. Thomas Nelson. ISBN 9781401685652. 305p.
Daphne had a promising career as a "nose" for a Parisian perfume maker, but she gave up her dream job for love. Then her fiancé left her at the altar on their wedding day. Now she's down in the dumps in Dayton, Ohio, creating scents for household products—even though her sense of smell seems to have disappeared. Juggling her despair, her professional ruse, and her budding feelings for her handsome boss may be more than she can handle.
Keywords: Humorous, Romantic.

Ashley Stockingdale series.

Ashley is a single patent attorney on the lookout for love. At age thirty-one, she's worried that she's never going to get married since all of the good guys seem to be taken, or they have some kind of deal-breaking flaw. This series follows Ashley's comic quest to find a mate who is everything she's looking for—and then some.

What a Girl Wants. 2007.

She's Out of Control. 2007.

With This Ring, I'm Confused. 2007.

Smitten series.

Written in conjunction with fellow authors Colleen Coble, Denise Hunter, and Diann Hunt, this series follows the lives and loves of the residents of Smitten, Vermont—the most romantic town in America.

Smitten. 2012.

Secretly Smitten. 2013.

Coble, Colleen.

Best known for her highly acclaimed historical fiction, Coble also writes contemporary women's fiction with a romantic feel, as well as romantic suspense.

Lonestar series.

Set in west Texas, this romantic suspense series features the lives of strong, independent Texan women and the men who love them.

Lonestar Sanctuary. 2008.

Lonestar Secrets. 2009.

Lonestar Homecoming. 2010.

Lonestar Angel. 2011.

Tidewater Inn. 2012. Thomas Nelson. ISBN 9781595547811. 320p.

Libby receives a surprise inheritance that is a dream come true—a historical inn on the picturesque shores of North Carolina's Outer Banks. But her dream quickly evaporates when her long-lost brothers and sisters reappear, claiming that the inn should be theirs. Then her best friend and business partner is kidnapped, and Libby is the prime suspect. It seems that her only hope may be to cut her losses and sell the inn, but she can't bear to part with her newfound home.

Keywords: Friendship, Gentle, Romantic.

Gunn, Robin Jones.

Gunn is a prolific author whose works include fiction for children, teens, and adults, as well as Christian-themed nonfiction.

Sisterchicks series.

Gunn's "sisterchicks" are the closest of friends, and the stand-alone novels in this series feature best friends who embark on adventures that strengthen their friendship as well as their faith.

Sisterchicks on the Loose. 2003.

Sisterchicks Do the Hula. 2004.

Sisterchicks in Sombreros. 2004.

Sisterchicks Down Under. 2005.

Sisterchicks Say Ooh La La! 2005.

Sisterchicks in Gondolas. 2006.

Sisterchicks Go Brit! 2008.

Sisterchicks in Wooden Shoes. 2009.

Henderson, Dee.

Dee Henderson writes romantic suspense novels with Christian themes, featuring characters in high-stakes occupations.

O'Malley Family series.

The O'Malleys are a family brought together by choice—they were all abandoned or orphaned as children. As adults, they've all chosen high-stakes careers in law enforcement, firefighting, or emergency medicine, allowing them to help strangers as they once helped one another.

Danger in the Shadows. 2002.

The Negotiator. 2001.

The Guardian. 2001.

The Truth Seeker. 2001.

The Protector. 2001.

The Healer. 2005.

The Rescuer. 2005.

Jennifer: An O'Malley Love Story. 2013.

Uncommon Heroes series.

This series features military men and women who rely on their love of God to sustain them.

True Devotion. 2008.

True Valor. 2008.

True Honor. 2008.

Kingsbury, Karen.

Prolific author Kingsbury writes faith-based fiction with contemporary settings, realistic characters, and strong emotional content. Not all of Kingsbury's novels are Christian women's fiction—she has several notable series featuring male protagonists—but many of her books are suitable for readers who enjoy romantic, issue-driven fiction with Christian content and themes.

The Chance. 2013. Howard Books. ISBN 9781451647037. 352p.

Ellie and Nolan are childhood friends, separated when Ellie's family moves to California. The two write letters to each other and bury them under an old oak tree, promising to return eleven years later to read them. When the time comes, both Ellie and Nolan are in very different places in their lives—Ellie is a struggling single mother and Nolan is a basketball star. Can they return to each other, and to the faith that used to sustain them?

Keyword: Romantic.

The Bridge. 2012. Howard Books. ISBN 9781451647013. 272p.

The Bridge, a bookstore in Franklin, Tennessee, has been a local institution for years. When a horrific flood, combined with declining sales, forces the store to shut down, its owners, married couple Charlie and Donna Barton, are devastated. Years later, Charlie is injured in an accident, and a couple who connected at the Bridge try to help Charlie rebuild his bookstore—and his life.

Keywords: Friendship, Romantic.

Baxter Family series.

Kingsbury's long-running series consists of several subseries, each following the members of the Baxter family as they grow in their faith.

Redemption. 2003.

Remember. 2003.

Return. 2003.

Rejoice. 2005.

Reunion. 2005.

Fame. 2005.

Forgiven. 2005.

Found. 2006.

Family. 2006.

Forever. 2007.

Sunrise. 2007.

Summer. 2007.

Someday. 2008.

Sunset. 2008.

Take One. 2009.

Take Two. 2009.

Take Three. 2010.

Take Four. 2010.

Leaving. 2011.

Learning. 2011.

Longing. 2011.

Loving. 2012.

Thompson, Janice.

Thompson writes in a variety of subgenres of Christian fiction, including historical fiction and romantic comedies.

Weddings by Bella series.

When thirty-year-old Bella inherits her family's wedding business, she's unprepared for the challenges, but she handles them with an open heart and a lot of laughs.

Fools Rush In. 2009.

Swinging on a Star. 2010.

It Had to Be You. 2010.

Backstage Pass series.

This comic series follows the goings-on behind the scenes of a popular sitcom.

Stars Collide. 2011.

Hello Hollywood. 2011.

The Director's Cut. 2012.

Warren, Susan May.

Warren writes romantic women's fiction with contemporary and historical settings.

Take a Chance on Me. 2013. Tyndale House. ISBN 9781414378411. 416p.
When Ivy Madison bids on Darek Christiansen in a bachelor auction, she is unaware of how they are connected. As the two get to know each other, she realizes that, three years ago, she was responsible for negotiating the release of the man responsible for the death of Darek's wife. But Darek feels like the family that Ivy has never had. Can the two overcome the challenges of their past and make a new life together?

Keyword: Romantic.

You Don't Know Me. 2012. Tyndale House. ISBN 9781414334844. 384p.
Annalise Decker has a dark secret: she was once a star witness in a high-profile criminal case, and she's been assigned a new identity and a new home in idyllic Deep Haven. When Annalise falls in love with a local real-estate agent, she must decide whether to reveal the truth about her past—even if it could endanger her future.

Keyword: Romantic.

The Shadow of Your Smile. 2012. Tyndale House. ISBN 9781414334837. 384p.
Noelle and Eli's twenty-five-year marriage is in shreds, and it seems like divorce is imminent. Then Noelle is in an accident that erases part of her memory, and she forgets both her marriage and her children. Is this a tragic loss, or an opportunity for the couple to reinvent their lives?

Keywords: Marriage, Romantic.

Historical Women's Fiction

Historical fiction is defined by the Historical Novels Society as novels "written at least fifty years after the events described, or have been written by someone who was not alive at the time of those events (who therefore approaches them only by research).[1] The novels listed in this section follow this definition of historical fiction, as well as the definition of women's fiction established in this book.

Historical fiction about women's lives is extremely popular and spans many time periods and settings. This is a small selection of novels in the genre, with a focus on twentieth-century American and European settings. A wider selection of historical novels featuring elements of women's fiction can be found in Sarah Johnson's two books on the genre, *Historical Fiction: A Guide to the Genre* (2005) and *Historical Fiction II: A Guide to the Genre* (2009).

Baker, Ellen.

Keeping the House. 2007. Random House. ISBN 1400066352. 544p.
A story within a story: one woman's struggles at the turn of the twentieth-century parallel with another woman's in the 1950s. Free-spirited Dolly doesn't have anything in common with the women in the quilting circle in the small Wisconsin town her husband has dragged her to live in. To pass the time, she becomes obsessed with the abandoned mansion on the hill and the family secrets hidden there. When she discovers one of the family members is secretly living in the house, Dolly transfers her attentions to him, with scandalous results.

Keywords: Self-Actualization, Thought-Provoking.

Brown, T. J.

Summerset Abbey trilogy.

Brown's romantic trilogy follows the wealthy Buxton sisters, Victoria and Rowena, and their friend Prudence, a governess's daughter who grew up with them. The three must learn to navigate the shifting social mores of pre– and post–World War I England.

Summerset Abbey. 2013.
Summerset Abbey: A Bloom in Winter. 2013.
Summerset Abbey: Spring Awakening. 2013.

Dilloway, Margaret.

How to Be an American Housewife. 2010. Putnam. ISBN 0399156372. 288p.
Inspired by the experiences of the author's mother, this novel follows Shoko, a young Japanese woman who marries a GI after World War II. Her brother is unable to forgive her for leaving and disowns her. Near the end

of her life, she longs to return home and reunite with her family, but she is too ill. She enlists her estranged daughter, Sue, to make the trip for her, and Sue learns about her mother's family secrets and heartbreak.

Keywords: Emotional, Family, Historical.

Domingue, Ronlyn.

The Mercy of Thin Air. 2005. Atria. ISBN 0743278801. 320p.
Rebellious flapper girl Raziela dies young in a swimming accident, leaving behind her college sweetheart, Andrew. Razi spends the next seventy years "in between" and wondering what happens to Andrew and his life after her. Her spirit "haunts" the young couple who buy her bookcase. Interwoven in the story are wonderful glimpses at what life in the Roaring Twenties must have been like for a smart, sassy young woman.

Keywords: Emotional, Romantic, Historical.

Garlock, Dorothy.

Dorothy Garlock writes romantic historical novels set during the early and mid-twentieth century. Her novels follow young women, usually from small midwestern towns, as they meet and fall in love with the man they will later marry. The romance is usually threatened by a villain of some sort.

The Moon Looked Down. 2010. Grand Central. ISBN 0446577944. 400p.
Sophie Heller is a German immigrant living in Victory, Illinois, during World War II. With many of the residents of the town mistrustful of Germans, Sophie and her family are the targets of harassment and attacks. When the attacks become life-threatening, Sophie wants to expose the perpetrators, but the personal cost is high. As Sophie grows closer to local teacher Cole Ambrose, she learns to rely on their combined strength to help her make the right decisions.

Keywords: Gentle, Historical, Romantic.

Stay a Little Longer. 2011. Grand Central. ISBN 044654020X. 384p.
Rachel Watkins runs a small boardinghouse and serves as the midwife for her small Minnesota town. World War I has devastated her close-knit family, and Rachel serves as the guardian for her orphaned niece, whose father died in the war. When Rachel falls in love with one of her boarders, they must learn to trust each other as an unspeakable threat to Rachel's security looms.

Keywords: Gentle, Historical, Romantic.

Keep a Little Secret. 2011. Grand Central. ISBN 0446540129. 384p.
Charlotte Tucker travels from Minnesota to Oklahoma in pursuit of her dream of being a teacher. Then a series of accidents threatens the well-being of the family that owns the ranch where Charlotte lives and teaches, and it is up to Charlotte to help Owen, a misunderstood ranch hand, solve the crime.

Keywords: Gentle, Historical, Romantic.

Horan, Nancy.

Loving Frank. 2007. Ballantine. ISBN 9780345494993. 384p.

When Mamah Borthwick Cheney meets Frank Lloyd Wright, both are happily married. Their scandalous affair shattered both of their marriages but set the stage for a surprising and intense love story that spans the globe.

Keywords: Historical, Romantic, Thought-Provoking.

McGraw, Erin.

The Seamstress of Hollywood Boulevard. 2008. Houghton Mifflin. ISBN 0618386289. 384p.

At the turn of the twentieth century, Nell marries at seventeen to escape her bleak farm life but finds she's traded one sad situation for another. A talented seamstress, she decides to leave her husband and two baby daughters behind and runs away to Hollywood. Once there, she quickly establishes herself as a master seamstress and invents a whole new persona. Twenty years later, her daughters show up on her doorstep, demanding answers.

Keywords: Family, Historical, Thought-Provoking.

McLain, Paula.

The Paris Wife. 2011. Ballantine. ISBN 9780345521309. 319p.

When Hadley Richardson falls in love with Ernest Hemingway, she falls fast and hard. Hadley soon finds herself half of one of the golden couples of Paris expat society in the 1920s, but she quickly realizes that her marriage is faltering.

Keywords: Historical, Marriage.

Morton, Kate.

Morton's deliciously Gothic stories border on saga, with hints of suspense and romance.

The House at Riverton. 2008. Atria. ISBN 9781416550518. 480p.

This atmospheric tale introduces ninety-nine-year-old Grace Reeves, who is forced to look back at her life and remember dangerous secrets involving the English family she worked for as a maid between the two world wars. At fourteen, Grace was sent to Riverton to work for the aristocratic Ashbury family. As time progressed, she learned of family secrets, including one involving herself, became a lady's maid to the two Ashbury sisters, and got caught in the middle of scandal.

Keywords: Historical, Saga.

The Distant Hours. 2010. Atria. ISBN 9781439152782. 576p.

The creepy Blythe sisters, society darlings of the 1920s, have been holding many secrets in their decaying English estate, and one of them directly concerns the young writer who has been sent to write a tell-all about the sisters and their fascinating lives.

Keywords: Historical, Romance, Saga.

 The Secret Keeper. 2012. Atria. ISBN 9781439152805. 496p.
As a teenager, Laurel is the witness to a shocking crime involving her mother. Years later, as her mother's ninetieth birthday approaches, Laurel and her siblings are called back to their family home. Laurel sees it as her final chance to ask her mother what happened that day, and the answer is more unexpected and troubling than Laurel could have imagined.

Keywords: Family, Historical, Saga.

Shaffer, Louise.

Looking for a Love Story. 2010. Ballantine. ISBN 978034550210-0. 320p.
The contemporary story of Francesca, a writer whose marriage unexpectedly crumbles, dovetails with the story of a Depression-era husband-and-wife vaudeville team. Francesca, stuck with writer's block on her second novel, is eager to work her way out of her sorrows. Spry ninety-year-old Chicky wants her parents' story to be told and hires Francesca to ghostwrite their memoirs. The two collaborate on a delightful love story as Francesca works out her own love life and family history.

Keywords: Family, Self-Actualization. Historical.

Shaffer, Mary Ann, and Annie Barrows.

The Guernsey Literary and Potato Peel Pie Society. 2009. Dial. ISBN 9780385341004. 290p.
This epistolary novel, set after the German Occupation of the island of Guernsey during World War II, follows the correspondence of author Juliet Ashton, who travels to Guernsey to write her novel, and the residents of the island, who are intent on sharing their stories of the Occupation.

Keywords: Gentle, Friendship, Historical.

Stockett, Kathryn.

The Help. 2009. Putnam. ISBN 9780399155345. 464p.
It's 1962, and young Eugenia, a.k.a. "Skeeter," wants to be a writer, so she starts to collect the stories of the black women in her town—the housekeepers and nannies who make Skeeter's racially charged Mississippi town run.

Keywords: Ensemble, Historical, Thought-Provoking.

Trigiani, Adriana.

Lucia Lucia. 2003. Random House. ISBN 1400060052. 256p.
Greenwich Village in the 1950s is the colorful setting for this novel, where Lucia, a good Italian girl, strikes out on her own in New York and becomes a talented

department store seamstress. Her fiancé and his mother have other plans, however, expecting her to quit working and become a meek wife and mother.

Keywords: Family, Historical.

Romantic Suspense

A basic definition of romantic suspense is a novel with a strong female protagonist who finds herself falling in love and escaping from some sort of peril (or solving a mystery). Elements from mystery, thrillers, and suspense novels combine with romance to create a story that does not fit comfortably in any of the genres it draws from. There is plenty of tension in romantic suspense, and that is the main appeal. There is a threat to the female protagonist, usually in the form of physical, mental, or emotional abuse. Romantic suspense can also differ—some stories are quite spicy and sexual, others focus on a mystery or a thriller element and less on the romance/sex.

Romantic suspense is tricky to classify as women's fiction, because while the books include strong female characters, the driving force behind the plot is the suspense or mystery, not the woman's relationships or small details of her life. However, romantic suspense has a good deal of crossover appeal, and readers who enjoy women's fiction may also enjoy these authors in particular.

Adler, Elizabeth.
Adler got her start in the glitz-and-glamour sagas popular in the 1980s but has since moved on to romantic suspense.

Mac Reilly series.
In this series, which features glitzy locales and a mix of humor, romance, and mystery, a TV actor Mac Reilly (he plays a detective) and his fiancée, Sunny, solve crimes. The feel is reminiscent of an old-time crime caper.

One of Those Malibu Nights. 2009.

There's Something about St. Tropez. 2009.

It All Began in Monte Carlo. 2010.

From Barcelona with Love. 2011.

Brown, Sandra.
Brown, one of the grand dames of women's fiction, has been writing romance and romantic suspense since the early 1980s. Her current focus is on single-title romantic suspense novels.

Low Pressure. 2012. Grand Central. ISBN 9781455501496. 480p.
When Bellamy Lyston is twelve years old, her sister is brutally murdered during a severe thunderstorm. Years later, Bellamy writes a pseudonymous

account of her sister's murder. When her identity is revealed, she is pursued by a stalker, who seems to have close ties to the case.

Keywords Romantic.

Lethal. 2011. Grand Central. ISBN 9781455501472. 480p.
When an accused mass murderer appears in Honor Gillette's backyard, she must make a quick decision to save both her life and the life of her four-year-old daughter. Lee Coburn insists on his innocence, and he believes that Honor's late husband hid something in the Gillette home that puts Honor and her family in further danger. Unsure of who to believe, Honor goes on the run, trying to outsmart her pursuers.

Keyword: Mothers and Daughters.

Tough Customer. 2010. Simon & Schuster. ISBN 1416563105. 400p.
Investigator Dodge Hanley always gets the job done—even if someone gets hurt in the process. But his latest job is more personal than usual, because it involves his daughter, who is being stalked by a mysterious man who will stop at nothing to get what he wants.

Keyword: Romantic.

Smash Cut. 2009. Simon & Schuster. ISBN 1416563083. 384p.
Creighton Wheeler is obsessed with movies, particularly crime scenes from movies. When his uncle is found dead, a local gallery owner and family friend fingers Creighton as the responsible party, setting a series of dramatic events into motion.

Keywords: Romantic, Southern.

Lowell, Elizabeth.

Lowell's prolific output includes novels in a variety of genres, from category romance to historical romance to thrillers, romantic suspense, and science fiction.

Beautiful Sacrifice. 2012. Morrow. ISBN 9780061629860. 400p.
Lina Taylor is an archaeologist specializing in Mayan culture. When several priceless Mayan artifacts go missing, it is up to Lina and Hunter Johnston, a sexy investigator with a secretive past, to solve the mystery.

Keyword: Romantic.

St. Kilda Consulting series.

This series, set among the employees of an elite security consulting company, blends elements of political thrillers, action-adventure novels, and steamy romance.

Always Time to Die. 2005.

The Wrong Hostage. 2006.

Innocent as Sin. 2007.

Blue Smoke and Murder. 2008.

Death Echo. 2010.

Michaels, Fern.

Sisterhood series.

The Sisterhood is a group of women who band together to exact vengeance when the justice system has failed them. The group begins when Myra Rutledge's daughter is killed by a drunk driver who escapes punishment by claiming diplomatic immunity. As the series progresses, a number of other women join Myra in her quest for justice.

Weekend Warriors. 2003.

Payback. 2004.

Vendetta. 2005.

The Jury. 2005.

Sweet Revenge. 2006.

Lethal Justice. 2006.

Free Fall. 2007.

Hide and Seek. 2007.

Hokus Pokus. 2007.

Fast Track. 2008.

Collateral Damage. 2008.

Final Justice. 2008.

Under the Radar. 2009.

Razor Sharp. 2009.

Vanishing Act. 2009.

Deadly Deals. 2009.

Game Over. 2010.

Crossroads. 2010.

Déjà Vu. 2010.

Home Free. 2011.

Gotcha! 2013.

Robards, Karen.

The Last Victim. 2012. Ballantine. ISBN 9780345535405. 336p.

Criminal pathologist Charlotte "Charlie" Stone has a personal tie to criminal minds. When she was a teenager, she witnessed the brutal murder of her best friend's family. Fifteen years later, Charlie is plagued by troubling visions, and a copycat crime has occurred. Can Charlie stop the murderer before he strikes again?

Keyword: Romantic.

Justice. 2011. Gallery. ISBN 9781439183700. 496p.

> After she witnessed the murder of the First Lady, attorney Jessica Ford was placed in the federal witness protection program. Jess may have changed her looks, but she isn't about to give up her work—much to the dismay of Mark Ryan, the Secret Service agent charged with keeping Jess safe. It quickly becomes apparent that someone is targeting Jess for an attack—but who is it, and can she and Mark foil their plot before something devastating happens?

> **Keyword:** Romantic.

Roberts, Nora.

Roberts's romantic suspense novels feature brave, independent women with fascinating jobs who find adventure and love while facing personal challenges. Her heroines don't sit back and wait for the man to do the rescuing—they are more than capable of saving themselves! Readers who enjoy the books listed here may also enjoy Roberts's In Death series, a futuristic police procedural/mystery series written under the name J. D. Robb.

Black Hills. 2009. Putnam. ISBN 9780399155819. 472p.

> Lil and Cooper have been friends since they met one summer, and their shared secret—the grisly discovery of the dead body of a hiker—forever cemented their friendship. As adults, they've drifted apart. Lil stayed on her family's land in South Dakota, making her living rehabilitating wildlife; Cooper is an investigator in New York. When Cooper returns home to care for his parents, the two are brought together again. Circumstances soon turn deadly as Lil realizes that someone is trying to derail her dream of opening a wildlife sanctuary, and Coop helps her figure out who is behind the mayhem.

> **Keyword:** Romantic.

The Search. 2010. Putnam. ISBN 9780399156571. 488p.

> After her fiancé is murdered by a serial killer, Fiona Bristow retreats into her work—training dogs for K9 search and rescue missions. When newcomer Simon Doyle appears with a difficult puppy, Fiona knows how to handle the dog but has problems with her feelings for the mysterious and very private artist. The life that Fiona has rebuilt for herself changes when a copycat killer emerges and Fiona's life is threatened once again.

> **Keyword:** Romantic.

Chasing Fire. 2011. Putnam. ISBN 97803991575448. 472p.

> Firefighting is a huge part of Rowan Tripp's life. She's a second-generation firefighter and smokejumper in the Montana wilderness, and her work is everything to her. After the tragic loss of her partner, the annual return to work is bittersweet, but she finds solace with Gull Curry, one of the rookies on the crew. When someone mysteriously seems to blame Rowan for her partner's death, their fledgling relationship is threatened—as is Rowan's life.

> **Keyword:** Romantic.

🎖 *The Witness.* 2012. Putnam. ISBN 9780399159121. 488p.

> Abigail Lowery is a mystery to her neighbors in her small Ozark town. She keeps to herself, works from home, and interacts infrequently with others. She's reclusive for a good reason: a brief period of teenage rebellion left her with a secret to hide. When Abigail piques the interest of the town's police chief, it sets into motion a series of events that will have far-reaching repercussions.

> **Keyword:** Romantic.

Outliers

Julia Alvarez's literary novels feature strong Hispanic women and have themes of identity and society, but her novels do not always center on women.

Charlene Baumbich's Dearest Dorothy series, featuring the quirky inhabitants of Partonville, Illinois, may be possible read-alikes for fans of gentle reads, but they are not strictly women's fiction because the large cast of characters also features men, and the plots are much more general.

Maeve Binchy's final novels started to stray from the women's fiction formula. You'll find most of her books in chapter 2, "Grand Dames of Women's Fiction," but in her four final novels the main characters are both men and women, and the stories are more about community than they are about individual relationships and personal growth.

Whitethorn Woods. 2007. Knopf. ISBN 9780307265781. 352p.

> The residents of tiny Irish village Rossmore band together when a planned highway threatens to cut through their beloved Whitethorn Woods. It's bad enough the solitude of the woods will be destroyed, but worse, it means the destruction of St. Ann's Well, a shrine thought to deliver miracles. With stories spanning generations, Binchy shows some of her best character work and gets the intimacies of small-town life spot-on.

> **Keywords:** Ensemble, Gentle.

Minding Frankie. 2011. Knopf. ISBN 9780307273567. 400p.

> When Noel's former fling contacts him to tell him she's dying of cancer, she also informs him that she's pregnant—but that it's not his. She's got no one else to turn to, so she asks the shiftless Noel to take responsibility for the child, a girl she wishes to name Francesca. When she dies shortly after the baby is delivered, Noel follows her wish and relies on his hometown family and friends to all help him take care of the baby girl.

> **Keywords:** Ensemble, Emotional.

1
2
3
4
5
6
7
8
9

A. S. Byatt is firmly in the literary fiction camp. Though her protagonists are usually women, her novels are more a snapshot of society and the times than they are about those women and their struggles.

MaryJanice Davidson's Queen Betsy series contains elements of chick lit, but these novels are decidedly paranormal romances.

Anita Diamant's literary fiction often features women, but her novels are spread out in different genres (i.e., historical) and do not have the same feel and emotional tone as contemporary women's fiction novels do.

Margaret Drabble (sister of A. S. Byatt) writes literary novels that feature women across ages and cultures dealing with complex family issues and emotions. However, the emotional pull of the story is not as important as the quality of her character studies, making her novels much more literary fiction than women's fiction.

Kaye Gibbons's literary fiction also does not have the same emotional "feel" as most women's fiction and tends to be more character studies.

Carol Goodman's novels are difficult to pigeonhole—they contain elements of mystery, suspense, romance, and history. But they always features richly drawn, strong women, and while the plots are focused on suspense and danger, the women's families and relationships play a major role as well, making them an interesting choice for women's fiction fans.

Charlaine Harris's paranormal novels feature female characters with a focus on romantic relationships and self-discovery, but they are so driven by the paranormal story line that they aren't part of the women's fiction genre.

Joanne Harris, because of her romantic novel *Chocolat*, is classified by many as a women's fiction writer, but her books run the gamut from literary to psychological suspense, and in most cases women's lives are not the heart of the story.

Alice Hoffman's novels feature strong and intelligent female characters who find their everyday lives disrupted by drama and/or magic. Her writing often has fairy-tale qualities and features magical realism, placing her in the literary fiction genre.

Jan Karon writes inspirational fiction, and more important, her novels are not women's fiction because the main character in her Mitford series is a male pastor, Father Tim.

Barbara Kingsolver is literary fiction. A case could be made for her novels *The Bean Trees* (1988), *Animal Dreams* (1990), and *Pigs in Heaven* (1993), because they do center on female characters; however, the plots are not driven by the relationships of the women.

Linda Lael Miller, a prolific romance author, was a tough call, but in the end her series romances really are pure romance. That's not to say that the contemporary ones wouldn't have appeal for some women's fiction fans, however.

Lisa See's historical fiction novels featuring Asian and Asian American women are really driven by the historical plotlines.

Jane Smiley's literary stories are not woman focused.

Anne Tyler writes male characters as often as she does women, and her works are more literary fiction than women's fiction.

Male Writers

We have our feet firmly planted in the "men don't write women's fiction" camp, but there are some who would argue the point. As we pointed out in the introduction, we have yet to read a women's fiction novel written by a man (maybe—see Douglas Kennedy's *Leaving the World*, below). On the whole, even when male writers use female protagonists, their stories simply do not have that nuance that gets into the character's head about what's going on in her life and they don't delve into her relationships and her emotions.

Robert Barclay's sentimental romantic stories are similar to Nicholas Sparks and would make great read-alikes, but they are not women-centered stories.

Chris Bohjalian writes literary fiction, and while his books often feature women as the main characters and sometimes center on women's issues, they are not solely focused on a woman's life and relationships. Several of his novels do make good read-alikes for those who enjoy issue-driven women's fiction, especially *Midwives* (1998) and *The Law of Similars* (2000).

Nicholas Evans's gentle, often animal-themed novels do not feature women as the main characters. He would be a good read-alike choice for readers looking for gentle reads.

Richard Paul Evans's sentimental tales often feature women, but they are more easily classified as general gentle reads. He would be a good read-alike choice for readers looking for gentle reads.

Judith Gould, one of the grand dames of glitz and glamour novels, is actually . . . two men! Who knew? Seeing as though Gould's particular brand of soap-opera romance has seen its heyday, we have not listed her books here, but she (he?) does at least deserve a mention.

Ad Hudler's brand of southern fiction will appeal to fans of women's fiction, but his leads are not female characters.

Douglas Kennedy's *Leaving the World* might, *just might*, be the one exception to the "no male authors" rule.

1

2

3

4

5

6

7

8

9

Leaving the World. 2010. Atria. ISBN 9781439180785. 512p.

This coming-of-age tale follows Jane, who vows to not live an unhappy life like her dysfunctional parents. She attends Harvard, becomes a professor, falls in love with a married man, and then falls in love with a man who cheats her out of her life savings, leaving her and their daughter bereft. Tired of being left by everyone she's loved, she soon decides to do the leaving.

Keyword: Thought-Provoking.

Sidney Sheldon's glitz-and-glamour, romantic suspense-esque novels have many fans, but there is little emotion or character development in them—they are almost pure story.

Nicholas Sparks's novels are romance, pure and simple. He often does not have a woman as the central character, either—men share the stage.

Note

1. Richard Lee, "Defining the Genre," Historical Novel Society, http://historicalnovelsociety.org/guides/defining-the-genre/, last accessed June 13, 2013.

Appendix A

Thirty Contemporary Women's Fiction Authors to Know

This list is not meant to be comprehensive; rather, it is a good starting place of authors a readers' adviser should be familiar with—particularly if you do not normally read women's fiction but serve readers who do.

If you get to know these authors, you'll have a very good sense of what the different varieties of women's fiction are all about.

Mary Kay Andrews

Elizabeth Berg

Maeve Binchy

Barbara Taylor Bradford

Meg Cabot

Jackie Collins

Claire Cook

Barbara Delinsky

Katie Fforde

Joy Fielding

Fannie Flagg

Jane Green

Emily Giffin

Kristin Hannah

Marian Keyes

Sophie Kinsella

Elinor Lipman

Terry McMillan

Sue Miller

Jacquelyn Mitchard

Jodi Picoult

Jeanne Ray

Luanne Rice

Anita Shreve

Danielle Steel

Nancy Thayer

Adriana Trigiani

Joanna Trollope

Jennifer Weiner

Marcia Willett

Appendix B

Read-Alike Lists

If You Like Elizabeth Berg

Elizabeth Berg writes contemporary stories about average, everyday women and families dealing with life in general. She has a good ear for dialogue and makes her situations realistic and familiar. Her novels deal with a variety of issues; for example, *Talk Before Sleep* (1994) is the story of a friendship tested by illness; while *Open House* (2000) showcases a woman dealing with divorce.

Then You Might Like

Ann Hood
> Hood's novels feature similar themes; much like Berg, she writes about women handling family issues, enjoying friendships, and dealing with the complexities of life.

Elinor Lipman
> Lipman is known for a sense of humor that's a little sharper than Berg's; however, her novels feature realistic, everyday women dealing with family and social issues. Her novels do a nice job of capturing their times, often acting as social satire.

Jeanne Ray
> Ray's novels also display more humor than Berg, but her stories feature families and mature women dealing with the everyday ups and downs of life. *Step-Ball-Change* (2002) and *Eat Cake* (2002) are good choices for Berg fans.

Luanne Rice
> Rice's novels feature strong, intelligent women dealing with life's everyday tragedies, much like Berg's. Family and friends are the showcased relationships in Rice's novels.

Anita Shreve

> Shreve is more literary than Berg, and her novels are much darker, but Berg readers may enjoy her stories of everyday women dealing with extraordinary circumstances.

Joanna Trollope

> Trollope's novels are set in an entirely different country than Berg's, but her novels all focus on average, middle-class women, dealing with anything from raising families to remarriage and other domestic dramas.

If You Like Maeve Binchy

Maeve Binchy writes gentle, light stories set in Ireland, often featuring a large cast of characters. Her characters are recognizable and true to life. Her settings have a delightful small-town feel, even when she's writing about Dublin. She focuses on the interactions between her (sometimes eccentric) characters.

Then You Might Like

Elizabeth Cadell

> Cadell is known for writing gentle romantic family stories. The plots of her novels often involve eccentric characters and an independent heroine. While they are more romantic in tone than Binchy, her characters and realistic situations will appeal to Binchy fans.

Fannie Flagg

> Flagg's stories may not be set in Ireland, but her small Southern towns featuring eccentric oddball characters are a good match for Binchy readers. Gentle and humorous, they evoke the same sense of community that Binchy is known for.

Lynne Hinton

> Hinton writes novels that are Christian fiction but feature strong women and issues that relate to family and friendship. Her Hope Springs trilogy features the very different ladies of a small North Carolina church, who begin the project of writing a cookbook and become unlikely friends. Also like Binchy, Hinton uses intertwining characters and subplots in this series.

Cathy Kelly

> While Kelly's novels are more contemporary and less gentle than Binchy, they do a wonderful job of capturing modern Ireland. Her stories focus more tightly on a smaller group of characters, as opposed to Binchy's style of incorporating many characters. Still, fans of Binchy will appreciate Kelly's touch with relationships and the everyday trials and tribulations of modern Irish women.

Rosamunde Pilcher

> Pilcher's novels feature large casts of characters—often extended families. This is very similar to Binchy. The English and Scottish settings will also appeal to Binchy fans. Pilcher's stories tend to be more romantic than Binchy.

Marcia Willett
> Willett's novels, set in the rural West Country English countryside, feature mature women and their families. Her sense of leisurely pacing matches Binchy's gentle style. *A Week in Winter* (2001), the charming story of an extended family dealing with the sale of the family farmhouse, would be a good choice for Binchy fans.

If You Like Barbara Taylor Bradford

Barbara Taylor Bradford's early heartwarming multigenerational sagas feature strong women who overcome obstacles to make it to the top.

Then You Might Like

Elizabeth Cadell
> Cadell is more of a gentle read than Bradford but was famous for her sweeping sagas, often set in exotic locales.

Catherine Cookson
> Cookson's sagas feature strong female characters, usually struggling with British class differences. Those spirited and likable heroines will appeal to Bradford's readers as well.

Belva Plain
> Plain is known for her sweeping, leisurely paced sagas featuring independent woman dealing with life.

Danielle Steel
> Several of Steel's novels are sagas and would appeal to readers looking for a long, intimate look at a woman's life, such as *Zoya* (1988) or *Granny Dan* (1999). Readers looking for the story of a woman's rise to fame would enjoy Steel's novel *Star* (1989).

Penny Vincenzi
> Vincenzi's novels are much more glitzy than Bradford's, however, her Spoils of Time trilogy is a saga that follows a high-powered family through the years.

If You Like Meg Cabot

Cabot's chick lit features snappy dialogue, self-deprecating characters, humorous situations, and romance.

Then You Might Like

Mary Kay Andrews
> While not chick lit, Andrew 's novels feature similar sassy characters and snappy dialogue that Cabot readers will enjoy.

Helen Fielding
> The chick lit originator, Fielding's Bridget Jones novels are sure to appeal to Cabot fans, particularly readers who enjoy Cabot's epistolary novels.

Marian Keyes
> Several of Keyes's chick lit novels, notably *Watermelon* (1998), share the same sense of wry humor that Cabot readers appreciate. Some of her later novels do get into darker themes.

Sophie Kinsella
> The books in Kinsella's Shopaholic series are sure bets for Cabot fans, as they are similar in pace, humor, and "fluff" factor.

If You Like Jackie Collins

Collins is known for over-the-top glitz and glamour. The lifestyles of the rich and famous are in full display in her novels, which usually feature plenty of steamy sex and soap-opera level drama as well.

Then You Might Like

Tilly Bagshawe
> Bagshawe's sexy, glitzy blockbusters are a modern millennial update to the famous glitz-and-glamour novels of the 1980s that made Collins so popular.

Olivia Goldsmith
> Several of Goldsmith's novels are set in the glamorous worlds of television, book publishing, and fashion.

Judith Krantz
> Krantz's rags-to-riches soap opera plots feature dazzling settings and characters in high-powered occupations. They are fast-paced stories of women struggling to get to the top, usually by any means necessary.

Danielle Steel
> Steel is much less gritty and dramatic than Collins, but her novels are packed with characters, subplots, and details that will appeal to those who like the "overstuffed" feel of a Collins novel.

Penny Vincenzi
> Vincenzi's glitzy novels cover the jet-setting lives of glamorous women and their high-powered families. Wildly popular in Britain, she is a good match for Collins fans, as her stories are packed with soap-opera level drama.

If You Like Fannie Flagg

Fannie Flagg is a great storyteller with a gentle sense of humor. Her novels, set in the South, feature small towns full of eccentric characters.

Then You Might Like

Maeve Binchy
> While Binchy does not have quite the same sense of humor as Flagg, readers who enjoy small-town settings with folksy characters will enjoy some of Binchy's novels, such as *Whitethorn Woods* (2006), the story of a town dealing with an impending highway cutting through it.

Cassandra King
> King's novels feature strong Southern women and are full of friendships, family relationships, and fun, often eccentric characters.

Ann B. Ross
> Ross's Miss Julia novels will offer Flagg's fans a familiar small-town setting, eccentric Southern characters, and gentle humor.

Haywood Smith
> Smith writes humorous fiction about sassy, older women. Her Red Hat trilogy will appeal to those who enjoy Flagg's sassy, mature characters.

Adriana Trigiani
> Trigiani's Big Stone Gap novels offer the same small-town, gossipy appeal with warm and familiar characters that Flagg's novels do.

If You Like Dorothea Benton Frank

Dorothea Benton Frank's novels take place in the Lowcountry coastal towns of South Carolina and feature independent, everyday women in realistic situations, often dealing with family and friends.

Then You Might Like

Cassandra King
> While not the same settings, King's novels feature strong Southern women and are full of friendships and family relationships, much like Frank's novels.

Mary Alice Monroe
> Monroe sets her novels in the same South Carolina coastal towns as Frank and also features women dealing with every day trials and tribulations.

Anne Rivers Siddons
> Siddons sets several of her novels in the same Lowcountry islands as Frank, and her novel *Low Country* (1998) is the story of the struggle between conserving natural beauty and coastal development.

Karen White
> White's Southern novels often take place in the same settings as Frank's novels, and also feature women dealing with family issues and friendships.

If You Like Jane Green

Not to be dismissed as fluff chick lit, Green's novels, usually set in Great Britain, feature young women dealing with friendships, jobs, family issues, and romantic relationships. While keeping a fun sense of humor, she tackles more serious issues, such as infidelity in her novel *To Have and to Hold* (2003) and different facets of motherhood in *The Other Woman* (2005) and *Babyville* (2000).

Then You Might Like

Barbara Delinsky
> While not on the same humor level as Green, Delinsky's character-driven novels of everyday women dealing with events have the same storytelling style as Green, and her earlier romances may also hold appeal.

Marian Keyes
> Keyes displays much of the same sense of wit that Green does, and her novels share similar British and Irish settings that will appeal to Green's readers.

Sophie Kinsella
> Kinsella's stand-alone novels, such as *Remember Me?*, the story of a woman who wakes up from an accident and can't remember the last three years of her life, will appeal to readers who enjoy Green's sense of humor. They are also set in Great Britain and feature likable characters.

Jennifer Weiner
> Weiner is known for giving her characters real personalities and quirks and for her sense of humor. Her intelligent style of chick lit is right on track with Green's more substantial take on the category.

If You Like Elinor Lipman

Lipman's novels featuring realistic women and comic humor deal with family and social issues. Her novels do a nice job of capturing their times, acting as social satire.

Then You Might Like

Claire Cook
> Cook's novels feature a good sense of humor, eccentric families, and everyday characters.

Patricia Gaffney
> Gaffney's novels feature smart and mature women and revolve around their friendships and family relationships. Her dialogue is clever, and the characters and situations are realistic. *Mad Dash* (2007), the story of a marriage that may or may not be over, is a good match for Lipman's fans of social satire.

Jane Heller
Heller's sense of humor is sharper than Lipman's, but she writes realistic characters and her romantic comedies feature sharp dialogue, funny situations, and strong female characters.

Lorna Landvik
Landvik has the same sense of humor as Lipman and writes about families and communities dealing with the world around them.

Mameve Medwed
Good friends with Lipman, Medwed writes in a very similar style. Her novels are contemporary and humorous and feature everyday women dealing with family relationships. Considered modern comedies of manners, they are also very character-led.

If You Like Jodi Picoult

Picoult's issue-driven fiction revolves around contemporary women and their families, dealing with a tragedy or some unforeseen, improbable situation. Her readers enjoy the thrill of getting to know ordinary people in extraordinary moral circumstances, with plenty of twists and turns.

Then You Might Like

Barbara Delinsky
Delinsky's issue-driven yet family-focused style would be a perfect fit for Picoult's fans.

Joy Fielding
Fielding's issue-driven novels center around ordinary women dealing with extraordinary circumstances and focus on complex issues such as divorce, child abductions, abusive relationships, and fatal illnesses.

Sue Miller
Miller is more literary than Picoult but still deals with the same sorts of serious subjects that people never think will happen to them and with families in crisis.

Jacquelyn Mitchard
Mitchard's issue-driven novels, such as *The Deep End of the Ocean* (1995) and *A Theory of Relativity* (2001) showcase families in turmoil dealing with shocking situations, much like Picoult's work.

Anita Shreve
Shreve's novels feature average characters dealing with extreme situations. A good choice for Picoult's fans would be *The Pilot's Wife* (1998), the story of a woman confronted with her husband's infidelity after his death.

If You Like Danielle Steel

Danielle Steel is one of the most well-known and most prolific women's fiction authors, with millions of copies sold. Her novels range in place and time but always focus on the lives and relationships of women. She tackles dramatic issues such as rape, child abuse, family secrets, and infertility and has a romantic tone to her stories.

Then You Might Like

Sandra Brown
>While she currently writes romantic suspense, Brown's early romances will appeal to Steel fans.

Barbara Delinsky
>Delinsky also blends romance with women's issues.

Eileen Goudge
>Goudge's novels feature women dealing with relationships, often broken friendships or family secrets. They often have to overcome obstacles to their happiness, which is a hallmark of Steel's fiction as well.

Kristin Hannah
>Hannah's novels tend to be more "tearjerkers" than Steel's, but her stories of family relationships and characters overcoming a variety of issues will appeal to Steel fans. She writes about love and loss, complicated relationships, family secrets, themes that Steel shares.

Santa Montefiore
>Montefiore, a U.K.-based author, writes romantic stories set in exotic locales, often including family secrets, betrayal, and epic love stories.

If You Like Joanna Trollope

Trollope's family stories featuring average, middle-class women, set in the modern English countryside appeal to readers looking for a good story and believable, familiar characters. Her contemporary domestic stories offer glimpses into everyday life and intelligent, complex characters.

Then You Might Like

Maeve Binchy
>Binchy's family stories, particularly early novels such as *The Glass Lake* (1994) and *Light a Penny Candle* (1982), will appeal to fans of Trollope's gentle storytelling style as well.

Rosamunde Pilcher
>Pilcher's multigenerational sagas, set in the Scottish and English countrysides,

have the same warm feel of Trollope's novels. *The Shell Seekers* (1987) and *September* (1990) would be good read-alike choices.

Luanne Rice
American author Rice's novels may have an entirely different setting than Trollope's but share the same contemporary domestic feel and share some of the same themes, such as facing responsibilities and the importance of family.

Marcia Willett
Willett's novels, set in the rural West Country English countryside, feature mature women and their families, and have many of the same characteristics of Trollope's domestic fiction.

If You Like Meg Wolitzer

Meg Wolitzer's women's fiction is smart and literary, featuring the intimate details of ordinary women's lives and relationships. Her novels also comment on women's roles in society.

Then You Might Like

Elizabeth Berg
Berg's novels focus on relationships, from friends to families to lovers. While not in the same literary style as Wolitzer, her stories about everyday life, tragedies large and small, and the search for happiness in its many forms would appeal to Wolitzer readers.

Elinor Lipman
Lipman's novels often deal with family and social issues. Her novels do a nice job of capturing their times, acting as social satire, which is very similar to Wolitzer's novels.

Jennifer Weiner
Much different in tone (more on the chick lit side than serious literary side), Weiner's smart writing and keen eye on society put her on par with Wolitzer and should appeal to readers who appreciate Wolitzer's social commentary but are looking for something more "fun." *Little Earthquakes*, an examination of motherhood from the view of four very different women, is a good example of this.

Appendix C

For Further Reading

Bouricious, Anne. *Romance Readers' Advisory: The Librarian's Guide to Love in the Stacks*. ALA Editions, 2000. Offers excellent readers' advisory suggestions for romance that translate to women's fiction as well.

Charles, John, and Shelly Mosely. *Romance Today: An A-to-Z Guide to Contemporary American Romance Writers*. Libraries Unlimited, 2006. Discusses the lives and works of more than 100 contemporary American romance writers

Hill, Nancy Milone. *Reading Women: A Book Club Guide for Women's Fiction*. Libraries Unlimited, 2012. Gathers and provides information on over 100 women's fiction titles published in the last ten years and offers brief summaries of an additional fifty titles.

Moyer, Jessica E., and Kaite Mediatore Stover, eds. *The Readers' Advisory Handbook*. ALA Editions, 2010. Excellent readers advisory advice on a varied number of topics.

Orr, Cynthia, ed. *Genreflecting: A Guide to Popular Reading Interests*, 7th ed. Libraries Unlimited, 2012. Contains a chapter on women's fiction.

Ramsdell, Kristin. *Romance Fiction : A Guide to the Genre*, 2nd ed. Libraries Unlimited, 2012. Discusses major categories of romance/women's fiction and offers tips for readers' advisory and collection development.

Saricks, Joyce G. *The Reader's Advisory Guide to Genre Fiction*, 2nd ed. ALA Editions, 2009. Includes an excellent chapter on "Women's Lives and Relationships."

Sheehan, Sarah E. *Romance Authors: A Research Guide*. Libraries Unlimited, 2010. Biographical and bibliographical information on over fifty romance authors.

Vasudevan, Aruna, ed. *Twentieth-Century Romance and Historical Writers*, 3rd ed. St. James Press, 1994. Profiles more than 500 authors who have made significant contributions to romance and historical writing.

Vnuk, Rebecca. *Read On—Women's Fiction: Reading Lists for Every Taste.* Libraries Unlimited, 2009. Annotated booklists of hundreds of contemporary women's fiction titles categorized according to five appeal characteristics.

Vnuk, Rebecca. *Women's Fiction Authors: A Research Guide.* Libraries Unlimited, 2009. Biographical and bibliographical information on over seventy-five contemporary women's fiction authors.

Zellers, Jessica. *Women's Nonfiction: A Guide to Reading Interests.* Libraries Unlimited, 2009. Guide to over 600 nonfiction titles by and about women.

Appendix D

Selected Online Resources

Women's Fiction–Specific Web Sites

Candy Covered Books. http://www.candycoveredbooks.com/. Last visited March 18, 2013. This site gathers reviews of chick lit and women's fiction titles.

Chick Lit Books. http://chicklitbooks.com/. Last visited March 18, 2013. Reviews, author interviews, rankings, and articles about chick lit.

Chick Lit Central. http://chicklitcentraltheblog.blogspot.com/. Last visited March 18, 2013. Features new women's fiction books, reviews, and author information, with a focus on independently published and e-only chick lit.

Chick Lit Club. http://www.chicklitclub.com. Last visited March 18, 2013. Features reviews and ratings of more than 1,500 titles by 725 authors, and 125 interviews.

Chick Lit Is Not Dead. http://chicklitisnotdead.com/. Last visited March 18, 2013. Features giveaways, interviews, author segments.

Chick Lit Plus. http://chicklitplus.com/. Last visited March 18, 2013. Book reviews and author information for best-selling and lesser-known chick lit authors.

Novelicious. http://www.novelicious.com/. Last visited March 18, 2013. U.K.-based site covering a variety of styles of romance and women's fiction.

Romance Writers of America. http://www.rwa.org/. Last visited March 18, 2013. Features descriptions of category types, reviews, and links to author Web sites.

Romantic Times Book Reviews. http://www.rtbookreviews.com/. Last visited March 18, 2013. Online magazine for romance and women's fiction readers, with articles, reviews, and title lists.

Smart Bitches, Trashy Books. http://www.smartbitchestrashybooks.com. Last visited March 18, 2013. Mostly covers romance, but women's fiction also makes appearances.

Women's Fiction Chapter of the Romance Writers of America. http://www.rwa-wf.com/. Last visited March 18, 2013. An excellent definition of women's fiction can be found here, as well as other interesting resources on the genre.

Women's Fiction Writers. http://womensfictionwriters.wordpress.com/. Last accessed March 18, 2013. Interviews and guest posts featuring women's fiction authors, as well as writing tips for up-and-coming authors.

Recommended General Fiction Web Sites

BookPage. http://bookpage.com/. Last visited March 18, 2013. BookPage is a monthly book review publication distributed through libraries and bookstores. The Web site features author interviews, book reviews, and articles of interest to readers.

Book Reporter. http://www.bookreporter.com/. Last visited March 18, 2013. Features reviews of newer titles across all genes and includes articles, author interviews, and feature spotlights.

Fiction DB.com. http://www.fictiondb.com/. Last visited March 18, 2013. Author book lists and descriptions of books across genres.

Articles of Interest

Bilston, Sarah. "The Death of Chick Lit." *Slate/Double X.com*, August 11, 2001. http://www.doublex.com/section/arts/death-chick-lit. Last visited March 18, 2013. Chick lit author Bilston suggests that the economy had a lot to do with the evolution of chick lit.

Coburn, Jennifer. "The Decline of Chick Lit." *San Diego Union-Tribune*. February 11, 2012. http://www.utsandiego.com/news/2012/feb/11/the-decline-of-chick-lit/?page=1#article. Last visited March 18, 2013. Coburn interviews authors, publishers, and booksellers to examine the changes to women's fiction.

Franklin, Ruth. "The READ: Franzen Fallout." *The New Republic*, September 7, 2010. http://www.tnr.com/article/books-and-arts/77506/the-read-franzen-fallout-ruth-franklin-sexism#. Last visited March 18, 2013. Franklin discusses the *New York Times*'s shameful treatment of women's fiction.

Groskop, Viv. "The Original Chick Lit." *The Telegraph*, May 13, 2011. http://www.telegraph.co.uk/culture/books/bookreviews/8509052/The-Original-Chick-lit.html. Last visited March 18, 2013. Discusses why the author believes best sellers from the 1950s are better than contemporary women's fiction.

Holmes, Linda. "The Death of Women's Fiction? We Beg to Differer. . . ." *NPR*, August 13, 2009. http://www.npr.org/blogs/monkeysee/2009/08/is_the_recession

_hurting_women.html. Last visited March 18, 2013. Holmes's reaction to Bilston's article (above) notes that all of commercial women's fiction does not fall into the same category.

Jackson, Chris. "All the Sad Young Literary Women." *The Atlantic*, August 20, 2010. http://www.theatlantic.com/entertainment/archive/2010/08/all-the-sad-young -literary-women/61821/. Last visited March 18, 2013. Jackson posts about reading books by female authors.

Krentz, Jayne Anne. "Are We There Yet? Mainstreaming the Romance." Keynote Speech, Bowling Green State University Conference on Romance, August 2000. http://www.krentz-quick.com/bgspeech.html. Last visited March 18, 2013. Romance author Krentz discusses mainstream, popular romance, much of which applies nicely to contemporary women's fiction as well.

Lusher, Adam. "Bookshop Changes 'Women's Fiction' Label after Appeal from 'Sisterhood'." *The Telegraph (U.K.)*, September 3, 2011. http://www.telegraph .co.uk/culture/books/booknews/8739104/Bookshop-changes-womens-fiction -label-after-appeal-from-sisterhood.html. Last visited March 18, 2013. British bookstore chain W. H. Smith decided to drop the shelf label "women's fiction" after customers complained about "condescending, pink fluffiness."

Meier, Diane. "Chick Lit? Women's Literature? Why Not Just . . . Literature?" *Huffington Post*, August 10, 2011. http://www.huffingtonpost.com/diane-meier/ chick-lit-womens-literatu_b_678893.html. Last visited March 18, 2013. Meier makes a case for not categorizing fiction, particularly if it's done with a condescending or negative tone.

Miller, Laura. "The Death of Chick Lit." *Salon*, February 22, 2012. http://www .salon.com/2012/02/23/the_death_of_chick_lit/singleton/. Last visited March 18, 2013. Miller discusses the rise and fall of chick lit but declares it's not quite dead yet.

Weiner, Jennifer. "Tuesday 9/10/2010." *A Moment of Jen* blog, September 10, 2010. http://jenniferweiner.blogspot.com/2010/09/back-in-august-when-jodi-picoult .html. Last visited March 18, 2013. Weiner recaps her "franzenfreude" experiences.

Author/Title Index

Subject Index

Friendship

Gentle

Marriage

Thought-Provoking

Workplace

About the Authors

REBECCA VNUK, MLS, is the editor for Reference and Collection Management at *Booklist*. She is the author of two previous Libraries Unlimited guides to Women's Fiction: *Read On . . . Women's Fiction* (2009) and *Women's Fiction Authors: A Research Guide* (2009). She received her MLS from Dominican University in 1998 and held several public library positions in Readers' Advisory, Collection Development, and administration. A longtime reviewer and collection development article writer for *Library Journal*, she was named their "Fiction Reviewer of the Year" in 2008. In 2010, Rebecca was both named a Library Journal Mover and Shaker and the recipient of the Public Library Association's Allie Beth Martin Award. In 2008 she co-created the Readers' Advisory blog *Shelf Renewal*, which can now be found at www.booklistonline.com. She also blogs (very) occasionally on her own pet project, http://womensfic.blogspot.com.

NANETTE DONOHUE, MS, LIS, is the Technical Services Manager at the Champaign Public Library, Champaign, Illinois. She received her MS in Library and Information Science from the University of Illinois at Urbana-Champaign in 2003. Nanette has reviewed fiction for *Library Journal* since 2005 and has served as *LJ*'s Fiber Crafts and Crafts columnist since 2008. She also reviews historical fiction and nonfiction for the *Historical Novels Review*. In 2007–2008, Nanette served as the president of the American Library Association's New Members Round Table. Her website is www.nanettedonohue.com.